Romeo - heartthrob
Juliet -

Mercutio
Tybalt

Nurs

Teaching Success Guide for the Advanced Placement Classroom

Muse - Verona

Romeo - Rosaline
- Juliet
Mercutio
Tybalt

Romeo *and* Juliet

Advanced Placement Classroom

Romeo *and* Juliet

Advanced Placement Classroom

R. Brigham Lampert

PRUFROCK PRESS INC.
WACO, TEXAS

Library of Congress Cataloging-in-Publication Data

Lampert, R. Brigham.
  Romeo and Juliet / R. Brigham Lampert.
    p. cm. -- (Teaching success guide for the advanced placement classroom)
  At head of title on cover: Advanced placement classroom.
  Includes bibliographical references.
  ISBN-13: 978-1-59363-322-6 (pbk.)
  ISBN-10: 1-59363-322-X (pbk.)
  1. Shakespeare, William, 1564–1616. Romeo and Juliet. 2. Shakespeare, William, 1564-1616—Study and teaching. I.
Title.
  PR2831.L36 2008
  822.3'3—dc22
                              2008014125

Edited by Lacy Elwood
Production Design by Marjorie Parker
Photos by R. Brigham Lampert
Figures 2, 3, and 4 from http://www.istockphoto.com

ISBN-13: 978-1-59363-322-6
ISBN-10: 1-59363-322-X

At the time of this book's publication, all facts and figures cited are the most current available; all telephone
numbers, addresses, and Web site URLs are accurate and active; all publications, organizations, Web sites, and
other resources exist as described in this book; and all have been verified. The authors and Prufrock Press make no
warranty or guarantee concerning the information and materials given out by organizations or content found at
Web sites, and we are not responsible for any changes that occur after this book's publication. If you find an error or
believe that a resource listed here is not as described, please contact Prufrock Press.

•AP and Advanced Placement Program are registered trademarks of the College Entrance Examination Board, which
was not involved in the production of, and does not endorse, this book.

Prufrock Press Inc.
P.O. Box 8813
Waco, TX 76714-8813
Phone: (800) 998-2208
Fax: (800) 240-0333
http://www.prufrock.com

Dedication

I would like to dedicate this book to my sons, Reid and Miles Lampert, who have so drastically and positively changed my life, and to those of my students at Jamestown High who shall one day become teachers themselves. A teacher without students is nothing.

Contents

Acknowledgments

Like the undertaking of any major project, my authorship of this book has been far from a strictly individual effort. There are numerous persons to whom I am greatly indebted for their assistance and promotion of this endeavor, intentional or not, and whom I would here like to thank: first and foremost, my wonderful wife Jennifer, without whose aid and encouragement this book simply would not exist; my parents, the Rev. Dr. Richard and Molly Ann Lampert, whose unceasing provision of excellent educational opportunities throughout my life certainly led in many ways to this assignment; Mr. Richard Meacock, my favorite teacher and first professional role model, without whose influence I would probably be neither a Shakespearean nor a classroom instructor today; Dr. Joyce VanTassel-Baska, past-president of the National Association for Gifted Children and my former advisor at The College of William and Mary, who repeatedly and generously provided me with opportunities to write professionally about a topic that I love; Ms. Lacy Elwood and the staff at Prufrock Press, with whom it has been my sincere privilege to work; and last but absolutely not least, my students, past and present, at Jamestown High School in Williamsburg, who shape me every day in far profounder ways than I could ever reciprocate. I am sincerely grateful to all of you.

Introduction

This book is not intended as a work of Shakespearean scholarship, nor is it supposed to be any kind of strictly academic exercise. Rather, I have aimed in writing this work to produce an extremely teacher-ready, user-friendly resource for those of us who wish to expand and enhance our classroom instruction of *Romeo and Juliet*. Additionally, I have specifically targeted in my planning the population of gifted and talented students who potentially benefit so very much from the rigors and joys of Shakespearean study. I do believe that the activities and assignments contained herein are likewise appropriate for gifted and nongifted classroom populations, but much of this book's content has been designed particularly to prepare students for success on the Advanced Placement (AP) Literature and Composition Examination, an assessment that requires preparation at an undergraduate level of difficulty. Thus, I have likewise assumed in preparing this book that its target population is one able not only to succeed, but also to thrive in such a rigorous course of study. Please note that the material included within this book does not constitute an official College Board curriculum, nor is it officially endorsed by the College Board. It is meant as a curricular supplement for use in Advanced Placement, International Baccalaureate, honors, gifted, and other likewise denoted advanced English and literature courses. Although this book is geared mainly toward a high school population, many of the activities can be adapted to fit advanced language arts classrooms at the middle school level.

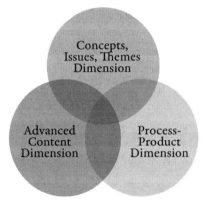

The Integrated Curriculum Model for Gifted Learners

Concepts, Issues, Themes Dimension

Advanced Content Dimension

Process-Product Dimension

Figure 1. Integrated Curriculum Model. Reprinted with permission from Joyce VanTassel-Baska and the College of William and Mary Center for Gifted Education. Copyright © 1987 Joyce VanTassel-Baska.

Bases in Scholarship and Standards

My work in designing Shakespearean curricula for gifted students began at the Center for Gifted Education at The College of William and Mary, in Williamsburg, VA. During 2 years, I designed *Navigator* teachers' guides for six Shakespearean plays, including *Romeo and Juliet*, based on the Center's—and particularly its director and my former academic advisor, Dr. Joyce VanTassel-Baska's—curricular model. Since first proposed by Dr. VanTassel-Baska (1986), the Integrated Curriculum Model (ICM) has gained widespread acceptance and use.

Emphasizing academic traditionalism, the ICM aims to provide gifted and talented students with (1) advanced content knowledge of a given scholastic discipline or subject, (2) opportunities to employ higher order thinking and processing skills in the acquisition and utilization or reinforcement of that content knowledge, and (3) applications to or considerations of major issues, themes, or ideas that are centrally or peripherally relevant to the given content, yet also applicable to the real world and/or otherwise interdisciplinary. These three dimensions of the ICM—the advanced content dimension, the process-product dimension, and the issues/themes dimension, respectively—compose the model upon which I have designed many of the activities in, as well as the full pedagogical scope of, this book. Figure 1 illustrates the most current visualization of the ICM's three distinct dimensions.

Additionally, I have attempted to design activities and assignments in accordance with national standards for English language arts instruction at the secondary level, both generally and more particularly, in AP Literature and Composition classes. I therefore chose for guidance in this endeavor two pedagogical compasses, the first of which was the National Council of Teachers of English's (NCTE) Standards for the English Language Arts (1996). Table 1 demonstrates the ways in which activities and assignments located within the five major chapters of this book accord with the NCTE's 12 standards.

I have aimed explicitly, moreover, to produce a resource specifically for AP Literature teachers of *Romeo and Juliet*, or for individual non-AP teachers or English departments that wish to scaffold their instructional strategies and content across grade levels, culminating ultimately in greater eventual success for AP students whose skills and knowledge bases have been built and strengthened over several years, rather than just one. Thus, the second pedagogical compass that I adopted was the College Board's (2007) AP English Literature and Composition Course Description, a document outlining what is expected and/or desired of AP English Literature teachers, students, and syllabi nationwide. Although the course description does not numerate instructional standards, á la NCTE, it does propose and outline numerous goals and requirements for instruction, according to which I have likewise designed my activities and assignments, as demonstrated in Table 2.

Please note that the AP English Literature and Composition Course Description lists three separate elements that are intrinsic to the close reading and study of a work of literature: (1) the experience of literature, (2) the interpretation of literature, and (3) the evaluation of literature. The College Board explicitly ties these three elements to particular approaches to reading and writing activities, and I have likewise imbedded them within the chapters and activities contained in this book. Please consider these elements as distinct from the actual goals and curricular requirements outlined in Table 2, yet inherently imbedded within them.

Organization of This Text

At the heart of this book, there are five chapters of activities and assignments designed to augment your classroom instruction of *Romeo and Juliet*. In truth, to deliver all of the lesson plans, dispense all of the assignments, and administer all of the assessments contained within these five chapters would take far longer than the time that most teachers allot for a single unit of literary study, Shakespearean or otherwise. Nevertheless, as any practiced instructor will admit, it is far better to be overplanned than underplanned. Thus, I have aimed to provide an overabundance of material from which any teacher of the play may cull as he or she sees fit.

Fronting these core pedagogical chapters are two more academic analyses of certain relevant aspects of Shakespeare's life ("Why Shakespeare?") and *Romeo and Juliet* ("Why *Romeo and Juliet*?"). Moreover, the core chapters are followed by a glossary of common literary terminology, an appendix (Appendix A) identifying a great number of literary devices and elements found throughout the play's

TABLE 1
Alignment With NCTE Standards for the English Language Arts

Standard	Ch.4 Reading Romeo and Juliet	Ch. 5 Understanding Romeo and Juliet	Ch. 6 Performing Romeo and Juliet	Ch. 7 Talking About Romeo and Juliet	Ch. 8 Writing About Romeo and Juliet
1. Read a wide range of texts for both intrapersonal and societal/cultural understanding, for the acquirement of new information, for response to society's needs, and for personal fulfillment.	✗	✗	✗	✗	✗
2. Read a wide range of literature to build an understanding of the universal human condition.	✗	✗		✗	✗
3. Apply various active linguistic strategies to comprehend, interpret, evaluate, and appreciate texts.	✗	✗	✗	✗	✗
4. Adjust spoken, written, and visual language methods to communicate effectively with various audiences for different purposes.			✗	✗	✗
5. Employ a wide range of writing strategies and elements to communicate effectively with different audiences for various purposes.		✗			✗
6. Apply knowledge of language structure, conventions, techniques, figurative elements, and genre to create, critique, and discuss texts.	✗	✗	✗	✗	✗
7. Conduct self-directed investigative research by gathering, evaluating, and synthesizing data from a variety of sources, then communicate those findings to an audience.					✗
8. Use various technological and information resources to gather and synthesize information and to create and communicate knowledge.					✗
9. Develop an understanding of and respect for diversity in human language use.	✗		✗	✗	✗
10. Non-native English speakers use their first languages to develop competency and understanding in the English language arts and curricula.					
11. Participate as knowledgeable, reflective, creative, and critical members of a variety of literacy communities.				✗	
12. Use spoken, written, and visual language to accomplish a variety of their own purposes.	✗	✗	✗	✗	✗

TABLE 2
Alignment With AP English Literature and Composition Goals/Curricular Requirements

Goal/Requirement	Ch.4 Reading Romeo and Juliet	Ch. 5 Understanding Romeo and Juliet	Ch. 6 Performing Romeo and Juliet	Ch. 7 Talking About Romeo and Juliet	Ch. 8 Writing About Romeo and Juliet
1. Intensive study of representative works by canonical Western authors from various time periods, engendering careful, deliberative reading and multiple interpretations.	✗	✗	✗	✗	✗
2. Interpretive, textually based analysis that considers a work of literature's structure, styles, and themes.	✗	✗	✗	✗	✗
3. Interpretive, textually based analysis that considers the social and historical values that a work of literature reflects and embodies.	✗	✗		✗	✗
4. Interpretive, textually based analysis that considers a work of literature's use of such elements as figurative language, imagery, symbolism, and tone.	✗	✗	✗	✗	✗
5. Opportunities to develop understanding of a work of literature, enabling students to discover what they think about their reading via informal, exploratory analytical activities.	✗	✗	✗	✗	
6. Opportunities to explain a work of literature via expository analyses that utilize textual details to develop and support interpretations of a text's meaning.	✗	✗		✗	✗
7. Opportunities to evaluate a work of literature's artistry and quality, and its social and cultural values, via argumentative analyses that draw upon textual details.	✗	✗		✗	✗
8. Instruction and feedback that help students develop a wide-ranging vocabulary used appropriately and effectively.	✗	✗	✗	✗	✗
9. Instruction and feedback that help students develop a variety of sentence structures, including appropriate use of subordination and coordination, in their writing.	✗				✗
10. Instruction and feedback that help students develop logical, coherent organization in analysis and writing, including specific techniques such as repetition, transitions, and emphasis.	✗				✗
11. Instruction and feedback that help students develop a balance of generalization and specific, illustrative detail in their analysis.	✗	✗	✗	✗	✗
12. Instruction and feedback that help students develop an effective use of rhetoric in writing and analysis, including such features as tone, voice, and appropriate emphasis in diction and syntax.			✗	✗	✗

first act, and lists of references and resources for further study of the Bard, his most popular and romantic play, and the education of the gifted and talented. Following are brief descriptions of the five core pedagogical chapters' contents.

Reading Romeo and Juliet

Unlike the other four pedagogical chapters, this one is organized chronologically, following the sequence of events in the play, act by act. I have organized it thusly because it contains assignments and assessments tied explicitly to particular moments and parts of the drama; plus, as the focus of this chapter concerns students' initial reading of *Romeo and Juliet*, it seems sensible that it be organized in the way in which all of us first encounter a literary work, from the front cover to the back.

The contents of this chapter that follow the play chronologically are of four main types: ideas for teaching higher level vocabulary through *Romeo and Juliet*; journaling questions for each of the play's scenes, which may be assigned for homework as a way to differentiate students' digestion and analysis of the drama; multiple-choice quizzes designed to mirror the multiple-choice portion of the AP English Literature and Composition Exam; and worksheets requiring students' performances of myriad tasks and consideration of various questions, structurally paralleling a generalized taxonomy of cognitive processes. Finally, a "precanned," ready-to-go lesson plan at the end of the chapter asks students to consider Tchaikovsky's musical adaptation of *Romeo and Juliet* in contrast to Shakespeare's original.

Understanding Romeo and Juliet

This second core chapter is rather dichotomous, containing two distinct approaches to appreciating *Romeo and Juliet* beyond a simple read-through of its action. The first portion of the chapter is devoted to Shakespeare's language, specifically its difficult syntax and figurative language. I identify many of the most common syntactical difficulties that new readers of the Bard encounter, addressing their apparent impenetrability and proposing ways to help students overcome such linguistic trials. I also briefly discuss Shakespeare's omnipresent use of figurative and otherwise difficult literary devices, although I later (in the Glossary and Appendix A) define, explain, and locate within *Romeo and Juliet* itself a plethora of those devices commonly used by Shakespeare.

In the chapter's second portion, I supply teachers with several mechanisms by which to help their students personalize their understandings of this play, its drama and conflict, and its characters. Writing prompts meant to engender bibliotherapy are followed in this respect by numerous worksheets that consider, and ask students to analyze, emotionally and otherwise, several of the most famous and/or most poignant quotations found in the text. Finally, two lesson plans are included to reinforce students' understanding of the Bard's mastery of the English language generally and, more particularly, of characterization; the first of these plans outlines in-class methodologies for demonstrating and considering the differences between Shakespeare's verse and everyone else's, while the second requires students to research medical histories of various cultures, then diagnose and prescribe remedies for several characters from the play according to their researched societies' practices.

Performing Romeo and Juliet

This chapter is devoted to the enactment of *Romeo and Juliet* and its major characters. As such, I first examine several aspects of stagecraft generally, defining and explaining key terms that students require an understanding of in order to engage "professionally" in the performance-based activities that follow. Additionally, two lesson plans highlight this chapter: one based upon and culminating in an analysis of the differences that ultimately arise from different students' (and, by association, practicing actors' and directors') interpretations and performances of a single scene; and another that guides students through the outlining of, preparation for, and enactment of two legal trials, of Juliet's Nurse and Friar Lawrence, respectively, both of whom are charged as accessories to murder.

Talking About Romeo and Juliet

This chapter focuses upon two methodologies for engaging students in discussions of the play: procedures and topics for both Socratic seminar discussions and interstudent debates. For each of these two types of activities, I include detailed explanations regarding various procedures, original mechanisms for assessing students' participation and success, and topics for discussion from which to choose. One Socratic seminar plan also highlights in detail a step-by-step approach to implementing classwide discussions, while another lesson plan engages students in a search for intertextuality between *Romeo and Juliet* and works of visual art, then has them present their conclusions orally to their peers.

Writing About Romeo and Juliet

This last of the core chapters explicates the fact that not all essay questions are equivalently aimed, posed, or administered. It highlights five distinct types of writing assignments and styles: 25-minute-long argumentative, judgmental essays resembling the writing section of the SAT; 40-minute-long analytical essays that mirror the AP English Literature and Composition Exam's essay portion; extended, college-length analyses of complex issues surrounding *Romeo and Juliet*; independent research projects that ultimately result in student presentations of their findings; and original creative-interpretive projects inviting students to personalize their reflections upon the play. For each of these types of assignments, I include numerous writing prompts and/or questions, as well as rubrics for assessment and additional ideas to maximize students' learning during their engagement in the writing process.

Notes on Citations

I have utilized, in writing this book, the traditional method of noting Shakespearean divisions into acts via capitalized Roman numerals, scenes via lowercased Roman numerals, and lines via standard numerals. The final couplet of *Romeo and Juliet*, then, is by this calculus denoted as Act V, scene iii, lines 320–321. When parenthetically citing quotations from this or other Shakespearean plays, however, I have adopted the American Psychological Association's (APA) consistent usage of standard numerals; hence, the same couplet is cited parenthetically as (5.3.320–321). Additionally, breaks between lines of metrical verse are noted within quotations by my use of slashes.

All excerpts from *Romeo and Juliet* that I quote in my text are taken from the Folger Shakespeare Library's revised paperback edition of the play (ISBN 0-7434-8280-8), edited by Barbara A. Mowat and Paul Werstine. All line numbers cited for these in-text quotations likewise correspond to the Folger edition's numeration, with the exception of excerpts contained on reproducible pages of this book, the lines of which are numbered independently.

Additionally, although my parenthetical citations generally follow the APA's guidelines for such, I have retained the literary tradition of citing lines of poetry not according to the pages of text on which they appear, but by the numbers of the quoted lines themselves. Therefore, although a poem's entry in my list of references lists the pages on which that poem appears in its text (e.g., pp. 10–11), I instead cite parenthetically within this book only the lines quoted (e.g., ll. 1–2). As such, any parenthetical citation following a quotation from a poem refers solely to the individual lines that I quote.

CHAPTER 2

Why Shakespeare?

Why teach Shakespeare?

Must this question even be asked? Everyone recognizes William Shakespeare's eminent place in the English literary canon. As in most of the United States, in Virginia, where I live and teach, it is impossible for one to gain licensure to teach English in any of the Commonwealth's public secondary schools without having taken at least one undergraduate Shakespeare course. There simply is no more commonly quoted or alluded to dramatist or author in the Western world, nor a storyteller with more films to his individual credit. The man helped invent the modern English language (the estimated number of words and phrases coined by the Bard is approximately 1,600, including such standards as *countless*, *majestic*, and *excellent*). Like a literary whirlpool, his dramatic corpus engulfs what is universal and essential in human philosophy, spirituality, and wisdom. With nothing but his mind and a quill pen, Shakespeare brought near to actual life such absolutely immortal persons as Hamlet and Falstaff, plus recreated the popularly accepted histories of Richard III, Henry V, and Julius Caesar, among others, whose stories we recognize largely, if not exclusively, thanks to this tradesman's son from Stratford. His name itself is a metonym for artistic culture.

In high school English courses, there simply is no better way to test students' interpretive mettle than to help them tackle a grandly demanding Shakespearean monologue or soliloquy. If you want to augment their vocabularies and help them to learn the irreplaceable linguistic value of prefixes and suffixes, then assign your students a syntactical exegesis of an excerpt from *King Lear*. Looking for a way to make cerebral philosophy relevant to the lives of modern teenagers? Present to them Hamlet's revelatory scene in the graveyard, which mixes such disparate ideological ingredients as Nietzschean nihilism and the lessons of Ecclesiastes into a philosophical statement that is totally pertinent to any young adult attempting to decide what to do with the rest of his or her life post-high school. Like many of the Bard's poems, "Sonnet 27" reads as if spoken impromptu by any adolescent discovering love (or infatuation) for the first time. And, in all of literature, is there any more joyful expression of young love's craziness than *A Midsummer Night's Dream*?

Yes, Shakespeare's language is difficult to read, especially for young adults unfamiliar with many modern conventions of formal English, much less with figurative verse written 400 years ago. His syntactical inversions, his verbal omissions, and his ambiguous referents all challenge the most fluent readers; his symbolism and metaphorical language puzzle the intellect even further. But, from such struggles arise large cognitive and academic benefits, especially for high-achieving gifted and talented students who, for the most part, are able to move through the prose of Hemingway and Poe without breaking the slightest intellectual sweat. He who can handle Shakespeare can read just about anything else, scholastic or otherwise.

Because you are currently holding this book, it is assumable that you already have a personal interest in teaching or better understanding the greatest writer in the history of the English language. Perhaps a more legitimate question, then, is, why choose *Romeo and Juliet*? That topic will be addressed at length in the next chapter.

In this chapter, I shall briefly consider elements of William Shakespeare's life and times. This book is not intended as a piece of historical scholarship; nevertheless, a basic understanding of Elizabethan England, both distinct from and pertaining to the theater, should enhance your appreciation of the social, political, and literary climate that produced such a magnificent pinnacle of English drama and poetry.

Shakespeare's England

It is a mistake to regard Shakespeare himself as some historical anomaly, an enlightened genius sprung unexpectedly from the darkness of an uncivilized people. By the reign of Queen Elizabeth in England, Johannes Gutenberg had long since invented the movable-type printing press, new translations of foreign literature, both contemporary and classical—many works of the latter had never previously been available—were streaming into the British Isles, and the educated upper crust of Tudor society, no longer composed exclusively of nobles, attended Cambridge and Oxford in droves. David Harris Willson (1972) described Elizabethan Englanders as "a young and vigorous people emerging from the Middle Ages into the warmer and more intense life of the Renaissance," the intellectual and artistic waves that had saturated European, not to mention English,

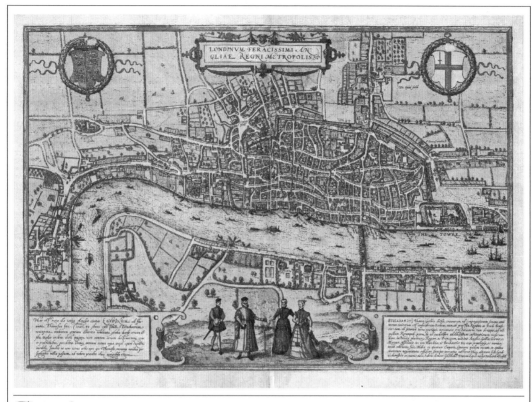

Figure 2. Seventeenth-century map of London.

society: "very much alive, alert to the world around them, not merely to grasp the main chance in a material way and to rise in the social scale, but to respond to intellectual and artistic impulses" (p. 314). Most scholars consider this period a golden age of English literature, as the proliferation of poems, dramas, and essays helped to popularize the very language itself as an acceptable tongue among even the wealthiest, most erudite members of society, those who had previously preferred French, considering English as the language of commoners.

On the other hand, by 1594, Copernicus's heliocentric theory of planetary orbits was only 50 years old, and Gioseffo Zarlino had fewer than 40 years previously defined the major and minor musical scales; there was no such thing as opera in 1594—Jacopo Peri's *Dafne*, regarded as the first of this genre, was still a few years off—and the English Colonies in North America did not yet exist, as Sir Walter Raleigh was but 10 years removed from his "discovery" of a new land named Virginia, in honor, of course, of the Queen herself. Nobody had ever heard of the political establishment Great Britain. And, the Internet? Well, suffice it to say that to many modern teenagers the England of Shakespeare and the waning Tudor dynasty may as well have been the Dark Ages. Compare, for example, the 17th-century map of London pictured in Figure 2 with a modern map of what hardly seems like, yet is, the same city; obviously, the physical growth thus depicted was paralleled over those 400 years by maturation in every other conceivable milieu.

Figure 3. Shakespeare's birthplace on Henley Street in Stratford.

Perhaps the most concisely descriptive synthesis of this social and political dichotomy between newness and antiquity, between forward motion and relative immaturity, again comes from Willson (1972), who wrote, "In some ways this was a childish age" (p. 315). Intellectual and artistic revolution, hopeful and energetic, was juxtaposed with a long and brutal war against the Spanish. Despite a stated and ostensible regard for matters of the Church, most of English society was secularly focused on the obtainment of wealth, on finery and social class, and on overseas expansion. The spread of philosophical humanism and skepticism butted heads with a well-recorded societal infatuation with shows, parades, colorful costumes, and bizarre monstrosities, natural and otherwise. In brief, Willson's childish England had become self-aware—of its capabilities, its potentials, and the diversity of its social body—but did not always control its own very human, somewhat egocentric impulses.

Shakespeare's Early Life

Into that England of vivacity and hope, on April 23, 1564, William Shakespeare was born in Stratford, a small town on the Avon River, in central England (see Figure 3). His parents, John and Mary Shakespeare, were financially stable, if not outright successful, but largely uneducated; John was of the yeoman class, a farmer and glove maker by trade, and Mary, as a female member of the gentry, was never privileged with formal education. It is presumable that young William attended the free Stratford Grammar School, principally studying Latin works by Ovid and Virgil, among others. As children generally left school at the age of 15, William probably took a job or apprenticeship of some kind in 1579, 3 years before his impregnation of Anne Hathaway, a local farmer's daughter 8 years his senior, led to their rushed matrimony and, 6 months later, 18-year-old William's fatherhood to his eldest daughter Susanna.

Other than the christening of Shakespeare's second and third children, twins Hamnet and Judith, in 1585, no further record of his life until 1592 survives. This period of roughly 10 years, from his marriage to a public slander of Shakespeare by writer Robert Greene, is commonly referred to as the "dark" or "lost period" of the Bard's life. Some scholars contend that he left Anne and their children and moved to London, crafting a career as both an actor and playwright; after all, Greene's criticism explicates William's public reputation by at least 1592. Other scholars believe that he joined the Royal Navy and traveled to Italy, among other destinations; why else would Shakespeare, they argue, have such an apparent firsthand knowledge of so many of his plays' Italian settings? Another plausible theory is that young William joined a traveling troupe of players and hit the road, journeying wherever the muse and money led, much as the company of players in *Hamlet* does. A rumor popularized shortly after his death claimed that Shakespeare was, during at least some of these years, a butcher of cattle! We may never find out exactly where the man went or what he did during this decade, but it is clear that by 1592, when he reappeared fully entrenched in London's theatrical world, he had become a rather respected playwright of six or seven works, probably including *Richard III* and *The Taming of the Shrew*.

Shakespeare's Theatrical Life

During William Shakespeare's youth, actors and playwrights were not regarded in English society as any kind of trustworthy, respectable, or even hygienic class of people. They performed either in traveling troupes, many of which are recorded as having passed through Stratford, or in large spaces such as private inn yards or public squares. No such troupe had its own permanent theater, and the most popular edifice for public entertainment was London's gallows, erected in 1571. It was not until 1576 that the first permanent performance theater, called simply the Theatre, was built by James Burbage in Shoreditch, a suburb of London. Other similar playhouses, most notably the Rose, soon followed, and the reputations, earnings, and lifestyles of theatrical professionals likewise improved as a result.

By 1592, when William Shakespeare resurfaced in written records, theater was a popular and potentially lucrative business. Certainly there were opponents, most notably Puritans, to the immoral behavior and lifestyles of playwrights, actors, and theatergoers, but Queen Elizabeth herself was a patron and fan, and it has been estimated that one in eight Londoners attended theatrical performances at least once weekly. It was illegal for women to act on stage, and playwrights, who aimed to sell several plays per year to acting companies or other theatrical producers, generally received no attendance royalties whatsoever for productions of their works; due to monetary constraints, actors almost never received full scripts of their productions, but were instead forced to work from lists of only their own cues and lines, remaining oblivious to other aspects of a given drama's complete scope. Moreover, these actors generally played multiple roles not only in one play, but in several plays simultaneously. Special effects were nearly impossible to create, and props were scanty. An easy professional life it was not. Nevertheless, careers based in the theater had become, at least in certain social circles, popular and appealing. Shortly following Shakespeare's reemergence in 1592, however, two major events occurred that transformed London's theatrical life permanently: an outbreak of plague forced the closings of all theaters for 2 years and Christopher Marlowe, Shakespeare's major competitor as a popular dramatist, was murdered at the age of 29.

Following the plague's decreed containment, in June 1594, Shakespeare joined the Lord Chamberlain's Men, with which company he performed for Queen Elizabeth herself numerous times, and began churning out plays at an incredible rate; *Romeo and Juliet* is dated as having been written during this period. By the time he purchased a familial coat of arms in 1596 and a mansion in Stratford in 1597, young William had become a wealthy and powerful man. During that same period, however, death struck the Shakespeare family repeatedly—that of his 11-year-old son Hamnet in 1596 and of his father in 1601—and the Bard began penning his most profound and darkest works, the Great Tragedies of *Hamlet*, *Macbeth*, and *King Lear*, among others. A movement in 1608 from the famed Globe Theatre (see Figure 4) to the more intimate, indoor Blackfriars Theatre likewise introduced the final period of Shakespeare's literary development, as well as provided him with inventive new possibilities for scene-setting and a higher class clientele. By 1612, he was a retired and wealthy resident of Stratford, but in 1616 he died of still-unknown causes, ironically on his birthday.

That his reputation has not only lasted, but grown exponentially over the last four centuries is obviously not unjustified. Arguably, his strongest and most unique literary ability was in characterization, an area in which all of his contemporaries struggled; while Marlowe's Doctor Faustus is as indistinct as a silhouette, characters such as Hamlet, Falstaff, and Lear are so individual as to be impossible to confuse with anyone else in literary history. His dramatic pacing and ability to engender suspense were unparalleled on the stage, and the philosophical, social, emotional, spiritual, and flat-out human relevancies of his greatest works are as

Figure 4. The reconstructed Globe Theatre on the south bank of the Thames River in central London.

timeless and inherent to our species as anything ever written in any culture. We may never see the likes of his linguistic inventiveness again, and the truest and most beautiful of his lines absolutely burn with the flames of poetry and ageless wisdom. Harold Bloom (1995), perhaps the most respected Shakespearean critic of our times, wrote succinctly and cogently an answer to the unnecessary question with which I opened this chapter. Why teach Shakespeare? Simply stated, in Bloom's words, "Shakespeare is the Canon" (p. 47). No other writer comes close.

Why *Romeo and Juliet*?

In 1623, seven years after William Shakespeare's death, John Heminge and Henry Condell, former professional associates of the Bard, published the First Folio edition of Shakespeare's plays, categorizing them into the genres of tragedies, histories, and comedies. In many cases still today, the lines separating these categories from one another are blurry; *Julius Caesar*, for instance, could certainly be classified among both the tragedies and the histories. Likewise, critical opinions and public receptions of many Shakespearean plays vary according to one's criteria and personal preferences. *Hamlet* is an undisputed masterpiece, yes, but the review of *The Tempest* that one hears is highly dependent upon the person of whose opinion you inquire. Nevertheless, descriptions and evaluations of particular entries in Shakespeare's dramatic corpus have never changed and are never likely to do so. To wit, *Romeo and Juliet* has always sat squarely among the high tragedies, exemplifying the genre as a whole, and since its initial public performances sometime in the mid-1590s, neither its popularity on stage and in print nor its emotional, social, and philosophical relevancies to playgoers and readers of many ages have ever diminished.

In fact, for more than 400 years *Romeo and Juliet* has almost certainly held the distinction of being Shakespeare's most widely popular play. Based largely on various versions of the Romeo and Juliet "legend" extant throughout the 16th century, it concerns a feud between two prominent families of Verona, Italy, circa the 1590s. The original cause of the feud between the Montagues and the Capulets is never divulged in the text, but all direct descendants, extended members, and even servants of both families are, at the play's inception, fully indoctrinated into the hate-your-enemy-without-question atmosphere of the conflict. Public demonstrations of the families' hatred for one another are implicitly quite common, moreover, as a seemingly fed-up Prince Escalus of Verona states in the play's first scene, further disruptions of the public peace as a result of the feud will be punished by death. The Prince's warning later plagues young Romeo Montague, who falls in love with 13-year-old Juliet Capulet at a masquerade ball, pledges his love to her that same night during the famous Balcony Scene of Act II, weds her secretly the next day, and in a rage slays her hot-headed cousin Tybalt following Tybalt's murder of Mercutio, Romeo's best friend. Importantly, both Mercutio's and Tybalt's murders occur in the streets of Verona, but as Romeo is found to have slain Tybalt retributively for Mercutio's murder, Prince Escalus punishes the newlywed not with execution, but with banishment to nearby Mantua. Juliet, however, enlists the Friar who performed their marriage ceremony to help her escape the unwanted, impending wedding that her parents (ignorant of her marriage to Romeo) have arranged to Paris, another nobleman of Verona. The Friar gives her a powerful elixir, which induces a coma-like state, yet makes Juliet appear outwardly dead. Her parents, thus believing her dead, bury Juliet in the Capulet family's sepulcher. Meanwhile, having mistakenly learned that his wife has died, Romeo procures instantaneously fatal poison, journeys to Juliet's sepulcher, and takes the poison seconds before Juliet awakes from her feigned death; she, perceiving that Romeo has in grief committed suicide, kills herself using his dagger. Sorrowfully, both families end the play with a public truce.

Even people who have never actually seen or read *Romeo and Juliet* are familiar with many aspects of this story. It has been filmed more times than any other Shakespearean drama save *Hamlet*, been adapted into multiple operas and at least one Broadway musical, inspired symphonic and balletic versions from such worldly musical giants as Tchaikovsky and Prokofiev, and, although such a figure is impossible to quantify, certainly eclipsed the Bard's other 37 canonical plays in its accruement of pop culture references. Images of the "star-crossed lovers"—especially of their emblematically tragic deaths—are recognized by people at the farthest reaches of the globe, and "Romeo, Romeo, wherefore art thou Romeo?" apostrophized from the most famous balcony in Europe (see Figure 5), is probably the single most identifiable line of English literature in the world.

Perhaps because of this popularity and ubiquity, Shakespearean teachers and scholars sometimes give Romeo and Juliet a backseat to other "grander" or "more cerebral" of the Bard's works. Especially in the highest level, most demanding English courses in high schools nationwide, *Hamlet* and *Macbeth* often are the tragedies of choice, with *Romeo and Juliet* consigned to earlier grades, where students cut their teeth on Elizabethan language before they are deemed ready to digest fully the Melancholy Dane and the Scottish play. Despite the quite appropriate reputations and value of those two masterpieces, such relegation of *Romeo* to the role of building block is rather shortsighted. After all, just because a story

Figure 5. Juliet's balcony in Verona, as seen from Romeo's vantage point.

is overwhelmingly popular does not mean that it somehow caters to a more common intellectual denominator than do works appealing largely to audiences with highly developed critical faculties. Perhaps, as in the case of this play, it simply means that just about anyone can relate in some way—experientially, vicariously, or otherwise—to the "misadventured piteous overthrows" of the world's most famous young lovers and the various persons and forces conspiring to keep them apart (Prologue, ln. 7).

Additionally, as I hope to demonstrate in this book, not only is the story of *Romeo and Juliet* compelling and relevant enough to grab and keep the attention of even the most intellectual of readers, but its text also is full of tools for teach-

Figure 6. The Adige River in central Verona, as seen from the Castelvecchio Bridge. Castelvecchio itself is on the right.

ers preparing their students for success on the AP Literature and Composition Exam and other similarly demanding assessments: a plethora of literary devices, innumerable philosophical conundrums ripe for consideration and conversation, and political and social issues as relevant today as they have ever been in any era. In brief, to quote Lady Capulet, "That book in many's eyes doth share the glory / That in gold clasps locks in the golden story" (1.3.98–99). Especially for classroom teachers of gifted, AP, and otherwise exceptional students of literature, there is gold within *Romeo and Juliet*; I hope that this book helps you to mine it.

Setting the Story

Located within a loop of the Adige River (see Figure 6), the city of Verona, Italy, has survived nearly 3,000 years of conquests, battles, and political occupations. Purportedly founded by the Euganei, who surrendered the city in 550 B.C., Verona today is a vibrant mixture of medieval and Renaissance architecture, modern urbanization and industrialization, and tourist attractions on one's way from Milan to Venice.

The city's history is spotted with residencies and visits by a veritable political and literary "who's who." After the Goths conquered Verona in 489 A.D., King Theodoric built a personal palace there, and Charlemagne likewise conquered the outpost in 774 (Julius Caesar also is rumored to have vacationed occasionally within the city). A Latin ode describes Verona's magnificence at that time, late in the first millennium A.D., when it served regularly as an Italian royal residence. Napoleon briefly occupied the city in 1797, and it was actually under Austrian control until 1866, when it officially and finally became a part of Italy, alongside the rest of Venetia, of which Verona is a provincial capital. Among other literati, Dante Alighieri almost certainly passed through, and Goethe and Stendhal both mention stays in Verona within their travel diaries. It also is rumored that Shakespeare, of course, may have visited the city during the infamous "lost period" of his life, of which we have few, if any, details and during which he perhaps first encountered the famously apocryphal feud between the Montecchi and Capelletti.

Many remnants of its ancient past stand today within the old, central section of the city, originally a Roman settlement (see Figure 7); in fact, many 2,000-year-old basalt-paved Roman roads still exist intact approximately 20 feet below the modern surface. Perhaps most notably, the Arena di Verona, the construction of which was completed circa 30 A.D., remains today one of the three largest Roman amphitheaters in Italy; only four arches (the Ala) remain of the Arena's outer rings, the remainder destroyed both by an earthquake in 1117 and by the ravages of time and war, but the amphitheater's acoustical properties are still so strong that annual outdoor operatic performances draw thousands to Verona from around the globe.

Numerous other Roman monuments likewise endure throughout the city, such as the Arco (Arch) de Gavi, built during the first century A.D., and the Porta Borsari and Porta Leonia, both ancient city gates built prior to 300 A.D. Various medieval basilicas similarly remain in use, as do various piazzas and palazzos, including the famed Piazza delle Erbe, the former site of a Roman forum. Larger and even more impressive, however, is the Piazza Brà (see Figure 8) at the heart of the ancient city, on the edge of which sits the remarkable Arena di Verona; numerous shops and cafes today line the Piazza, centered upon a fountain but focused upon the Arena, and you'd be pressed to find anywhere in Verona a more delectable serving of tiramisu, especially during the first intermission of *Madama Butterfly* or *La Bohème*.

The Casa di Giulietta (Juliet's House; see Figure 9) is one block away from the Arena, the courtyard of which is accessible only through a tiny alleyway marked by the graffiti of thousands of romantically literary lovers. Although built during the 20th century, Juliet's balcony, which overlooks a golden statue of Shakespeare's heroine, is among the most famous balconies in the world (upon which you can have your picture taken for 5 euros), and despite the admittedly inauthentic nature of the quite-touristy Capelletti courtyard, its romantic Renaissance ambience certainly brings the Bard's story to life.

A proud, old soldier upon the banks of the Adige River, Castelvecchio ("Old Castle" in Italian; see Figure 10) stands as one of the most solid examples of 14th-

Figure 7. The author below a Roman archway on the streets of Verona.

century Gothic architecture in Italy; built between 1354 and 1376, the castle boasts seven towers, a grand keep, an erstwhile moat, and even a fortified "escape bridge" across the Adige River, constructed in the 1350s by the tyrannical Della Scala patriarch just in case of rebellion by the Veronese populous. Constructed on the probable location of a former Roman fortification, Castelvecchio and its bridge have been nearly destroyed twice, in 1796 by the Napoleonic French and in 1945 by retreating Nazi troops, but both were thankfully restored following World War II. Today, a museum of Romanesque artwork and metalwork resides within Castelvecchio's walls.

Figure 8. The Piazza Brà fronting the Arena di Verona.

Figure 9. Looking down on Giulietta's statue in the Capelletti courtyard.

Figure 10. The author atop Castelvecchio's battlements. Note the signature M-shaped merlons, which run along nearly the entire length of the castle.

Because *Romeo and Juliet* is set in the 1590s, it is certainly valuable for both students and teachers of the play to visualize Verona's many ancient monuments and aesthetic characteristics. Having visited or seen pictures, for example, it is not hard for one to envision Romeo and Tybalt fencing atop Castelvecchio's grand stone fortifications, to imagine Prince Escalus addressing the feuding Veronese scattered across the Piazza Brà, or to conceive of the famous balcony scene, Romeo exclaiming, having scaled the high walls of Via Cappello 23, "But soft, what light through yonder window breaks? / It is the East, and Juliet is the sun" (2.2.2–3). A magnificent setting, certainly, for a magnificent romance.

Cast of Major Characters

Part of the enduring appeal of *Romeo and Juliet* is certainly attributable to its very real adolescent familiarity; the eponymous characters, for instance, are inherently and enduringly relatable to gifted students worldwide, themselves full of passionate overexcitabilities and adolescent hormones. What high schooler has not imagined his or her own youthful rebellion against one's familial traditions and rules? What teenager has never dreamed of a passionate romance born quite literally "at first sight," powerful enough to engender, as its immediate expression, a perfectly spoken love sonnet? Who does not know persons as familiar and common as Mercutio and Tybalt, both riotous instigators of trouble, albeit in very different ways? If *Hamlet*'s defining adjective is "mature," then *Romeo and Juliet* is contrarily best described as "youthful"; its conflicts, its emotional expressions, its rebellious schemes, and even its outcome overflow with the passion and possibility of young adulthood. This fact alone sets the play apart from the rest of Shakespeare's corpus as not only appropriate, but also near-essential for instruction in secondary English courses.

Romeo Montague

One of the play's title characters, young Romeo matures before the audience's eyes throughout the drama, progressing from a stereotypically melancholic, lovesick adolescent in the first act to a more mature and devoted husband and lover by the play's midpoint. He is first characterized indirectly for the audience in Act I, scene i, reported as a wistful, withdrawn young man; the cause of this melancholy is Rosaline, the quite indistinct maiden for whom Romeo pines and who is discussed but never actually seen on stage. Romeo's immediate emotional oscillation upon seeing Juliet—"O, she doth teach the torches to burn bright!" (1.5.51)—indicates his romantic immaturity, as do his somewhat cliché first expressions of passion to Juliet via a Shakespearean sonnet, which she coauthors, and his rapturous, infatuated outpouring in the balcony scene of Act II, scene ii. He hastes Lawrence to marry them the next morning as well, demonstrating youthful impatience, but by the time he aims for concord between Tybalt and Mercutio in Act III, Romeo's emotional maturity evidently is growing. Moments later, however, he loses his cool and vindictively, unthinkingly slays Tybalt, a clear sign that he has more maturation to undergo; his response to news of his own banishment, described by Lawrence as "womanish . . . wild acts [that] denote / The unreasonable fury of a beast," is a similar example of rash, hysterical behavior (3.3.120–121). Although it is difficult to label his suicide in the play's final scene as mature, this final act certainly demonstrates Romeo's determination and devotion to his bride; no longer is he the wistful and wishy-washy romantic neophyte of Act I, but a passionate and strong-willed young man, even if he demonstrates it in a decidedly unproductive way.

Juliet Capulet

The other eponymous lover, Juliet is notably more mature than her husband throughout the play, despite her relative youth (13 years old). Her intelligence and implicit experience are evident as soon as she meets Romeo at the Capulets' ball; "You kiss by th'book," she tells him, ambiguously characterizing both herself and young Montague (1.5.121). Though just as ecstatic as Romeo during the balcony scene, Juliet is ostensibly more prudent than he, recognizing their celeritous rapture as "too rash, too unadvised, too sudden, / Too like the lightning, which doth cease to be / Ere one can say 'It lightens,'" pressing for marriage as a potential solution to their familial dilemma (2.2.125–127). She is, nevertheless, an archetypal young girl in love, excitedly impatient for and enraptured by her lover, whom she adores more than all the world, as evidenced by her euphoric soliloquy in Act III, scene ii. Her most outstanding characteristic, however, is probably her courage, evidenced both by her resistance to her father and mother's plans for her future—a resistance that she enacts by wedding the son of their enemies behind their backs!—and by her willing acquiescence to Friar Lawrence's plan, requiring her, in effect, to be buried alive within the family crypt. In the play's final scene, just as determined as Romeo in the face of overwhelming misfortune, she exhibits her courage and, arguably, heroism by joining her husband in the afterlife rather than accepting a predetermined life devoid of love.

Lord and Lady Montague

Despite their inherently important positions within the plot and surrounding the chief conflict of *Romeo and Juliet*, Lord and Lady Montague appear but rarely and briefly, always in response to a public outburst concerning their familial feud with the Capulets. Although Lord Montague is apparently no less hot-headed than anyone else involved in the rivalry—"Thou villain Capulet!" he exclaims in Act I, scene i, brandishing his own sword and struggling to get in on the action (81)—both he and his wife are just as obviously concerned and loving parents of Romeo, as evidenced particularly in Act I, scene i and Act V, scene iii, wherein Montague reports his wife's death caused by woe: "Grief of my son's exile hath stopped her breath" (219). Lord Montague, too, expresses sympathy and remorse at the play's conclusion, offering to build a statue of Juliet from pure gold.

Lord and Lady Capulet

The patriarch and matriarch of the House of Capulet appear in the play more often and are more strongly characterized than their Montague counterparts. Lord Capulet seems benign and pacific in the play's first act, resisting Paris's requests for Juliet's immediate hand in marriage and preventing Tybalt from attacking Romeo, who has crashed the Capulets' ball. His quick temper shows itself soon enough, however, as he furiously lambasts Juliet for her resistance in Act III to marrying Paris, then expedites their wedding one act later, referencing her "peevish self-willed harlotry" (4.2.14). Lady Capulet, on the other hand, always incites the audience's abhorrence; she responds coldly and insensitively to Juliet's reservations toward Paris as a potential husband, and she screams for bloody retribution following Romeo's murder of her nephew Tybalt: "Prince, as thou art true, / For blood of ours, shed blood of Montague. . . . Romeo slew Tybalt; Romeo must not live" (3.1.156–157, 190). Believing that Juliet has died in Act IV, scene v, Lady Capulet sobbingly laments the "Accursed, unhappy, wretched, hateful day!" (49), but by this time the audience's capacity for sympathy toward Lady Capulet is perhaps largely muffled, especially because she and her husband throughout the drama play well their roles as instruments of fate, unintentionally hastening the deaths of their own daughter and her beloved.

Juliet's Nurse

Perhaps best played or understood as a well-meaning friend and confidante who ultimately lacks the integrity to stand up for herself or her young charge, Juliet's Nurse initially appears as a very likeable character, a ribald storyteller, and comedic straight-woman to Mercutio in Act II, scene iv. In fact, it is unlikely that Romeo and Juliet actually would wed when they do without assistance from the Nurse, who serves them as a matchmaking intermediary. Following Tybalt's murder, when Lord and Lady Capulet inform Juliet of her betrothal to Paris, the Nurse immediately but weakly comes to her aid—"You are to blame, my lord, to rate her so," she tells Capulet (3.5.176)—but, when faced with her employers' furious and threatening rigidity 50 lines later, she isolates the girl and loses face as a congenial character by timidly, insensitively recommending that Juliet ignore her union with Romeo and marry Paris: "O, he's a lovely gentleman! / Romeo's a dishclout to him" (3.5.231–232). Although well-intentioned and affable when not under pressure, Juliet's Nurse eventually becomes one of the least sympathetic characters in the play, a meddlesome comic who simply bites off more trouble than she can politically or emotionally chew.

Friar Lawrence

A male counterpart to Juliet's Nurse, Friar Lawrence comes off initially as an amiable and respectable clergyman, urging that Romeo and Juliet proceed patiently and prudently through their courtship, rather than rush into the marriage that he nonetheless immediately performs. Ironically, his ineffectual morality soon shows itself when he, like the Nurse, ostensibly caves under the political pressure induced by his meddling union of the rival families. He silently accepts Juliet's seemingly inevitable bigamous marriage to Paris in Act IV, scene i, then undermines that arrangement and the Capulets' parenthood by deviously formulating the plan whereby Juliet feigns suicide, hoodwinking all of Verona with "poison" supplied by the Friar himself! Finally, his utter lack of integrity is demonstrated in the final scene, as he fearfully abandons Juliet and Romeo, whom he recognizes as dead, to the fate unleashed by his own deceitfulness: "Come, I'll dispose of thee / Among a sisterhood of holy nuns," he yells to her within the crypt, "Stay not to question, for the watch is coming" (5.3.161–163). Disgraceful, to say the least.

Tybalt, Kinsman to the Capulets

[handwritten margin note: Symb. + Psych.]

An apparently minor character who actually plays a critical role in *Romeo and Juliet*, Tybalt, Juliet's cousin, is the catalyst for two (nearly three) brawls between the Montagues and Capulets, the last of which causes his own and Mercutio's violent deaths, plus the banishment of Romeo and the sequence of events that inevitably eventually resolve the tragic drama. He is hungrily belligerent at every appearance and, more so than any other character in the play, symbolizes the unreasonable feud between the warring families, as well as the tragedy's ubiquitous cruel irony. ". . . thou art a villain," he tells Romeo only moments before his own death (3.1.62). Actually, if anyone in this tragedy of circumstance can be characterized as a villain, beyond the "crossed" stars and Fates, then Tybalt himself fits that bill.

Mercutio   *[handwritten: emotional, loyal, die-charming { whimsical / temper / combative]*

Other than the eponymous lovers, Mercutio, kinsman to the Prince, is by far the most engaging and memorable character in the drama. His astoundingly vulgar sense of humor upstages even the Nurse's, and his buoyant attitude toward everything not named Capulet is evident from his first spoken line, responding to Romeo's torpid statement of lovesickness for Rosaline: "Nay, gentle Romeo, we must have you dance" (1.4.13). Despite this generally delightful disposition, Mercutio angers quickly, and his belligerence rivals Tybalt's, a characteristic on account of which both gallants ultimately are killed. His two most famous statements demonstrate well his dichotomous personality, on the one hand pleasurably, whimsically inventive and on the other fiercely combative: respectively, his Queen Mab monologue of Act I, scene iv, and his viciously bitter declaration of "A plague o'both . . . houses!" upon being slain (3.1.111). Ironically, it is the combination of these two halves of his personality that truly lead to his death, for while he enters parlay with Tybalt lightheartedly at the beginning of Act III, enjoying verbal disputes as much as ribaldry, the escalated banter and his aggressive temper eventually get the best of him when he draws and fences. Truth be told, Mercutio has little cause to avenge his murder by calling a plague on either warring house more so than on himself.

Paris

County Paris is a nobleman who wishes throughout the play to wed Juliet. He is confident and prudent, approaching Lord Capulet repeatedly to request this betrothal. Whether what he actually feels for Juliet can be called love is debatable; certainly his emotions for her do not approach the sincere, overpowering passion exhibited by Romeo, against whom he is rightly juxtaposed. The difference between these two young suitors is in no way better exhibited than by a consideration of their distinct language in wooing or speaking of Juliet, for while both are introduced as utterly conventional lovers—like Romeo, Paris is compared to a book, by Lady Capulet in Act I, scene iii—Paris's romantic expressions never escape predictable formality as Romeo's quickly do. Compare, for example, their respective farewell vows to Juliet at the Capulets' crypt: "Sweet flower, with flowers thy bridal bed I strew," Paris apostrophizes, "Which with sweet water nightly I will dew" (5.3.12–14), paling to the passion of Romeo's determined oath, "O, here / Will I set up my everlasting rest / And shake the yoke of inauspicious stars / From this world-wearied flesh! Eyes, look your last" (5.3.109–112). Paris is no villain, surely, but even his most honorable attempt at heroism, confronting Romeo before Juliet's tomb, is snuffed out quickly by the genuineness of zealous young love.

Prince Escalus

The Prince's name, Escalus, is divulged by Shakespeare nowhere but in the stage directions announcing his first entrance, in Act I, scene i; it is a Latinized version of *Della Scala*, the name of Verona's royal family throughout the late 13th and 14th centuries. It often is remarked that Escalus himself serves little function in the drama but to symbolize civic law and order. He lacks any personality distinct from such officialism, yet he ironically expresses solemn regret and accepts personal blame for, in his estimation, decisions leading directly to the deaths of Romeo, Juliet, Mercutio, and others; "I, for winking at your discords too, / Have lost a brace of kinsmen. All are punished," he tells the assembled Montagues and Capulets at the drama's conclusion (5.3.304–305). Nevertheless, Prince Escalus's chief function in the drama is to introduce the condition of Romeo's banishment that ultimately engenders the tragic denouement. Like many other characters in *Romeo and Juliet*, Escalus, despite his lofty position, simply plays, albeit unwittingly, his role as an instrument of the "crossed" stars.

Themes and Motifs of Note

As with all Shakespearean plays, there is more to *Romeo and Juliet* than just its plot. One of the many reasons for Shakespeare's supreme position in the English literary canon is his constant incorporation of philosophy into his dramas; we don't just attend a performance of *Macbeth*, for example, to witness a story concerning the fall of a powerful, overly ambitious nobleman, but also to consider, right alongside the Bard himself, the very natures of power, ambition, guilt, and loyalty as they truly exist within our world and ourselves. Although rarely overtly didactic with his themes, Shakespeare consistently incorporated these philosophical and sociological statements about human life into his plays, a rule to which *Romeo and Juliet* is no exception.

On the other hand, the commonness of *motifs*, recurring symbols that gather importance as they accumulate throughout a narrative, varies among plays. Arguably more common in Shakespeare's tragedies and romances than in his histories and comedies, such symbols can be read as grand artistic strokes, not necessarily as philosophical or even as tied to real life as themes are, yet much more powerful than simple one-off metaphors. Strong intertextuality sometimes exists with various plays' usage of similar motifs, and students' recognition and understanding of them absolutely grows with exposure to numerous Shakespearean works (I include the sonnets here), especially those works composed together or near one another during the Bard's career.

This collection represents the major themes and motifs in *Romeo and Juliet*, although other, less significant examples remain ripe for analysis.

Love Doesn't Conquer After All

Romeo and Juliet's most obvious theme is, paradoxically, also its most debatable. Although the passionate love that Romeo and Juliet feel for one another is inarguable, the way in which the outcome to which it leads them should be viewed—positively or negatively—absolutely is arguable. To generations of romantics raised on incalculably numerous popular incarnations of the "love conquers all" cliché (just check out the daily paper's slate of cookie cutter "date movies" for proof of the sentiment's omnipresence), the eponymous couple's bitterly ironic demise is especially tragic. The truth, of course, is that we *want* Romeo and Juliet to wind up together, regardless of their circumstances: happily remaining in Verona, exiled to Mantua, secretly eloped to who-knows-where . . . it doesn't matter, so long as their perfect, fairy tale love continues to exist, rendering all extraneous aspects of their lives insignificant and proving to the audience once again that true love will always win the day. Well, *A Midsummer Night's Dream* may satisfy that appetite, but the slate of opponents to such a happy ending in this play—their disapproving families, enacted civic laws, and even the "inauspicious stars" themselves—simply overwhelm their chances and our sentimental wishes (5.3.111). Yes, this incredibly powerful love does end Italy's most famous family feud, but it takes the unnecessary deaths of children to do so, and whether or not we agree that such a positive flicker of hope outweighs the darkness of the denouement, it is clear by the Prince's summative couplet—" . . . never was a story of more woe / Than this of Juliet and her Romeo"—that this drama is no fairy tale (5.3.320–321).

The Past Against the Future

Chaucer's Miller comically opined that "youthe and elde is often at debaat," an observation ostensibly true throughout *Romeo and Juliet*. Its clearest exposition, of course, is the fact that the young lovers both defy their parents not only in wedding one another, but also in falling in love in the first place. Additionally, however, this antagonism between age and youth is present in Lord Capulet's initial rebuttal of Paris, himself believably younger than Capulet, who cites Juliet's lack of age as the reason why she is not yet "ripe to be a bride" (1.2.11). Capulet likewise rebukes Tybalt as "goodman boy" and "a saucy boy" when the latter aims to disrupt the family ball by attacking Romeo (1.5.86, 94). Juliet's Nurse and the Friar begin on the side of youth, truly, but even Lawrence's introduction in the play is full of language that calls attention to his elder distinctness from young Montague: the two repeatedly refer to each other as "Father" and "son"; upon learning of Romeo's infatuation with Juliet, Friar Lawrence generally chides "Young men" whose "love then lies / Not truly in their hearts, but in their eyes" (2.3.71–72); and the scene's closing interchange—"I stand on sudden haste," pleads Romeo, to which Lawrence replies, "Wisely and slow. They stumble that run fast" (2.3.100–101)—absolutely exclaims the prudence and superiority of age. Eventually, of course, even the Nurse and the Friar, the play's two sympathetic and cooperative elders, abandon the young lovers to their fate.

Examination through a wider lens illuminates this theme's most critical and clear expression. Although Romeo and Juliet's love represents not only youth, but also the future—implying a generalized hope, plus particular familial reunion and growth (i.e., children of their own)—what prevents such progress is their families' hatred, so historical and ingrained that neither the cause nor the time of its inception is ever divulged, if even remembered. In short, the past prevents the potential future from occurring, creating instead an imminent future that may include sorrowful regret and reconciliation, but will be totally devoid of love.

The Futility of Fighting Fate

Although Shakespeare courts ancient Greek traditions, his dramatic inventiveness prevents our categorization of *Romeo and Juliet* as a fully extrapolated Greek tragedy. Nevertheless, there is as clear a sense here as in anything by Sophocles that the protagonists are fighting a predestined, unavoidable end. The drama is bookended, of course, by explications of that fact: the first Prologue famously characterizes the lovers as "star-crossed" from the get-go (6), and Romeo settles, in the last scene, on their coupled deaths as the only way to "shake the yoke of inauspicious stars / From this world-wearied flesh." (5.3.111–112). In between, the audience is reminded of that improvidence by such parallelism as Romeo's remark that "Two of the fairest stars in all the heaven" attract the gaze of Juliet (2.2.15), who later hypothesizes that were night itself to "Take [Romeo] and cut him out in little stars," its own augmented beauty would outshine even the sun (3.2.24). More explicitly, Romeo calls himself "Fortune's fool!" (3.1.142) and later resolves to "defy you, stars!" (5.1.25). Such references to divinely imposed destiny, direct and indirect, pepper the text.

Unlike Oedipus or Creon, however, neither Romeo nor Juliet meets that unavoidable end on account of what is commonly called a fatal flaw, but what in the Greek tragedies is more accurately identified as *hamartia*, an excess in one particular aspect of personality that ultimately leads the protagonist to an agonizingly obvious self-immolation (hamartia also can refer to a mistake the character commits that leads to some form of destruction). Lear and Macbeth arguably suffer from such characteristic excessiveness, but Romeo and Juliet's inevitable demise seems entirely undue to anything other than the Fates' arbitrariness. Even Juliet acknowledges that "Fortune, Fortune, all men call thee fickle" (3.5.60). Probably this unjustified improvidence makes the outcome, in most readers' estimations, all the more tragic, and the lovers' unavoidable march to it even more excruciating and unnerving to behold.

Omnipresent Irony

Defined generally as a difference between one's expectation and reality, irony is all over the place in *Romeo and Juliet*. Romeo meets the girl of his dreams, only to discover that she's his enemy by birthright. The two wed nevertheless, only to discover soon that Juliet is betrothed to another suitor of her parents' choosing. Attempting in public to pacify the combatants of their familial war, thereby engendering reconciliation, Romeo brings about nothing but murder, vengeance, and banishment. And of course, the hero, believing the feigned death of his bride, tragically takes his own life just moments before she awakes from a long nap, at which point she arises expecting to run away with him, but finds instead that actual suicide is the only agreeable next step. Dozens of smaller examples of irony can be unearthed from the text, but we hardly need to find their sum in order to get Shakespeare's apparent message: despite our best intentions and strongest hopes, nothing in life ever turns out quite how we envision it will.

Speed

diction for quick pass. of time

Romeo's first lines in the play concern the passage of time, particularly its slowness: "Ay me, sad hours seem long" (1.1.165). Immediately, Shakespeare's diction emphasizes quickness—"Was that my father that went hence so fast?" Romeo asks Benvolio in the very next line—and the Bard continues to emphasize accelerated and lost time through the rest of the tragedy. Mercutio complains in Act I, scene iv that Romeo et al. "burn daylight," and once the group arrives at the Capulets' ball, Lord Capulet's incredulous response to an acquaintance's age likewise emphasizes time's hasty flight (44). In the famous balcony scene, Juliet worries that Romeo's oaths are "too rash, too unadvised, too sudden, / Too like the lightning, which doth cease to be / Ere one can say 'it lightens'" (2.2.125–127), foreshadowing Friar Lawrence's advisement in the next scene that the lovers should proceed "Wisely and slow [for] They stumble that run fast" (2.3.101) and subsequent caution that "Too swift arrives as tardy as too slow" (2.6.15).

Ironically, time's rapidity plays as crucial a role in ensuring the play's tragic outcome as does any one character. The Friar concocts his rash plan as a response to Capulet's unexpected decision to expedite Juliet and Paris's marriage, a temporary quarantine delays Father John in bringing Romeo news that his wife is but feigning death, a setback that proves critically costly, and the lovers' agonizingly unnecessary suicides could be prevented by Lawrence's arrival at the Capulets' sepulcher just moments earlier. The most obvious instrument of the infamous stars "crossed" against the lovers, time, particularly its unceasing acceleration throughout the play, acts as a vice, tightening the pressure on Romeo and Juliet until the last scene, when just a few lost seconds make all of the difference between a potentially happy ending and the dreadful denouement that is.

Light and Dark

The ageless literary symbols of light and darkness get considerable airplay in *Romeo and Juliet*, although sometimes rather ambiguously. Upon first apprehending Juliet's beauty, Romeo famously remarks, "O, she doth teach the torches to burn bright!" (1.5.51), a judgment later echoed by his description of the Capulets' tomb as "A lantern . . . For here lies Juliet, and her beauty makes / This vault a feasting presence full of light" (5.3.84–86). Later, when awaiting a tryst with her new husband, Juliet summons both night and Romeo by stating that her expected "day in night . . . wilt lie upon the wings of night / Whiter than new snow upon a raven's back" (3.2.18–20). Archetypal portrayals of light as positive and darkness as negative are sometimes inverted, however, such as by Romeo's ironic statement when leaving his bride at daybreak, "More light and light, more dark and dark our woes" and Juliet's desire for darkness to descend quickly, allowing her secret rendezvous with Romeo to occur (3.5.36). Even more strikingly, illumination is frequently equated with violence, as in Juliet's rather gruesome proposal that were night to apprehend Romeo at death and "cut him out in little stars, / . . . he [would] make the face of heaven so fine / That all the world [would] be in love with night" (3.2.24–26).

Allusions to heavenly bodies are especially common. Soliloquizing in the balcony scene alone, Romeo compares Juliet, directly or indirectly, to the sun, the stars, daylight, and a "bright angel" (2.2.29). Paradoxically, though, such references often present mixed views of heavenly illumination as either positive or negative, peaceful or aggressive; immediately after calling Juliet "the sun," for example, Romeo entreats her / it to "Arise . . . and kill the envious moon" (2.2.3–4). Shakespeare consistently presents daybreak as woeful, moreover: the first dawn reportedly sees Romeo moping about after Rosaline, the third forces him to leave his beloved's bed and flee to Mantua, the fourth sunrise marks the Nurse's discovery of the apparently dead Juliet, and on the final morning, immediately following the lovers' suicides, "The sun for sorrow will not show his head" (5.3.317). And, we cannot forget, of course, that this apparently inevitable denouement is all the fault of the "inauspicious stars" themselves (5.3.111). Just what Shakespeare is trying to say with such a mixed bag of references and connotations is debatable, but their commonness and massive interpretability make them, if nothing else, absolutely worthy of our critical attention.

Conclusion

I hope that this chapter has convinced you not only of the thematic and symbolic depth of this wonderful play, but also of its appropriateness for instruction in upper level English classes. The next five chapters detail various techniques for engaging your students in a demanding, differentiated, and ultimately enjoyable study of *Romeo and Juliet*, beginning with Chapter 4, which concerns students' initial reading of the drama.

Reading *Romeo and Juliet*

This chapter contains activities and assignments to guide students through the initial process of reading *Romeo and Juliet*. Unlike those to come, this chapter is organized according to the play's five acts, through which students' reading obviously will proceed. For each act, I have included assignments, quizzes, and worksheets that aim not only to augment students' understanding of the plot and characters, but also to require engagement of the text and higher level thinking, and thus to prepare them for the type of in-depth observation and analysis required by the AP Literature and Composition Exam. Specifically, I have provided teachers with the following components for each of the five acts: vocabulary analysis, journaling questions, taxonomical worksheets, and AP-style quizzes.

Vocabulary Analysis

One of the major difficulties facing inexperienced students of Shakespeare concerns his diction (syntax is another common cause of difficulty, but I consider it separately in the next chapter). In his literary corpus, Shakespeare utilized approximately 21,000 different words, many of which, of course, are archaic or otherwise unfamiliar to even the most well-read of modern adolescents. As a result, one of the biggest boons that encountering Shakespeare offers such students is the opportunity to improve their own vocabularies, as well as their understanding of the ways in which words and languages are formed and evolve.

Believing that linguistic instruction, especially instruction designed to build vocabulary, is always more effective when it is both student-directed and contextualized in taught curricula, I here include a vocabulary web—Figure 11—that students can use as a template for their investigations of diction.

As students proceed through *Romeo and Juliet*, they should pick out words that either are incomprehensible or interesting to them, then utilize the web in Figure 11 as an organizational mechanism for further research. For each of the five acts, I have suggested words that students commonly find confusing; teachers may wish to assign analyses of them prior to reading the acts and scenes in which they occur, thereby anticipating and inoculating students against such difficulties before they arise.

Additionally, there are many creative ways in which classroom teachers can "publicize" or spread students' products utilizing the vocabulary web, helping all members of a given class to benefit from the scholarship of individual learners. Bulletin boards, simple pair-and-shares, collected linguistic folios or mini-dictionaries, and oral presentations to one's own or other classes are all highly feasible options for further "using" the knowledge that students garner through their own usage of this web.

Vocabulary lists for each of the five acts are included in Table 3. The list provides reference points to where each word occurs in the text.

Journaling Questions

When I teach Shakespeare to my own AP Literature students, I always ask them to complete journaling assignments on nights when they read for homework. Daily reading quizzes following such homework assignments are useful, certainly, but do not always ensure that students both read fully and give their entire attention to a given night's assignment. Asking them to respond analytically to their readings, however, requires that they mine Shakespeare's scenes for particularly telling details and quotations; interpret characters' motivations, tones, and actions; pay close attention to symbolism and literary devices; and ultimately report their findings in well-organized, strongly supported short essays. Such journal entries prove to be exceptional practice for the kinds of quick thinking and analytical writing that students are required to produce on the AP Literature and Composition Exam itself. If you have students with special needs who need adaptations for journaling activities (or just need a break from essay writing), you may wish to offer alternative options, such as blog entries of their thoughts to allow for keyboarding accommodations to handwriting difficulties, detailed drawings with notations explaining their decisions and pointing to textual references, or recordings of the student speaking aloud his or her ideas, perhaps in a podcast format that his or her classmates can download (tape recorders and microphones that attach to iPods and other mp3 players are handy for this, as are various computer

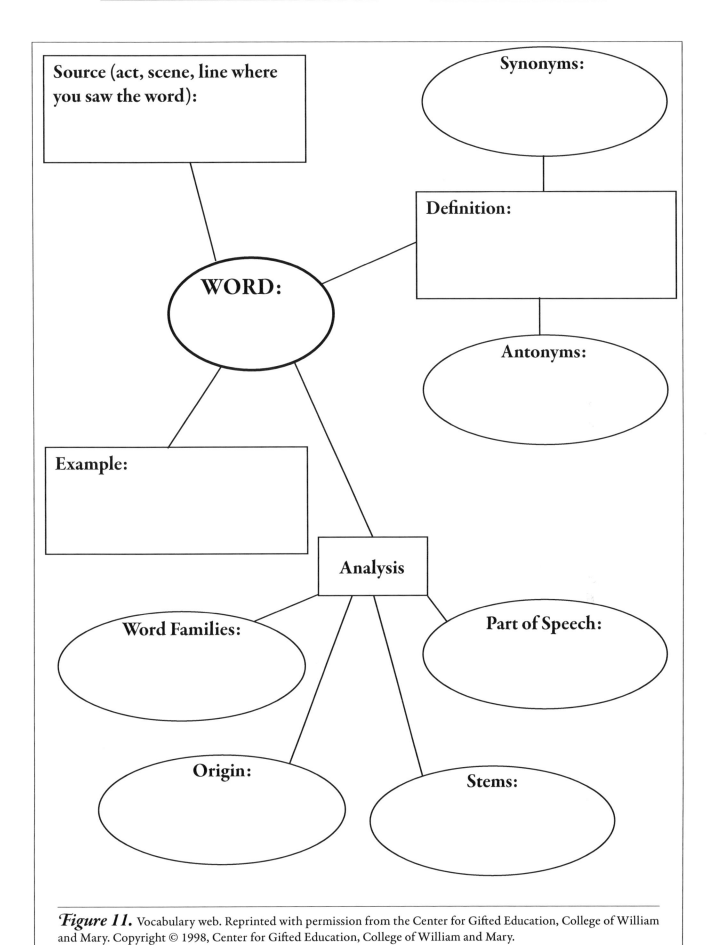

Source (act, scene, line where you saw the word):

Synonyms:

Definition:

WORD:

Antonyms:

Example:

Analysis

Word Families:

Part of Speech:

Origin:

Stems:

Figure 11. Vocabulary web. Reprinted with permission from the Center for Gifted Education, College of William and Mary. Copyright © 1998, Center for Gifted Education, College of William and Mary.

TABLE 3
Vocabulary Lists for Romeo and Juliet

Act I	Act II	Act III	Act IV	Act V
piteous (1 Prologue.7)	extremity (2 Prologue.14)	addle (3.1.25)	immoderate (4.1.6)	presage (5.1.2)
naught (1 Prologue.11)	purblind (2.1.15)	zounds (3.1.50)	inundation (4.1.12)	apothecary (5.1.40)
choler (1.1.3)	demesnes (2.1.23)	appertaining (3.1.64)	prorogue (4.1.49)	penury (5.1.52)
partisan (1.1.74)	invocation (2.1.30)	bandying (3.1.90)	arbitrating (4.1.64)	caitiff (5.1.55)
pernicious (1.1.86)	vestal (2.2.8)	lenity (3.1.128)	surcease (4.1.99)	cordial (5.1.90)
cankered (1.1.97)	livery (2.2.8)	martial (3.1.169)	abate (4.1.122)	obsequies (5.3.16)
withal (1.1.114)	discourse (2.2.13)	dexterity (3.1.171)	peevish (4.2.14)	mattock (5.3.22)
augment (1.1.135)	entreat (2.2.16)	amerce (3.1.200)	gadding (4.2.17)	inexorable (5.3.38)
portentous (1.1.144)	bestride (2.2.34)	amorous (3.2.8)	behest (4.2.20)	haughty (5.3.49)
importune (1.1.148)	wherefore (2.2.36)	garish (3.2.27)	enjoined (4.2.20)	unhallowed (5.3.54)
shrift (1.1.162)	henceforth (2.2.55)	eloquence (3.2.36)	prostrate (4.2.21)	interred (5.3.87)
transgression (1.1.192)	alack (2.2.76)	bedaubed (3.2.61)	provision (4.2.39)	ensign (5.3.94)
propagate (1.1.194)	enmity (2.2.78)	bier (3.2.66)	orison (4.3.3)	sunder (5.3.100)
assailing (1.1.221)	prorogued (2.2.83)	dissembler (3.2.94)	loathsome (4.3.47)	abhorred (5.3.104)
posterity (1.1.228)	fain (2.2.93)	tributary (3.2.113)	environed (4.3.51)	paramour (5.3.105)
forsworn (1.1.231)	perjury (2.2.97)	calamity (3.3.3)	solace (4.5.53)	inauspicious (5.3.111)
languish (1.2.50)	idolatry (2.2.120)	usurer (3.3.133)	beguiled (4.5.61)	contagion (5.3.157)
scant (1.2.106)	repose (2.2.130)	reconcile (3.3.161)	melancholy (4.5.92)	churl (5.3.168)
fortnight (1.3.17)	procure (2.2.152)	jocund (3.5.9)	lour (4.5.100)	descry (5.3.187)
stint (1.3.53)	beseech (2.2.158)	affray (3.5.33)	prate (4.5.139)	sovereign (5.3.202)
disposition (1.3.70)	osier (2.3.7)	divining (3.5.54)	pestilent (4.5.149)	ambiguities (5.3.225)
lineament (1.3.89)	predominant (2.3.30)	runagate (3.5.94)		forbear (5.3.229)
margent (1.3.92)	distempered (2.3.35)	dram (3.5.95)		direful (5.3.234)
prolixity (1.4.3)	ere (2.3.52)	vexed (3.5.100)		scourge (5.3.302)
hoodwink (1.4.4)	intercession (2.3.58)	beseech (3.5.111)		
ambling (1.4.11)	sallow (2.3.74)	conduit (3.5.134)		
visage (1.4.30)	doting (2.3.87)	minion (3.5.156)		
cote (1.4.31)	rancor (2.3.99)	prudence (3.5.179)		
wanton (1.4.35)	minim (2.4.23)	puling (3.5.195)		
midwife (1.4.59)	lamentable (2.4.32)	stratagem (3.5.221)		
courtier (1.4.77)	cheveril (2.4.85)			
benefice (1.4.86)	mar (2.4.118)			
ambuscade (1.4.89)	bawd (2.4.132)			
anon (1.4.90)	shrived (2.4.186)			
begot (1.4.105)	topgallant (2.4.193)			
forfeit (1.4.118)	prating (2.4.203)			
knave (1.5.32)	clout (2.4.209)			
sirrah (1.5.34)	sententious (2.4.214)			
nuptial (1.5.41)	perchance (2.5.3)			
antic (1.5.64)	pinioned (2.5.7)			
solemnity (1.5.65)	bandy (2.5.14)			
disparagement (1.5.79)	poultice (2.5.68)			
semblance (1.5.83)	countervail (2.6.4)			
mannerly (1.5.109)	gossamer (2.6.18)			
	blazon (2.6.26)			

Note. All references to line numbers are based on the Folger edition of the play [Shakespeare, W. (1992). *Romeo and Juliet* (Rev. ed., B. A. Mowat & P. Werstine, Eds.). Washington, DC: Folger Shakespeare Library. (Original work written 1594)].

programs, including Microsoft Word's notebook feature and Apple's ⟨
software).

I do not grade these entries using any extraneous rubric, but sim,
swiftly assess students' responses based upon three criteria: length and ⟨
their utilization of textual support, and the "correctness" of their analyses.
last criterion is subjective, of course, especially because the questions themsel\
generally are quite open-ended, but it allows me to discount responses that simply
don't fly based upon evidence and/or sensibleness. Over the course of one unit of
Shakespearean study, such entries accumulate within students' journals, eventually
providing both a much more substantive measure of pupils' engagement with text
than reading quizzes, and an excellent resource for later, in-depth review of the
play and its important elements.

Lists of potential questions for each of the five acts are included below.

- *Act I, scene i:* When the play opens, Sampson and Gregory, two servants of the house of Capulet, are walking along the public streets armed with swords and bucklers; later, the Lords of the Houses of Montague and Capulet enter their servants' melee, although they never actually come to blows. What kind of an atmosphere do these and other such details convey to an attentive audience?

- *Act I, scene ii:* In this scene, Paris and Romeo are juxtaposed. Paris speaks only to Lord Capulet, while Romeo speaks only to Capulet's Servingman and to Benvolio. Based upon the minimal characterization offered in this scene, compare and contrast these two young men: How are they apparently alike, and how are they seemingly different?

- *Act I, scene iii:* Juliet in this scene speaks with two matronly figures: her Nurse and Lady Capulet, who actually is her birthmother. These two older women apparently have very different personalities and relationships with Juliet, not to mention priorities and observable senses of social grace. Compare and contrast these two mother-figures: How are they seemingly the same, and how are they different?

- *Act I, scene iv:* In scene iv, we encounter Mercutio, one of the most successful scene-stealers in all of Shakespeare's plays. Despite his apparent vulgarity and hysterical unpredictability—or perhaps because of them—many readers adore this character. Well, as the saying goes, one never gets a second chance to make a first impression. Based upon this first encounter with Mercutio, what is *your* impression of the man and his personality? How do you respond to him, either emotionally or intellectually?

- *Act I, scene v:* As demonstrated in scene v, not all members of the Capulet household are alike, especially regarding their varied responses to Romeo Montague's uninvited appearance at their feast. Consider all of the members of the Capulet household who actually recognize or interact with Romeo in this scene: What do their distinct responses to or interactions with him imply about their personalities or priorities?

- *Act II, Chorus, scene i:* The definition of dramatic irony is a difference between what characters on stage believe or perceive and what their audience, observing or reading a scene, recognizes as fact. Pick out particular examples of dramatic irony here: Why and how do the details or quotations that you choose fit this definition?

- *Act II, scene ii:* Figurative language, such as metaphors, similes, and analogies, often is used to express emotions or relationships that are difficult, if not impossible, to communicate fully using common, denotative language. In scene ii, the famed balcony scene, Romeo and Juliet commonly and clearly demonstrate this usage of figurative language to convey the otherwise inexpressible aspects of their love. How and when do they do so? Pick out and analyze as many examples as you can find of the use of figurative language in this scene.

- *Act II, scene iii:* One of the strongest themes conveyed in *Romeo and Juliet* concerns the opposition of maturity and youth, a conflict that is portrayed in scene iii both through dialogue and through the characters' personal responses to particular events and ideas. Find examples in this scene of this opposition of youth and agedness: What does Shakespeare seem to be saying about their antagonism (i.e., either how does he himself or how do his characters—perhaps unintentionally or indirectly—side in this conflict of age)?

- *Act II, scene iv:* There are many common responses to scene iv among readers and playgoers, but perhaps the most common is laughter, for portions of this scene are inherently comedic. Where and from what causes does this humor originate? Pick out particularly comedic moments and dissect them, ascertaining their emotional, social, physical, or verbal underpinnings (exactly what it is about these specific moments that makes us laugh).

- *Act II, scene v:* Scene v affords the audience an excellent portrait of the relationship between Juliet and her Nurse, as well as of the two characters' distinct personalities. How does Shakespeare in this scene characterize these two, both as separate individuals and as a pair?

- *Act II, scene vi:* This scene exhibits Friar Lawrence's personality perhaps more strongly than it does either Romeo's or Juliet's. How is he characterized by Shakespeare in scene vi, and what can you tell about the Friar's personality and thoughts based upon his dialogue?

- *Act III, scene i:* Suffice it so say that things go downhill in this first scene of Act III! In your estimation, who or what is to blame for the sudden devolution of both the public peace and the potentially happy future envisioned at the end of Act II? Support your response by citing particular events in scene i.

🕮 *Act III, scene ii:* Like the previous one, scene ii is a passionate rollercoaster, carrying its characters between emotional extremes at a very rapid pace. How did Shakespeare pull off such oscillation convincingly? What particular moments or aspects of this scene make the characters' emotional fluctuations and responsive dialogue believable?

🕮 *Act III, scene iii:* The majority of scene iii is comprised of Friar Lawrence's response to Romeo's heartbroken hysteria. In any staged drama, the delivery of dialogue, considered distinctly from actual spoken words, is a mechanism by which actors can sway an audience's emotions and thoughts; in this scene, particularly, it is very clear just how Lawrence should deliver the lines that he is given to speak. As such, consider both his words and his implicit or assumed delivery: Does Friar Lawrence speak for you as a reader in this scene, echoing your own thoughts and expressions, or does he speak in contrast to them? Cite particular dialogic examples to support your answer.

🕮 *Act III, scene iv:* Although only 38 lines long, this scene is among the most important in the play thus far. Why? Make sure that in answering this question you predict possible outcomes or effects of this scene's events and decisions.

🕮 *Act III, scene v:* Among the literary devices that Shakespeare utilized most commonly in *Romeo and Juliet* was *juxtaposition*, the placement of contrary objects or images side by side in order to evoke a particular reaction or symbolic effect. In scene v, he creates many such juxtapositions: of light and dark, of day and night, and of air and earth, just to name a few. What are some of the reactions or symbolic effects that he thereby engenders (i.e., what do such juxtapositions actually *do* here, and why are they important)?

🕮 *Act IV, scene i:* The first scene of Act IV demonstrates well the statement that words are not necessarily a reflection of a speaker's true feelings. Much verbal irony, a difference between what one says and what one actually means, is exhibited in scene i, but there also is much legitimate dialogue spoken, words that truly denote—often powerfully—what their speaker is feeling. Find examples of both kinds of language in this scene: that which does not convey a speaker's honest feelings, and that which does. How does the actual diction, the words that Shakespeare chose for his characters to speak, differ in both cases?

🕮 *Act IV, scene ii:* Lord Capulet's anger is seemingly pacified in scene ii, but how, exactly? Members of his household seem to know, probably from experience, how to assuage the man's fiery temper. Judging from this scene, what such tactics do they enact to do so, and why do they apparently work?

🎕 *Act IV, scene iii:* Three fourths of this scene is composed of Juliet's fearful soliloquy, most of which is itself made up of strongly connotative imagery, language that engages or recreates the five senses. What examples of imagistic language in her soliloquy are the most powerful or evocative, in your estimation, and considering the context of scene iii, why do they strike the emotional or intellectual chords that they do?

🎕 *Act IV, scene iv:* Even if removed entirely from its contextualized placement at this moment of *Romeo and Juliet*, the dialogue of scene iv would still convey clearly an atmosphere of anxious anticipation and feverish work. How, exactly, does Shakespeare create that effect here? Consider in your answer not only the characters' diction, but also their syntax.

🎕 *Act IV, scene v:* Numerous times in this individual scene both characters and their audience are subjected to an emotional process of buildup and subsequent release, buildup and release, buildup and release. How many instances of this flux can you identify in scene v, and what is their overall effect on an audience watching or reading, especially considering its context near the end of the play's dramatic arc?

🎕 *Act V, scene i:* As *Romeo and Juliet* draws near its resolution, Shakespeare implies more strongly than ever that things are not what they seem or should be. In scene i, he conveys this impression not only through plot events, but also connotatively and subtly in characters' speech, through two distinct literary devices: *personification*, the attribution of human characteristics to inhuman things, and the use of *metaphor*. What particularly relevant or symbolic examples of these devices can you find, and how do they contribute to the overall atmosphere of the play at this point in time?

🎕 *Act V, scene ii:* Throughout the play, Shakespeare has implied, if not outright stated, that Romeo and Juliet's inevitably tragic end will be a result of fate, fortune, destiny, supernatural improvidence, and so on. How does scene ii, although only 30 lines long, apparently confirm that opinion, providing proof that the stars really may be "crossed" against these young lovers?

🎕 *Act V, scene iii:* Performances of plays on Elizabethan stages, like Shakespeare's own Globe Theatre, were almost universally devoid of set decorations. Thus, stage directions and props were important during dramatic productions as ways for actors, directors, and stage managers to imply the settings of particular scenes without actually having to pay for and construct them. The final scene of *Romeo and Juliet* is an excellent example of Shakespeare's incorporation of props and stage directions to this effect. What examples of such utilization can you find, and what aspects of the scene's hypothetical set do they imply?

Taxonomical Worksheets

Worksheets as a genre of student practice and/or assessment often get a bad rap from teachers of the gifted, who perhaps see them as prepackaged busywork for instructors lacking the creativity or energy to design their own assessments or engage their classes interpersonally. I have no such essential problem with worksheets, so long as they are truly demanding instruments that eschew tediously repetitive exercises in order to stretch students' intellectual reasoning, practices of scholarship, and creative faculties instead. To this end, I have designed and included five worksheets—one for each act of *Romeo and Juliet*—that reward students for engaging in cognitively and creatively demanding tasks in consideration of and response to the play. Briefly stated, because I have focused these worksheets around the concept of taxonomically organized intellectual processes, the more challenging the task that a student completes, the more he or she is to be rewarded in the grade book.

These worksheets are not based strictly upon any single taxonomy of cognitive processes, although they certainly resemble them all in their requirement of academic tasks that escalate in incremental difficulty. Students who wish to earn the highest marks on these worksheets are obligated to ratchet up their analytical and creative performances grade by grade, level by level, completing not only the task attached to the mark that he or she desires, but also those assignments "below" it on the worksheet. Wholly, highly motivated students who successfully complete these worksheets in their entireties and thereby earn "A" grades are forced to digest and respond to *Romeo and Juliet* in a myriad of ways, demonstrating everything from their comprehension of basic events to their ability to formulate and defend judgmental hierarchies concerning extremely subjective ethical topics.

There surely are a number of correct or otherwise legitimate ways in which students can answer the questions or complete the tasks on these worksheets; there is not just one "right answer" in each case. The exception, of course, is the simplest task, the one required of students who wish to earn a "D-"; it does require textual details in response to a simple fact-based assignment. As such, teachers should regard each student's answers and responses individually, considering their legitimacy in relation to the text itself, not in relation solely to other students' answers and responses.

When assessing students' products, pay attention to tasks and questions that require the consideration of multiple parts (e.g., the fulfillment of a given task *plus* the provision of textual support for that task). Students who complete only half of an assigned task's requirements should not receive credit for the completion of that task. Moreover, students should be required to complete all of the tasks and answer all of the questions listed below the one for which they wish to earn the highest grade; do not just award a student an "A" for completing the "A" assignment, but make him or her complete all of the others, as well. In this way, teachers not only can ensure that learners experience and engage in a large variety of cognitive processes, but they also can guarantee that students consider multiple areas and details of the act in question, rather than just one isolated scene or event.

The taxonomical worksheets can be found at the end of this chapter, on pages 51–60.

AP-Style Quizzes

On the AP Literature and Composition Exam, students are required to read short passages of prose and poetry, then correctly answer questions that demand precise understanding and excellent analysis of their literary devices, authors' intentions, overarching themes, and holistic structures. This section of the examination puts students under tremendous pressure to manage their time well, as it usually involves approximately the same number of multiple-choice questions as it allows students minutes in which to answer them (usually 60 questions in 60 minutes). Allowing one minute per question, absolutely no time is left for students to devote to reading, annotating, and considering the excerpts themselves! Needless to say, this multiple-choice section is not one that AP Literature students should approach cold; practicing on instruments that mimic the section's format and level of difficulty helps students to develop time and stress management techniques, test-taking strategies, interpretive-analytical skills, a strong knowledge base, and general comfort with the demanding assessment.

I have designed these AP-style quizzes with just such mimicry (and eventual test-taking benefit) in mind. They are *not* to be considered reading quizzes to assess students' understanding of assigned homework, but rather pop quizzes to be administered respectively at the completion of each of the play's acts. If teachers administer them in this way, then students' cognitive performances will escalate in difficulty act by act; the quiz concerning a passage from Act I, for example, requires students almost exclusively to identify particular literary devices, while its counterpart regarding a passage from Act V demands that they demonstrate holistic understanding of the excerpt and ability to analyze the meaning of its distinct parts. I also have included suggested time limits for all quizzes, which, if followed, should similarly help students to develop comfort with the intense pressure under which they will be placed by the AP Exam.

The AP-style quizzes are included at the end of this chapter, on pages 61–70. Detailed answers to the quizzes are included on pages 71–76.

Lesson Plan 1: Tchaikovsky's Symphonic Version of *Romeo and Juliet*

The activity in this lesson plan asks students to compare Peter Tchaikovsky's famous Overture-Fantasy *Romeo and Juliet* to the plot and dramatic elements of Shakespeare's play. The lesson aims to help students focus on a totally different expression of the emotional undercurrents running throughout Shakespeare's plot, in musical contrast to the spoken dialogue of the play, and review the entirety of *Romeo and Juliet*'s action.

The complete lesson plan for this activity is included on pages 48–50.

Conclusion

This chapter concludes with the reproducible pages for each of the acts' taxonomical activities and the AP-style quizzes. The next chapter will provide multiple activities for understanding *Romeo and Juliet* as a meaningful work of art, helping students move beyond basic comprehension and identification of key themes and elements, into a deeper, more personal ownership of the play as a relevant human document.

Chapter Materials

Tchaikovsky's Symphonic Version of *Romeo and Juliet*

- **Purpose/Objective:** This activity is a comparison of Peter Tchaikovsky's famous Overture-Fantasy *Romeo and Juliet* to the plot and dramatic elements of Shakespeare's play. As such, it is an attempt both to access students' musical intelligence and to allow them an opportunity to synthesize disparate media's portrayals of the same dramatic themes. Moreover, it aims to help them focus on a totally different expression of the emotional undercurrents running throughout Shakespeare's plot, in musical contrast to the spoken dialogue of the play, and review the entirety of *Romeo and Juliet*'s action.

- **Placement:** This activity should be conducted near the end of the students' study of *Romeo and Juliet*, after they have finished reading the play and thus digested the full scope of Shakespeare's plot.

- **Materials Required:** A recorded copy of Tchaikovsky's Overture-Fantasy *Romeo and Juliet* is necessary for this activity. There are many such versions extant and readily available from various merchants.

- **Duration:** This activity should occur over approximately 45 minutes of one class period.

- **Lesson Plan:**

  1. *Anticipatory Set:* At the beginning of the activity, ask students to pair with partners and, working together, list in their notebooks or on a separate piece of paper the major events of Acts I–V of the play, simply as a matter of review. They also can refer to these critical moments of the plot while listening to Tchaikovsky's piece during the activity.

  2. *Communication of Objective:* Many students previously will have heard of Peter Tchaikovsky, and an understanding of his life is probably unnecessary for their engagement in this activity, so it is enough simply to inform the class that it will be listening for nearly 20 minutes to a "symphonic poem" by the composer, in which he conflates into one musical movement various parts of Shakespeare's *Romeo and Juliet*. As if solving a riddle, students are to listen to the Overture-Fantasy with the play's plot in mind, attempting to pick out and list in their notebooks what sections of the musical piece correlate with moments or events found in the Shakespearean drama.

3. *Listening Time:* Depending upon the pace of the recording that you choose, the entire Overture-Fantasy should run between 18 and 19 minutes. Some of the major sections of Tchaikovsky's *Romeo and Juliet*, as well as musical identifiers and potential parallels in Shakespeare's play, are listed in Table 4. As they listen, students should record in their notebooks the times at which different musical motifs appear and/or "events" occur, then theorize as to what portions of Shakespeare's plot they correlate.

4. *Discussion:* Ask the students to organize their chairs and desks in a circle, then discuss what they thought occurred during the first portions of the musical piece. This discussion should grow organically, as certain students comment upon others' ideas along the lines of, "No, I thought that part was later (or earlier), when these certain instruments played in such a way." You might wish to play once again certain motives or portions of the music as the discussion proceeds in order to aid students' justifications and considerations. At the end of the discussion, it is important to point out to the class that there is no one right answer, *per se*, as even musical critics are not able to pinpoint Tchaikovsky's exact intentions regarding parallels between his Overture-Fantasy and Shakespeare's plot; this comment should reinforce the validity of all students' usage of the musical intelligence and their individual interpretations.

Closure: Once students have returned desks and chairs to their orthodox positions, you may wish to ask them to complete another musical-interpretive activity, albeit a more personal one. Replay the Love Theme from Tchaikovsky's Overture-Fantasy and ask them to write in their notebooks what thoughts and images from their own lives pass through their minds as they listen. For the sake of authenticity, it may be important to inform the students prior to doing so that they will not be asked to share their responses; rather, they will remain totally private in their notebooks. The effect of this self-reflection, of course, will be a synthesis of the plot and drama of *Romeo and Juliet*, the emotions expressed by Tchaikovsky, and the students' experiences as high schoolers (i.e., the personalizing of their reading experience).

TABLE 4
Tchaikovsky's Musical Themes and Motifs

Approximate Time	Common Name	Musical Identifier	Potential Parallel
0:00	Hymn Theme	Low clarinets and bassoons, anguished-sounding strings	The Prologue; the inception or background of the Montague-Capulet feud; the "crossing of stars" against Romeo and Juliet
1:30	n/a	Strumming harp	The Prologue; one common theory is that the Friar is about to "tell" the lovers' story
5:00	Vendetta or Fate Theme	Short, vigorous, perhaps angry motives; full orchestra playing	The initial portrayal of the Montague-Capulet feud in Act I; "crossing of stars"
7:15	Sighing Theme	Muted strings	Romeo's feelings for Rosaline and of despair prior to meeting Juliet
8:00	Love Theme	Surging, romantic string melody	The meeting of Romeo and Juliet
9:00	n/a	Love Theme dies down fully	The balcony scene, wedding, or lovers' separation
10:00	Developmental Section	Combination of motives from the Vendetta and Hymn Themes, perhaps march-like in rhythm, culminating in a cymbal clash	The ongoing struggle between the lovers' families, punctuated by the murders of Mercutio and Tybalt
13:00	Love Theme	Same as earlier, but interrupted near 14:30 by "angry" sounds	The Friar's plan to aid Romeo and Juliet, interrupted by misdelivery of the letter
16:00	"Broken" Love Theme	Same motive over funereal drum taps in the timpani	Romeo's final speeches before taking the poison
18:00	n/a	Resumed harp strumming, new cadential version of the Love Theme, ecstatically surging	The reunion of the two families in tragedy; light emerging from darkness

Name: _____   Date: _____

Taxonomical Worksheet for Act I of *Romeo and Juliet*

Please use only the spaces provided to the right of each task/question.

To get an **A** on this assignment, you must answer this question, plus all of the ones below.	Consider the physical setting of the play's first act in Verona, Italy, as well as the physical setting of each scene in the act. Could these five scenes take place anywhere and be just as effective dramatically? Please judge whether these physical settings are actually important to the events of the act, and if you consider them important, the degree of their importance. In the space to the right, justify your evaluation.	
To get a **B+** on this assignment, you must complete this task, plus all of the ones below.	The Prologue of the play is justly famous both as a perfect Shakespearean sonnet and as a summation of the entire play's action. In the space to the right, compose a new prologue that serves the same summative purpose, albeit only for the events of the play's first act. Your new prologue, however, should remain a Shakespearean sonnet, utilizing iambic pentameter perfectly over exactly 14 lines, maintaining the rhyme scheme of a Shakespearean sonnet: ABAB CDCD EFEF GG.	

To get a **B-** on this assignment, you must complete these three tasks, plus all of the ones below.	Although they do not come to blows, when Lords Montague and Capulet draw their swords in scene i, preparing to enter the servants' melee, they effectively sanction such public outbursts by members of their respective houses. Please analyze this moment of the play, determine how exactly they communicate this sanctioning of public disruption, and then explain whether you believe that it is done inadvertently.	
To get a **C** on this assignment, you must accomplish this task, plus the ones below.	Romeo and Juliet's initial exchange of words at the Capulets' party in scene v (lines 93–110) comprise an extended (18-line) Shakespearean love sonnet. A true sonnet, however, has exactly 14 lines. Please choose four lines from these 18 to cut in order to create a true Shakespearean love sonnet, then justify your choices of all four lines.	
To get a **D+** on this assignment, you must complete this task, plus the one below.	When the play opens, Sampson and Gregory, two servants of the house of Capulet, walk along the public streets armed with swords and bucklers. Please explain what kind of an atmosphere this small detail conveys immediately to an attentive audience, and why it does so.	
To get a **D-** on this assignment, you must accomplish this task.	In scene iv of this act, Mercutio delivers his famed "Queen Mab" monologue. Dividing your product into two halves—physical characteristics and actions—please list the characteristics of the fairy queen that Mercutio offers in his speech.	

Name: _____ Date: _____

Taxonomical Worksheet for Act II of *Romeo and Juliet*

Please use only the spaces provided to the right of each task/question.

To get an **A** on this assignment, you must answer this question, plus all of the ones below.	Shakespeare writes dialogue in a variety of styles in this act: (1) rhyming couplets in iambic pentameter, (2) unrhymed (blank) iambic verse, and (3) nonmetrical prose. Justifying your claims by referring to particular examples of each style, assess his purposes in doing so. In other words, why does Shakespeare have some characters speak metrically and others not, some rhyme and others not? Examine various combinations of these three dialogic styles found in Act II and judge his possible artistic purposes in all cases.	
To get a **B+** on this assignment, you must complete this task, plus all of the ones below.	At the beginning of scene iv, Mercutio and Benvolio discuss Tybalt's letter to the Montagues' house, in which he challenges Romeo to a duel. Imagining Tybalt's complaints against Romeo (his justification for this challenge), compose a version of that very letter, written as a Shakespearean sonnet, utilizing iambic pentameter perfectly over exactly 14 lines, maintaining the rhyme scheme of a Shakespearean sonnet: ABAB CDCD EFEF GG. Make sure in your sonnet-letter to refer clearly to the transgressions against you and your household that Romeo has made.	

To get a **B-** on this assignment, you must complete this task, plus all of the ones below.	Like the previous act, Act II begins with a prologue, a sonnet spoken by the Chorus. The dramatic purposes of these two prologues, however, are entirely quite distinct. Compare and contrast the two sonnet-speeches, distinguishing between their different purposes by analyzing the diction and tone of each.	
To get a **C** on this assignment, you must accomplish this task, plus the ones below.	Both Friar Lawrence and Juliet's Nurse are characterized quite clearly in Act II. Citing particular lines as textual support for your claims, compose brief character sketches of both characters, highlighting their personalities and eccentricities as exhibited in this act.	
To get a **D+** on this assignment, you must complete this task, plus the one below.	Certainly the most famous scene in the play is this act's second scene, the balcony scene. Explain Juliet's meaning in her extended consideration of Romeo's name, from lines 36 to 52, identifying the way in which this speech is emblematic of the ill fate or bad luck against which the lovers' relationship is set.	
To get a **D-** on this assignment, you must accomplish this task.	In scene iv, Mercutio deliberately, though playfully, insults Juliet's Nurse. Identify three such statements or comments that Mercutio makes either to or about the Nurse, and explain why they are insulting or derogatory.	

Taxonomical Worksheet for Act III of *Romeo and Juliet*

Please use only the spaces provided to the right of each task/question.

<table>
<tr>
<td>To get an A on this assignment, you must answer this question, plus all of the ones below.</td>
<td>

Despite Romeo and Juliet's passionate love for one another, almost every condition or character in the play is set or, in Act III, turns against the young pair: their families, the government of Verona, their trusted friends and allies, the all-too-quick passage of time itself, and the fated destiny set forth by the stars.

Do you think that this fact, therefore, characterizes the lovers as "heroic"? Please evaluate both your personal definition of heroism generally, then use it as a gauge to evaluate whether Romeo and Juliet qualify, as of the end of Act III, as heroic.

</td>
<td></td>
</tr>
<tr>
<td>To get a B+ on this assignment, you must complete this task, plus all of the ones below.</td>
<td>

In contrast to its common usage in reference to a particular field of mathematics, the word *calculus* simply means "an organized system of evaluation, categorization, or other judgment."

At the end of scene i, Prince Escalus interrogates the bystanders to the deadly fray regarding various persons' guilt. Regardless of the Prince's decision in the text, please construct a "calculus of culpability," which you should use to rank characters' levels of blameworthiness for Mercutio's death. You should judge Romeo, Tybalt, and Mercutio himself, of course, but also consider other, more peripheral, persons to blame.

</td>
<td></td>
</tr>
</table>

To get a **B-** on this assignment, you must answer this question, plus all of the ones below.	Juliet begins the first 33 lines of scene ii with an appeal to the "gentle night" for speed in descending. An archetypal symbol throughout ages and cultures, nighttime is often associated by humans with scariness, danger, evil, and even death. Analyze Juliet's soliloquy that opens scene ii, especially its apparent dramatic irony. Particularly considering scene i's events, why is it ironic?	
To get a **C** on this assignment, you must accomplish this task, plus the ones below.	At the end of the act, her hopes and dreams having been disregarded, if not shattered, by her parents and the Nurse, Juliet decides to appeal to Friar Lawrence for help. In the space to the right, please write what you imagine her petition to Lawrence might be. Make sure to pay attention not only to her reasons, but also to her emotional tone.	
To get a **D+** on this assignment, you must complete this task, plus the one below.	In scene iii, Friar Lawrence responds to Romeo's lamentations by telling him, in brief, to "snap out of it and cheer up." Please explain Friar Lawrence's perspective, highlighting all of the reasons why, in his estimation, Romeo should cease being sorrowful.	
To get a **D-** on this assignment, you must answer this question.	By the end of Act III, both Romeo and Juliet are sentenced by authority figures to futures that they despise. What are those sentences, exactly, and when are they to be enacted (how much longer do Romeo and Juliet have together)?	

Name: _____   Date: _____

Taxonomical Worksheet for Act IV of *Romeo and Juliet*

Please use only the spaces provided to the right of each task/question.

<table>
<tr><td>To get an A on this assignment, you must accomplish this task, plus all of the ones below.</td><td>Imagine that you are Juliet, having just been told by your father that tomorrow you will be forced to marry a man whom you do not love. What would you do?

Please list all of the options that you believe are open to you—these options should be realistic in light of the world of Shakespeare's plot, as of Act IV, scene ii—and evaluate their respective levels of reasonability. Then choose which of these options you, as Juliet, would choose.</td><td></td></tr>
<tr><td>To get a B+ on this assignment, you must complete this task, plus all of the ones below.</td><td>In scene ii, Lord Capulet expedites Paris and Juliet's engagement by directing everyone "to church tomorrow." Friar Lawrence, by now, has already devised a plan to save Romeo and Juliet's relationship, but now the time is suddenly much truncated!

Juliet's Nurse apparently is no longer so inclined as Lawrence is to interfere with the Capulets' plans for their daughter, but if she were, then now would be an appropriate time for her to intervene.

Please devise an alternate plan for escape/rescue, as if it were the Nurse's, and explain why its success is at this point more realistic than Lawrence's.</td><td></td></tr>
</table>

To get a **B-** on this assignment, you must answer this question, plus all of the ones below.	Many playgoers, readers, and students throughout centuries undoubtedly have been puzzled by Shakespeare's insertion at the end of Act IV of some seemingly irrelevant dialogue among Peter and three hired musicians. What do you believe that Shakespeare's purpose was for including this dialogic aside? In the space to the right, present your hypothesis and support it logically.	
To get a **C** on this assignment, you must accomplish this task, plus the ones below.	During the first 44 lines of scene i, Friar Lawrence both speaks with and listens to a discussion between Paris and Juliet. Throughout these conversations, the Friar is probably both displeased and quite worried. Why? In the space to the right, compose an interior monologue for the Friar, verbalizing what you imagine him to be thinking to himself during this section of text.	
To get a **D+** on this assignment, you must complete this task, plus the one below.	In a long soliloquy in scene iv, Juliet expresses hesitation to enact her role in Friar Lawrence's plan. In the space to the right, please restate in your own words all of her reasons for this hesitation, plus explain how this soliloquy demonstrates Juliet's vivid imagination.	
To get a **D-** on this assignment, you must answer this question.	In scene i, Friar Lawrence concocts a plan to aid Romeo and Juliet. What are the specific details of that plan, and who is responsible for enacting which portions of it?	

Taxonomical Worksheet for Act V of *Romeo and Juliet*

Please use only the spaces provided to the right of each task/question.

To get an **A** on this assignment, you must accomplish this task, plus all of the ones below.	Who or what is truly to blame for the tragic outcome of this drama? Consider all of the factors, establishments, and persons to whom culpability might legitimately be attached, and, in the space to the right, rank them in descending order, from the most blameworthy to the least. Be sure to justify your hierarchical placements both with logic and with references to the text itself.	
To get a **B+** on this assignment, you must complete this task, plus all of the ones below.	*Romeo and Juliet* commences, of course, with the Chorus's spoken prologue, a perfect sonnet that famously sets the stage for Shakespeare's grand tragedy. The Chorus speaks likewise at the beginning of Act II, but then disappears for the rest of the drama. In the space to the right, compose an appropriate epilogue for the Chorus to speak at the closing of *Romeo and Juliet*. Make sure to retain the iambic pentameter and rhyme scheme of a true Shakespearean sonnet, and keep in mind the literary purpose of an epilogue, as distinct from that of a prologue.	

To get a **B-** on this assignment, you must complete this task, plus all of the ones below.	Romeo and Juliet meet their ends because of many different factors and events, some of which can accurately and simply be labeled bad luck or poor coincidence, or perhaps the inevitability of their "star-crossed" destinies. Friar John's inability to reach Romeo, as reported in scene ii, is just such an event. Restate the factors that delay John's travel and appraise them as either a stroke of bad luck or a symbol of the lovers' inescapable destiny.	
To get a **C** on this assignment, you must accomplish this task, plus the ones below.	At the beginning of this act's third scene, Romeo gives Balthasar a letter, which the servant is to deliver to Lord Montague the next morning. This letter reappears at the end of the play, presented by Balthasar to the Prince instead. Based on the characters' brief discussions in this scene of the letter's subject, please write, á la Romeo, what you imagine its contents may be.	
To get a **D+** on this assignment, you must complete this task, plus the one below.	The play's conclusion changes considerably the relationship between the Montague and Capulet families. Please explain the outcome of the tragedy, as summarized in the last 21 lines of the play, as well as what Prince Escalus implies will happen next to or for the families.	
To get a **D-** on this assignment, you must answer this question.	In Act V, three persons die. Who, and by what means does each one perish?	

AP-Style Multiple Choice Quiz
Romeo and Juliet, Act I

Directions: This quiz consists of a selection from *Romeo and Juliet* and questions regarding its content, form, and style. After reading the excerpt, choose and circle the best answer to each question.

Note: Pay particular attention to the requirement of questions that contain the word EXCEPT.

Read the following excerpt carefully before choosing your answers. **Suggested time: 10 minutes.**

	Lady Capulet:	—Tell me, daughter Juliet,
		How stands your disposition to be married?
	Juliet:	It is an honor that I dream not of.
Line	**Nurse:**	An honor? Were not I thine only nurse,
5		I would say thou hadst sucked wisdom from thy teat.
	Lady Capulet:	Well, think of marriage now. Younger than you
		Here in Verona, ladies of esteem,
		Are made already mothers. By my count
		I was your mother much upon these years
10		That you are now a maid. Thus, then, in brief:
		The valiant Paris seeks you for his love.
	Nurse:	A man, young lady—lady, such a man
		As all the world—why, he's a man of wax.
	Lady Capulet:	Verona's summer hath not such a flower.
15	**Nurse:**	Nay, he's a flower, in faith, a very flower.
	Lady Capulet:	What say you? Can you love the gentleman?
		This night you shall behold him at our feast.
		Read o'er the volume of young Paris' face,
		And find delight writ there with beauty's pen.
20		Examine every married lineament
		And see how one another lends content,
		And what obscured in this fair volume lies
		Find written in the margent of his eyes.
		This precious book of love, this unbound lover,
25		To beautify him only lacks a cover.
		The fish lives in the sea, and 'tis much pride
		For fair without the fair within to hide.
		That book in many's eyes doth share the glory
		That in gold clasps locks in the golden story.
30		So shall you share all that he doth possess
		By having him, making yourself no less.
	Nurse:	No less? Nay, bigger. Women grow by men.
	Lady Capulet:	Speak briefly. Can you like of Paris' love?
	Juliet:	I'll look to like, if looking liking move.
35		But no more deep will I endart mine eye
		Than your consent gives strength to make it fly.

1. Lines 6–10 contain all of the following EXCEPT
   (A) alliteration
   (B) assonance
   (C) consonance
   (D) meter
   (E) end rhyme

2. Lines 24–25, like lines 28–29, contain an example of
   (A) feminine rhyme
   (B) masculine rhyme
   (C) internal rhyme
   (D) slant rhyme
   (E) enjambment

3. Lines 20–31 are written in
   (A) prose
   (B) rhyming couplets
   (C) dramatic irony
   (D) a soliloquy
   (E) an apostrophe

4. All of the following words accurately describe the comparison in lines 17–29 EXCEPT
   (A) figurative language
   (B) metaphor
   (C) conceit
   (D) analogy
   (E) simile

5. The difference between line 27 and line 34 regards
   (A) dialogue vs. monologue
   (B) euphony vs. cacophony
   (C) epithet vs. epilogue
   (D) connotation vs. denotation
   (E) prose vs. verse

6. Lines 31–32 present a good example of
   (A) personification
   (B) an allusion
   (C) an oxymoron
   (D) a pun
   (E) a refrain

7. The Nurse's description in line 13 is closest to
   (A) a stereotype
   (B) synecdoche
   (C) a refrain
   (D) an allusion
   (E) an epithet

8. Lines 34–36 can best be understood as stating
   (A) that Juliet will consider Paris only superficially and only because she is being forced
   (B) that Juliet would rather run away than be married to a man whom she does not love
   (C) that the Nurse and Lady Capulet's approval of Paris has unnerved Juliet
   (D) that Juliet now likes the idea of Paris as her potential future husband
   (E) that Juliet understands her own inability to choose a suitable husband

AP-Style Multiple Choice Quiz
Romeo and Juliet, Act II

Directions: This quiz consists of a selection from *Romeo and Juliet* and questions regarding its content, form, and style. After reading the excerpt, choose and circle the best answer to each question.

Note: Pay particular attention to the requirement of questions that contain the word EXCEPT.

Read the following excerpt carefully before choosing your answers. **Suggested time: 10 minutes.**

Juliet:
The clock struck nine when I did send the Nurse.
In half an hour she promised to return.
Perchance she cannot meet him. That's not so.
O, she is lame! Love's heralds should be thoughts,
5 Which ten times faster glides than the sun's beams,
Driving back shadows over louring hills.
Therefore do nimble-pinioned doves draw Love,
And therefore hath the wind-swift Cupid wings.
Now is the sun upon the highmost hill
10 Of this day's journey, and from nine till twelve
Is three long hours, yet she is not come.
Had she affections and warm youthful blood,
She would be as swift in motion as a ball;
My words would bandy her to my sweet love,
15 And his to me.
But old folks, many feign as they were dead,
Unwieldy, slow, heavy, and pale as lead.

Line indicates lines 5, 10, and 15 in the margin.

1. All lines in this selection are written in perfect iambic pentameter EXCEPT
   (A) lines 5 and 15
   (B) lines 8 and 15
   (C) lines 13 and 15
   (D) lines 14 and 15
   (E) lines 15 and 16

2. Juliet's tone in this selection can best be described as
   (A) laconic
   (B) sensible
   (C) fastidious
   (D) anxious
   (E) affable

3. The majority of this selection can be described accurately as
   (A) free verse
   (B) blank verse
   (C) a narrative poem
   (D) rhyming couplets
   (E) a Shakespearean sonnet

4. Lines 7–13 contain all of the following literary elements EXCEPT
   (A) a simile
   (B) an allusion
   (C) a metaphor
   (D) an anachronism
   (E) figurative language

5. Lines 16–17 incorporate all of the following literary elements EXCEPT
   (A) assonance
   (B) consonance
   (C) alliteration
   (D) feminine rhyme
   (E) masculine rhyme

6. In this selection, Juliet emphasizes
   (A) a difference between youths and their elders
   (B) Cupid's responsibility for the sun's arc
   (C) Love's musical quality
   (D) an association of age with darkness
   (E) the way in which sunlight travels more quickly than do thoughts

7. In this selection, Juliet is apparently speaking
   (A) at noon
   (B) at nine in the morning
   (C) to her Nurse
   (D) to Cupid
   (E) in the presence of Romeo

8. Lines 9–10 contain
   (A) an allusion
   (B) internal rhyme
   (C) enjambment
   (D) parallelism
   (E) personification

9. In this selection, Juliet characterizes her Nurse as
   (A) celeritous
   (B) sluggish
   (C) conscientious
   (D) elevated
   (E) exacting

10. It is probable that Juliet speaks these 17 lines as
    (A) a monologue
    (B) a soliloquy
    (C) an epithet
    (D) an apostrophe
    (E) an analogy

Name: _____   Date: _____

AP-Style Multiple Choice Quiz
Romeo and Juliet, Act III

Directions: This quiz consists of a selection from *Romeo and Juliet* and questions regarding its content, form, and style. After reading the excerpt, choose and circle the best answer to each question.

Note: Pay particular attention to the requirement of questions that contain the word EXCEPT.

Read the following excerpt carefully before choosing your answers. **Suggested time: 9 minutes.**

> **Juliet:**
> Gallop apace, you fiery-footed steeds,
> Toward Phoebus' lodging. Such a wagoner
> As Phaeton would whip you to the west
> *Line*   And bring in cloudy night immediately.
> 5   Spread thy curtain close, love-performing night,
> That runaways' eyes may wink, and Romeo
> Leap to these arms, untalked of and unseen.
> Lovers can see to do their amorous rites
> By their own beauties, or, if love be blind,
> 10   It best agrees with night. Come, civil night,
> Thou sober-suited matron all in black,
> And learn me how to lose a winning match
> Played for a pair of stainless maidenhoods.
> Hood my unmanned blood, bating in my cheeks,
> 15   With thy black mantle till strange love grow bold,
> Think true love acted simple modesty.
> Come, night. Come, Romeo. Come, thou day in night,
> For thou wilt lie upon the wings of night
> Whiter than new snow upon a raven's back.
> 20   Come, gentle night; come, loving black-browed night,
> Give me my Romeo, and when I shall die,
> Take him and cut him out in little stars,
> And he will make the face of heaven so fine
> That all the world will be in love with night
> 25   And pay no worship to the garish sun.
> O, I have bought the mansion of a love
> But not possessed it, and, though I am sold,
> Not yet enjoyed. So tedious is this day
> As is the night before some festival
> 30   To an impatient child that hath new robes
> And may not wear them.

1. In lines 26–28, there is an implied comparison between monetary purchases and
   (A) real estate
   (B) possession
   (C) marriage
   (D) sunlight
   (E) tedium

2. In lines 17–25, Juliet presents numerous juxtapositions of
   (A) lightness and darkness
   (B) wholeness and incompleteness
   (C) heaven and earth
   (D) snow and stars
   (E) love and violence

3. Lines 1–4 utilize mythological allusions to emphasize
   (A) Juliet's detestation of violence
   (B) Juliet's impatience at the sun's slowness
   (C) parallels between modern and ancient cultures
   (D) the importance of a classical education
   (E) the swiftness with which the sun rises

4. In this selection, Juliet indirectly compares herself to
   (A) night
   (B) a raven
   (C) the stars
   (D) a child
   (E) a blind matron

5. Lines 10–11 contain an example of
   (A) an epithet
   (B) a simile
   (C) personification
   (D) enjambment
   (E) a paradox

6. The phrase "day in night" (line 17) can be understood as all of the following EXCEPT
   (A) Juliet's joy at Romeo's arrival tonight
   (B) Juliet's wakefulness during this night
   (C) the positive nature of this night
   (D) the new beginning that this night symbolizes
   (E) Juliet's desire that dark night quickly accede to light day

7. The phrase "untalked of and unseen" (line 7) emphasizes
   (A) the secrecy surrounding Romeo and Juliet's relationship and interactions
   (B) the quietness with which daytime gives way to the night
   (C) the lack of attention paid to the actions of runaways
   (D) the social taboo of discussing young Veronese ladies' nightly actions
   (E) the snowfall that Juliet expects this night

8. The implication of lines 20–25 is that Juliet considers Romeo
   (A) unfaithful to their marriage
   (B) more beautiful than the heavens themselves
   (C) ungentle, and thus worthy of education by night
   (D) a potential cause of Juliet's death
   (E) a gift from heaven to her

Name: _____   Date: _____

AP-Style Multiple Choice Quiz
Romeo and Juliet, Act IV

Directions: This quiz consists of a selection from *Romeo and Juliet* and questions regarding its content, form, and style. After reading the excerpt, choose and circle the best answer to each question.

Read the following excerpt carefully before choosing your answers. **Suggested time: 9 minutes.**

	Peter:	Musicians, O musicians, "Heart's ease," "Heart's ease." O, an you will have me live, play "Heart's ease."
	1st Musician:	Why "Heart's ease"?
Line	**Peter:**	O, musicians, because my heart itself plays "My heart is full."
5		O, play me some merry dump to comfort me.
	1st Musician:	Not a dump, we. 'Tis no time to play now.
	Peter:	You will not then?
	1st Musician:	No.
	Peter:	I will then give it you soundly.
10	**1st Musician:**	What will you give us?
	Peter:	No money, on my faith, but the gleek. I will give you the minstrel.
	1st Musician:	Then I will give you the serving-creature.
	Peter:	Then will I lay the serving-creature's dagger on your pate. I will carry no crochets. I'll *re* you, I'll *fa* you. Do you note me?
15	**1st Musician:**	An you *re* us and *fa* us, you note us.
	2nd Musician:	Pray you, put up your dagger and put out your wit.
	Peter:	Then have at you with my wit. I will dry-beat you with an iron wit, and put up my iron dagger. Answer me like men.
		[*Sings.*] *When griping griefs the heart doth wound*
20		*And doleful dumps the mind oppress,*
		Then music with her silver sound—
		Why "silver sound"? Why "music with her silver sound"? What say you, Simon Catling?
	1st Musician:	Marry, sir, because silver hath a sweet sound.
25	**Peter:**	Prates.—What say you, Hugh Rebeck?
	2nd Musician:	I say "silver sound" because musicians sound for silver.
	Peter:	Prates too.—What say you, James Soundpost?
	3rd Musician:	Faith, I know not what to say.
	Peter:	O, I cry you for mercy. You are the singer. I will say for you.
30		It is "music with her silver sound" because musicians have no gold for sounding.
		[*Sings.*] *Then music with her silver sound*
		With speedy help doth lend redress. [*He exits.*]
	1st Musician:	What a pestilent knave is this same!
35	**2nd Musician:**	Hang him, Jack. Come, we'll in here, tarry for the mourners, and stay dinner. [*They exit.*]

1. In lines 1–15, Peter's and the 1st Musician's interaction is mainly
   (A) somber
   (B) abstract
   (C) antagonistic
   (D) cooperative
   (E) disinterested

2. The majority of this selection is written in
    (A) iambic pentameter
    (B) irregular meter
    (C) ballad stanzas
    (D) blank verse
    (E) prose

3. In this selection, Peter's tone is or becomes
    I.   sorrowful
    II. heated
    III. lighthearted

    (A) I only
    (B) II only
    (C) I and III only
    (D) II and III only
    (E) I, II, and III

4. The word "minstrel" (line 11) and the phrase "serving-creature" (line 12) are best understood as
    (A) insults
    (B) threats
    (C) compliments
    (D) absent persons
    (E) tangible objects

5. This selection's comic element is created by
    I.   puns
    II. banter
    III. a riddle
    IV. characterization

    (A) I and III only
    (B) II and III only
    (C) I, II, and III only
    (D) II, III, and IV only
    (E) I, II, III, and IV

6. The song that Peter sings in this selection declares
    (A) that musicians are rich of spirit, but monetarily poor
    (B) that music is a poor substitute for gold
    (C) that musicians commonly depress their listeners
    (D) that music can lighten one's heavy mood
    (E) that music is best when performed hastily

7. "Heart's ease" (lines 1–3) is best understood as
    (A) a prayer
    (B) a song's title
    (C) Peter's mood
    (D) a term describing a particular musical quality
    (E) the name of this selection's group of musicians

Name: _____ Date: _____

AP-Style Multiple Choice Quiz
Romeo and Juliet, Act V

Directions: This quiz consists of a selection from *Romeo and Juliet* and questions regarding its content, form, and style. After reading the excerpt, choose and circle the best answer to each question.

Note: Pay particular attention to the requirement of questions that contain the words NOT or EXCEPT.

Read the following excerpt carefully before choosing your answers. **Suggested time: 7 minutes.**

Romeo [*Opening the tomb.*]:
A grave? O, no. A lantern, slaughtered youth,
For here lies Juliet, and her beauty makes
This vault a feasting presence full of light.—
Death, lie thou there, by a dead man interred.
                                  [*Laying Paris in the tomb.*]
Line
5   How oft when men are at the point of death
Have they been merry, which their keepers call
A light'ning before death! O, how may I
Call this a light'ning?—O, my love, my wife,
Death, that hath sucked the honey of thy breath,
10   Hath had no power yet upon thy beauty.
Thou art not conquered. Beauty's ensign yet
Is crimson in thy lips and in thy cheeks,
And death's pale flag is not advancèd there.—
Tybalt, liest thou there in thy bloody sheet?
15   O, what more favor can I do to thee
Than with that hand that cut thy youth in twain
To sunder his that was thine enemy?
Forgive me, cousin.—Ah, dear Juliet,
Why art thou yet so fair? Shall I believe
20   That unsubstantial death is amorous,
And that the lean abhorrèd monster keeps
Thee here in dark to be his paramour?
For fear of that I still will stay with thee
And never from this palace of dim night
25   Depart again. Here, here will I remain
With worms that are thy chambermaids. O, here
Will I set up my everlasting rest
And shake the yoke of inauspicious stars
From this world-wearied flesh! Eyes, look your last.
30   Arms, take your last embrace. And, lips, O, you
The doors of breath, seal with a righteous kiss
A dateless bargain to engrossing death.
                                  [*Kissing Juliet.*]
Come, bitter conduct, come, unsavory guide!
Thou desperate pilot, now at once run on
35   The dashing rocks thy seasick weary bark!
Here's to my love. [*Drinking.*] O true apothecary,
Thy drugs are quick. Thus with a kiss I die.

1. Which of these does NOT evidence apostrophe?
   (A) "true apothecary" (line 36)
   (B) "thee" (line 15)
   (C) "thou" (line 4)
   (D) "bitter conduct" (line 33)
   (E) "flesh" (line 29)

2. Lines 8–13 can best be summarized by
   (A) Juliet does not appear dead
   (B) Juliet is beautiful in apparent death
   (C) Juliet is not dead
   (D) Juliet is colorful
   (E) Juliet is apparently breathing

3. In this selection, Romeo states or implies that
   I.   men about to die often are unusually cheerful
   II. death can never truly conquer young love
   III. in death, he can escape his "star-crossed" curse
   IV. all men are masters of their own eternal destiny

   (A) I only
   (B) I and II only
   (C) I and III only
   (D) II and III only
   (E) I, II, and IV only

4. In this selection, Romeo characterizes or describes death as all of the following EXCEPT
   (A) intangible
   (B) a ship
   (C) a lover
   (D) a bargainer
   (E) a soldier

5. In this selection, Romeo compares Juliet to
   I.   a military objective
   II. a candle in a lantern
   III. a kidnapped lover

   (A) I only
   (B) II only
   (C) I and II only
   (D) II and III only
   (E) I, II, and III

6. Lines 29–32 do NOT exhibit or contain
   (A) parallelism
   (B) alliteration
   (C) apostrophe
   (D) a metaphor
   (E) an allusion

Quiz Answers

Act I

1. **E.** Alliteration is exhibited in lines 6–10 by the phrases "Younger than you" (6), "made already mothers" (8), and "your mother much upon these years" (9), all of which are also examples of consonance. Assonance is exhibited by such excerpts as "think *of . . . Youn*ger" (6), "lad*ies* of est*eem*" (7), and "*By my* count" (8). All five lines are written in metrical iambic pentameter, but none of them exhibit end rhyme.

2. **B.** Masculine rhyme, the rhyming of multiple syllables at the ends of words, is demonstrated by lines' 24 and 25 rhyming of "lover" and "cover," as well as by lines' 28 and 29 rhyming of "glory" and "story."

3. **B.** Lines 20–31 are written in rhyming couplets, mixing feminine and masculine rhymes.

4. **E.** The comparison in lines 17–29 of Paris to a well-bound book can be labeled many things. It qualifies as a conceit because the metaphor is a bit stretched; Lady Capulet tries a bit too hard, perhaps, to make this somewhat silly comparison work. It is simultaneously a metaphor and an analogy, because Paris and the book are compared via their similarities. Moreover, all of the above classifications fall under the larger umbrella of figurative language, yet nowhere in Lady Capulet's comparison does either the word "like" or the word "as" appear, thereby disqualifying the comparison as a simile.

5. **B.** Probably the most difficult question on this quiz, this one requires that students hear the combinations of sounds produced by lines 27 and 34. Juliet's spoken line 34, "I'll look to like, if looking liking move," contains an abundance of hard "k" sounds in proximity, mixed with gentle "l" sounds; the combination is both awkward and difficult to say aloud, a definitive example of cacophony. On the other hand, line 27 mixes both the soft "f" and "w" sounds, plus includes only one long vowel sound, in the last word. It is much easier to say and pleasing to the ear, a clear example of euphony. In determining this answer, students may find the technique of process of elimination quite useful.

6. **D.** In line 31, Lady Capulet concludes her conceited analogy by stating that were Juliet to "have" Paris, then she would certainly be "no less" well-off than she would be otherwise, the implication of which is that Paris would prove a socially appropriate match for her. In line 32, however, Juliet's Nurse either mistakes Lady Capulet's meaning or twists it intentionally, remarking, "No less? Nay, bigger. Women grow by men," referring instead of social class to pregnancy. Shakespeare, therefore, puns upon the word *less*.

7. **E.** In line 13, the Nurse describes Paris as "a man of wax," a compliment that is hardly stereotypical, instead implying the man's exceptionality. She does not repeat the description, disqualifying it as a refrain, nor does it imply a smaller part of something larger, therefore disqualifying synecdoche as a potential answer. It alludes to nothing in particular, yet is perhaps a phrase that was in common use in Elizabethan discourse to describe "molded" young men. Via process of elimination, students should conclude that an epithet is the only classification of this phrase that even somewhat fits.

8. **A.** Juliet's response to her mother's entreaty to consider Paris lacks commitment and enthusiasm, stating specifically that she'll "look to like" him "no more deep . . . Than [her mother's] consent gives strength to make [her examination of Paris] fly" (34–36). In other words, she tells Mom, "I'll look at this guy, mother, but only because you're making me."

Act II

1. **C.** Line 15, at only four syllables long, is obviously not written in iambic pentameter, so the key to answering this question is to find the other line that is not exactly 10 syllables long. Line 13, in fact, contains 11 syllables, none of which is contracted to fit the pentameter.

2. **D.** Anyone's tone reveals his or her attitude toward a subject; it should be clear from this passage that Juliet's attitude toward the Nurse is anxious, if not perturbed.

3. **B.** There is no regular pattern of end rhyming in this passage, so the last pair of potential answers clearly can be eliminated; likewise, the fact that Juliet is not narrating a story of any kind removes its potential description as a narrative poem. Down to the options of free verse and blank verse, students need only ask themselves if the lines are written metrically. Yes, the lines almost uniformly are written in iambic pentameter, classifying the excerpt as blank verse.

4. **D.** Juliet states in lines 12–13 that were the Nurse more youthful, she would move as rapidly "as a ball," a clear simile. Her mention of Cupid in line 8 qualifies as an allusion to Roman mythology, and her description of "the highmost hill / Of this day's journey" is a metaphor (9–10). Both metaphors and similes are examples of figurative language, as is Juliet's image of "nimble-pinioned doves draw[ing] Love" in line 7. There is no anachronism in this passage.

5. **E.** Line 16 contains the assonant phrase "old folks" and words "feign" and "they." The words "Folks" and "feign" also utilize consonant alliteration, and the repetition of the "l" sound in line 17, "Unwieldy, slow . . . and pale as lead" qualifies as another example of consonance. The end-rhymed

words "dead" and "lead" are only one syllable each, and their predecessors, "were" and "as," do not rhyme, so this couplet is a clear example of feminine, not masculine, rhyme.

6. **A.** Juliet concentrates throughout the first half of this passage on her Nurse's tardiness, which she attributes in the second half to her relatively advanced age, finally extrapolating the Nurse's example as representative of all "old folks" and their sluggishness (16).

7. **A.** Juliet states in line 1 that it was "nine when [she] did send the Nurse," but that "Now is the sun upon the highmost hill / Of this day's journey," further clarifying that "from nine till twelve / Is three hours long" (9–11). Obviously, Juliet is speaking at noon.

8. **E.** The description in lines 9–10 of the sun as "upon the highmost hill / Of this day's journey" is a metaphoric comparison, but its implicit depiction of the sun as a traveler mounting a hill recalls humanness. Moreover, none of the other potential answers works at all here.

9. **B.** The last three potential answers to this question make no sense at all in consideration of this passage, so students need only know that celerity is the opposite of sluggishness to discount its viability. The Nurse is portrayed by an anxious Juliet as tardy, slow, and sluggish.

10. **B.** This speech, taken as a whole, is certainly neither an epithet nor an analogy, and were Juliet to apostrophize it, we can assume that she would address the object or figure to whom she is speaking; she obviously does not here. Therefore, this question truly tests students' knowledge of the difference between a monologue, which is spoken to others onstage, and a soliloquy, which is best described as thinking aloud. She addresses no one in this speech, but we recognize that she awaits someone who is absent and her words seem akin to legitimately anxious thoughts.

Act III

1. **C.** Speaking metaphorically of her marriage to Romeo, Juliet states that she has "bought the mansion of a love" (26) and describes herself as "sold" (27). Students may think initially that any of the first three answers are potentially legitimate, but the keyword "comparison" in this question disqualifies the first two distracters, as real estate is the good being purchased, while possession is not so much compared as contrasted with monetary purchases. Juliet is implicitly comparing monetary purchases to marriage here.

2. **A.** Line 17's phrase "day in night," is only the first juxtaposition of light and dark images in lines 17–25. The others are Juliet's depiction of "new snow upon a raven's back" (19) and the antagonism between a star-filled

night and "the garish sun" in lines 24–25. All of these juxtapositions utilize images of light and dark.

3. **B.** The point of lines 1–4 is Juliet's desire that night would quickly descend, a point clarified by her references to "Phoebus' lodging" and the fast-driving Phaeton (3). Phoebus is a Latinized form of Apollo, the Greek sun god who drives a chariot pulled by "fiery-footed steeds" (1), and Phaeton is his son, who "would whip [the steeds] to the west," where the sun sets.

4. **D.** In the last full sentence of this passage, Juliet proclaims that in awaiting her nighttime tryst with Romeo this day feels as tedious "As is the night before some festival / To an impatient child," implying that she herself is analogous to that child (29–30).

5. **C.** By addressing the "civil night" as "Thou sober-suited matron all in black," Juliet clearly personifies it (10–11).

6. **E.** The third directive in line 17—"Come, night. Come, Romeo. Come, thou day in night"—is ambiguous, of course. We might understand the "day" as a period of wakefulness, as joyful or positive (i.e., light, the subsequent product of a dawn). Regardless, and especially because the entirety of this soliloquy concerns Juliet's impatience at night's slow arrival, it is clear that she does not want daylight to come again quickly.

7. **A.** Students must find the antecedent of the participial phrase "untalked of and unseen" to answer this question (7). It modifies Romeo, and particularly his leaping to Juliet's arms once "love-performing night" has descended.

8. **B.** Some readers and audience members find the imagery of lines 20–25 a bit disturbing, especially since Juliet expresses a desire that Romeo be "cut . . . out in little stars" when she herself "shall die" (21–22). Her true focus, however, is not the implicit violence of the act, but the effect of Romeo's effectively becoming starlight, that "he will make the face of heaven so fine / That all the world will be in love with night / And pay no worship to the garish sun" (23–25). Stated otherwise, Juliet finds Romeo more beautiful than the heavenly bodies themselves.

Act IV

1. **C.** When asked to play "Heart's ease" at Peter's request, the 1st Musician responds, "'Tis no time to play now" (6), to which Peter replies, "I will then give it you soundly" (9), a threatening statement of violence akin to the proverbial "knuckle sandwich." In line 11, moreover, Peter calls the 1st Musician a common "minstrel," who in turn rebuts the inhuman "serving-creature" Peter with this insult (12). Finally, in lines 13–14, Peter threatens to use "the serving-creature's [i.e., his own] dagger" to "*re* you, [and] *fa* you," once again implying physical violence, this time by bringing

the conversation around once again to music. Clearly, this interaction is antagonistic.

2. **E.** There is no metrical pattern whatsoever regularized, if even present, in this dialogue. It is clearly written in prose; moreover, the other four potential answers all involve poetic meter.

3. **E.** Peter's tone is sorrowful when he tells the musicians that he needs them to play "Heart's ease" because "my heart itself plays 'My heart is full,'" so he needs "comfort" (3–5). It becomes heated when he threatens the resistant musicians with violence, and it is lighthearted when he avoids paying them and playfully jests that "musicians have no gold for sounding" (30–31).

4. **A.** Peter refers to the hired musician as a common "minstrel," thereby insulting him; the minstrel in turn calls Peter a "serving-creature," which is likewise an insult (11–12).

5. **E.** The 1st Musician puns in response to Peter's threatening question, "Do you note me?" by stating matter-of-factly, "An you *re* us and *fa* us, you note us," referring to music rather than to observation (14–15). The entire interaction can be labeled banter among the four characters, while its second half is dominated by Peter's riddle to the three musicians. Finally, both the quick-tempered but playful Peter and the dim-witted 3rd Musician— "Faith, I know not what to say"—are characterized clearly, if briefly, in this dialogue (28). All four elements of humor are present here.

6. **D.** Peter's song concerning music's "silver sound" (21) states in its first two lines that "griping griefs" and "doleful dumps" can overtake a person's mood (19–20). However, its last couplet declares that music, to such an afflicted person, "With speedy help doth lend redress," or relief.

7. **B.** Peter requests that the three musicians "play 'Heart's ease'" because "[his] heart itself plays 'My heart is full'" (2–4). It should be clear to students that while "My heart is full" may be a description of Peter's mood, "Heart's ease" is clearly a song, a "merry dump" (5) that he wishes played in order to lighten that mood.

Act V

1. **E.** The "true apothecary" addressed in line 36 is not present in the Capulets' crypt, and Romeo addresses the intangible "bitter conduct" in line 33. The pronouns "thou" (4) and "thee" (15) refer to Death itself and Tybalt, who is dead, respectively. However, Romeo just mentions, but does not address, "flesh" in line 29; apostrophe requires a direct address, so the answer is E.

2. **B.** Romeo admits that death "hath sucked the honey of [Juliet's] breath, / [But] Hath had no power yet upon [her] beauty" (9–10). Moreover,

he states that "Beauty's ensign yet / Is crimson in [Juliet's] lips and . . . cheeks," adding that "death's pale flag" is not visible there (11–13). This last reference may entice students to infer that Romeo believes that Juliet is not dead, but it is death's paleness (i.e., its coloration) that is absent, not death itself. The first, second, and fourth choices are all potentially legitimate answers to this question, but the most correct answer is B.

3. **C.** Romeo abstractly considers "A light'ning before death" (7), his phrase for the merriness that sometimes comes upon men "at the point of death," which mirrors statement I (5). He later asserts that finally, in his "everlasting rest," he will "shake the yoke of inauspicious stars / From this world-wearied flesh!" a clear paraphrase of statement III (27–29). He never remarks upon statements II and IV even somewhat.

4. **B.** Romeo's description of "unsubstantial death [as] amorous" (20) comments upon its intangibility and personifies death as a lover, while his decision to "seal with a righteous kiss / A dateless bargain to engrossing death" depicts it as a bargainer (31–32). His allusions to "Beauty's ensign" and "death's pale flag," as well as his statement to Juliet, "Thou are not conquered" (11–13) recall soldiery, but he refers to himself, not to death, as a "seasick weary bark," a ship (35).

5. **E.** Romeo's statement that "death's pale flag is not advancèd" (13) to the lips and cheeks of Juliet, who is "not conquered," portrays his wife as death's military objective (11). He describes the Capulets' "vault [as] a feasting presence full of light" (4), "a lantern," because Juliet lies within it (1); thus, Juliet herself is analogously a candle, illuminating the vault. Moreover, he apostrophizes to Juliet that "unsubstantial death is amorous, / And . . . keeps / Thee here in dark to be his paramour," portraying his bride as a lover kidnapped by death itself (20–22).

6. **E.** By addressing and directing his own eyes, arms, and lips successively in lines 29–30, Romeo employs parallelism and engages in apostrophe. Particularly, the direction that he gives his eyes, "look your last," contains alliteration (29). He also describes his lips as "The doors of breath" (31), a certain metaphor, yet he alludes to nothing specific in lines 29–32.

Understanding
Romeo and Juliet

There is, of course, a thin line between the reading of Shakespeare's plays and the comprehension of them. It obviously does students little good simply to read the words on the page, but not to understand what they signify or demonstrate. Much overlap exists, therefore, between the content of the previous chapter, "Reading *Romeo and Juliet*," and this one; many of the activities in that chapter logically could be placed in this one, and vice-versa. Nevertheless, I have attempted to distinguish between activities and assignments that require students' reading and comprehension of the play's action and artistry at an introductory "surface" level and, in this chapter, at a deeper, cognitively more demanding one. Additionally, while the previous chapter was organized according to the play's five acts, this one, as well as all subsequent chapters, is organized by topic of inquiry.

This chapter contains more thorough explications of some of *Romeo and Juliet*'s linguistically difficult and artistically literary aspects, as well as writing prompts requiring students not only to digest what characters say and do, but also to relate such utterances and actions to their own lives, synthesizing Shakespeare's play with elements of the modern teenage (and potentially larger) world. If the contents of the previous chapter required students to encounter and absorb the play's dramatic action, then these activities are designed to focus their intellectual and reflective lenses more sharply, addressing the potentially personal questions, "So what? Why is this play relevant to my life?" Through an examination firstly of Shakespeare's demanding but worthwhile-to-master syntactical patterns and creative linguistic devices, and secondly of his timeless emotional, social, and political relevancies, I hope to help you provide your students with answers to these questions.

Difficulties With Shakespeare's Syntax

Dealing with Shakespeare's massive and sometimes unorthodox vocabulary is one problem commonly facing modern readers, but interpreting his similarly challenging syntax, the way in which he uses and combines the words that he chooses, is a different beast altogether. Consider, for example, this statement to Juliet by her father, Lord Capulet, taken from Act III, scene v:

> In one little body
> Thou counterfeits a bark, a sea, a wind.
> For still thy eyes, which I may call the sea,
> Do ebb and flow with tears; the bark thy body is,
> Sailing in this salt flood; the winds thy sighs,
> Who, raging with thy tears and they with them,
> Without a sudden calm, will overset
> Thy tempest-tossèd body. (135–142)

Technically, that's one English sentence, spread over eight lines of verse. Perhaps the most common difficulty that young readers and students of Shakespeare encounter results from an inexperience with dramatic verse; they read the text line-to-line, probably expecting each given line to make sense by itself, independent of its neighbors. If read in this way, then much of Shakespeare's writings will not make sense.

Line 140 above, for example, simply reads, "Who, raging with thy tears and they with them"; it is composed of nothing but a relative pronoun and a participial phrase, plus another at the end in which the verb isn't even stated, but simply implied! Moreover, 3 of the line's 10 syllables—"thy," "they," and "them"—sound alike and serve confusingly similar syntactic purposes. The relative pronoun that opens the line is here separated from any kind of referent, and 3 more of Shakespeare's 10 syllables are just as meaningfully indistinct, the conjunction "and" and the repeated preposition "with." Any student of the Bard who simply takes line 140 at face value, independent of its dramatic context and neighboring lines, would construe a meaning either close to nothingness or, at most, misleadingly incorrect. Students should be directed to fight their perhaps natural inclination to read Shakespeare's verse in this way, looking instead for the often unusually long sentence structures of which his text is constructed. Line 140 makes much more sense, of course, if encountered in the context of the entire sentence spanning lines 135–142.

Once students do get into the habit of reading Shakespeare sentence-to-sentence rather than line-to-line, however, he still challenges them with numerous syntactical and linguistic difficulties that, although at least common within his literary corpus, are nonetheless problematic for speakers and writers of modern English. Of the most tricky of these are syntatical inversion and word omission, discussed below.

Syntactical Inversion

Standard English syntax generally requires that, in most clauses, nouns be placed before verbs, which are placed before their direct objects. Shakespeare often inverts this order, engendering much consternation among readers who cannot easily follow the flow of his sentences. In line 138 above, for example, Shakespeare writes, "the bark thy body is." Even if students recognize that a bark is a type of sailboat, they are liable to get tripped up by this unorthodoxly inverted syntax, for while today we would simply say to Juliet, "Your body is a boat," Shakespeare places the object *before* the subject, which ultimately is followed by its verb.

He commonly inverts the order of nouns and verbs, too. Consider a short excerpt from Act II's balcony scene, stretching from line 67 to line 84. Kicking off this span of 18 lines, Juliet asks Romeo, "How camest thou hither, tell me, and wherefore?" (2.2.67). The archaic words "camest," "hither," and "wherefore" potentially confuse students enough by themselves, but throw in the inverted noun and verb, "camest thou," and young readers may not have a clue what this line asks. Additionally, the predicate of this sentence's initial clause actually is split by the subject; modern speakers would ask, "How did you come here?" but Shakespeare effectively moves the "you" between "come" and "here," asking instead, "How camest thou hither," another latent booby trap.

Shakespeare continues this dialogue using common word order for 10 more lines, then hits his readership with Romeo's "Alack, there lies more peril in thine eye / Than twenty of their swords. Look thou but sweet, / And I am proof against their enmity" (2.2.76–78). The archaic usage of "but" and "Alack," plus the perhaps puzzling word "enmity," might throw readers off, but the proximate inversions "lies more peril" and "look thou but sweet" are even more likely candidates. Six lines later, Juliet asks Romeo, "By whose direction found'st thou out this place?" laying for readers the same traps engendered by the line "How camest thou hither," but adding the prepositional phrase "By whose direction" at the sentence's beginning, prior to its referent (2.2.84). No wonder Elizabethan English is so troublesome to read!

Word Omission

Returning to our example of Capulet's long statement to Juliet in Act III, scene v (see p. 78), we see two clear examples in lines 139–140 of another Shakespearean syntactical oddity that puzzles inexperienced readers. In both of these lines,

"Sailing in this salt flood; the winds thy sighs, / Who, raging with thy tears and they with them," the Bard omitted a verb, instead implying its existence as a function of his parallelism in this long sentence. The first missing verb is "are," which technically should be found between "winds" and "thy" in line 139. Shakespeare instead chose, for the sake of retaining his iambic pentameter, to omit the verb, assuming that his audience would recognize its implicit functionality, based upon the previous line, "the bark thy body is," wherein he makes a similar comparison to the one found in line 139, yet does include the verb, "is" (3.5.138). Line 140 contains a similar omission, in this case of the verb "raging," which is implied by the parallel structure of the comparisons "raging with thy tears and they [i.e., the tears, raging] with them [i.e., Juliet's sighs]." If both of these verbs were replaced in this couplet, then it would read, "the winds [are] thy sighs, / Who, raging with thy tears and they [raging] with them," which would be more easily comprehensible, especially if a reader were to read the rest of the sentence, wherein Capulet states that Juliet's heaving sighs will capsize her metaphorically storm-tossed bark. Such verbal omissions are not uncommon in Shakespeare's language, so helping students to spot, accept, and bypass them when reading is a critical step toward building their understanding and appreciation of his artistry.

Figurative Language and Other Artistic Devices

Even more difficult for young Shakespearean scholars to digest than his syntactical "traps," however, is the Bard's consistent usage of figurative language to emphasize the points that he wishes to convey. Again consider Capulet's long statement to Juliet in lines 135–142 of Act III, scene v. Rather than saying outright something along the lines of, "Wow, you sure are crying hard, Juliet," which is actually all that this sentence denotatively communicates, Lord Capulet creates a complicated analogy, whereby he compares Juliet to a sailboat tossed about during a storm, in danger of capsizing due to the roughness of the sea (i.e., Juliet's tears), the "little" (135) size of the boat itself (her body), and the raging winds (her sighs).

Anyone who has ever taught Shakespeare surely has been asked the very legitimate question, "Why doesn't he just say what he means?" The most sincere answers to this question, that he is being either "dramatic" or "artistic" with his language, are certainly true, yet probably as reductively unsatisfying to us, the teachers, as to our students. Nevertheless, Shakespeare's incorporation of artistic literary devices into his characters' dialogue absolutely heightens both their own and the audience's emotions, paints more vivid imagery and creates meaningful dramatic subtext, and, wholly, allows the Bard to "say" much more than he is actually "saying." The audience's difficulty lies in the interpretation of such devices, of course; yes, we get a much clearer picture of just how the heartbroken Juliet looks and ostensibly feels via Capulet's description of her in lines 135–142 than we would were he simply to say, "You're crying hard," but unless we actually pore over his figurative lines in order to interpret the analogy, we are liable to think that all of a sudden he's just describing some boat in a storm, without apparent cause in the dialogue to mention it.

The first step to understanding how such literary devices and elements augment the play's drama and action is to understand them independent of the text itself. As such, I include on pages 175–186 a glossary of literary terminology describing and demonstrating such devices and elements.

Moreover, although it is useful for students to understand and be able to define these literary devices and elements in isolation, their true analytical utility arises only when they are contextualized in studies of actual literature. If students can find examples of hyperbole in Romeo's monologues, for example, then they are more liable to understand the purpose of the device as a mechanism for portraying intense emotion.

It is unfeasible to pick out every occurrence in *Romeo and Juliet* of each of these literary devices. Nevertheless, I have culled many of the clearest examples of them from the play's first act in Appendix A, found on pages 187–200, hoping to help you identify them for your students as you proceed through the drama together. There are certainly more occurrences of each device within Act I, waiting to be mined, but this appendix should provide you and your students with an excellent foundation upon which to build your contextualized understanding of Shakespeare's literary devices.

Lesson Plan 2: Art? Not Art?

After you review some (or all) of the literary devices present in Shakespeare with your students, you can incorporate the lesson plan on pages 86–89. This activity requires students to compare and contrast two pairs of poetic excerpts, the first a pair of love poems and the second a set of romantically descriptive verse, extracted from Elizabethan plays.

Self-Reflective Prompts

My personal belief regarding the modern value of ancient literature is that any piece of writing, regardless of how historically "priceless" it may be considered, truly does students little lasting good to read or understand unless it contributes in some meaningful way to their own understandings of themselves and their lives. Questions regarding a narrative's plot, characters, conflicts, or symbolism pale, I think, in comparative importance to the most important inquiry posed by teenagers encountering any book, play, or poem in English class: "What does this have to do with me?" If we as teachers can help our students to answer this question meaningfully and sincerely for themselves, then we do them the largest educational service possible by helping them to understand the *personal* value of a literary education.

It is always important, I therefore feel, to allow students a chance to reflect upon their literary studies not as artifacts from bygone eras and places, disengaged from the modern world of teenagers, but as mirrors to be considered honestly and individually, capable of demonstrating just how connected to the great human family any adolescent truly is, no matter how disconnected from it he or she may feel.

The following questions offer students just such an opportunity to examine themselves in the adolescent mirror that is *Romeo and Juliet*. I do not believe that when students are assigned to consider these topics their responses should be assessed, perhaps not even collected or read by the teacher; privacy, after all, engenders honesty. You might wish to ask students to spread out around the classroom, writing individually and silently upon a given topic for 10 minutes, after which time they could pack their responses away and move on to something else. On the other hand, you could assign these self-reflections for homework just as easily. Regardless of the pedagogical way in which you choose to administer these prompts, I do advise that you attempt to create a safe environment for students' self-reflection, one in which they do not feel threatened by impending grades, the thought of their peers critiquing their responses, or perhaps even you, the teacher, reading their personal statements. Especially for gifted teenagers full of rampant emotional overexcitabilities, a place to write considerately, honestly, and safely is a very valuable place, and certainly worth protecting.

- Which of the play's characters do you feel that you understand best and/or can connect with most easily? Explain why.

- What or whom do you personally feel is to blame for the tragic deaths of Romeo and Juliet? On whom or what is the lion's share of culpability to be placed?

- For many people, *Romeo and Juliet* is a singularly powerful expression of the overwhelmingly wonderful force of young love. Have you ever been in love with, or even just attracted to, someone else and felt similarly to the way the Bard's young lovers feel? If you're not sure, then what suggests that perhaps you have? In either case, do you think that the beautiful poetry of Shakespeare's amorous text is an accurate verbalization of such feelings (i.e., did he actually capture in this play the essence of being in love)?

- Some people find in *Romeo and Juliet* a depiction of the dangers of overprotective or overcontrolling parents. Have you personally ever felt caught between loyalties to your family and to another person or responsibility? If so, then what were the circumstances, and how did you ultimately deal with the situation?

This play is a consideration, among other topics, of the role of government as an arbiter of private lives and disputes. In the Verona of *Romeo and Juliet*, violence is both public and rampant, and the authorities only seem to step in when conflicts have potentially escalated beyond control! Can you relate to this lack of authoritarian discipline in your life or world? Do you think that more or less management of violence is necessary, both in Shakespeare's play and in the real world in which you live?

Lesson Plan 3: Apothecary's Cabinet

This lesson plan requires students to engage in several higher order cognitive processes and activities, including historical research, anachronistic application of the findings of that research to several characters from the play, and creatively visual representation of that applicative synthesis. Wholly, the lesson will both enhance students' study of *Romeo and Juliet* and reinforce their understanding of Shakespeare's distinct characters.

The complete lesson plan for this activity is included on pages 90–93.

Quotation Identification and Analysis

It is difficult to dispute the statement that for many years, scholarly recognition of famous quotations from the Bard's plays has been a cultural currency of not only academic Shakespeareans, but also educated readers of all kinds. The following worksheets provide teachers with a methodology for helping students to build personal caches of such famous quotes' significances and probable usages, focusing upon their logistical importance, dramatic or emotional substance, philosophical implications, and relevancy to contemporary culture. Overall, students' consideration of these quotes from *Romeo and Juliet* should help them to develop a deeper understanding of the play's significance to their own lives and their worlds, perhaps causing them to see the drama not as an Elizabethan relic, nor as a tragic and syrupy romance gone awry, but as a poignant commentary upon politics, both modern and timeless, upon ageless sociological tendencies and truths, and even upon the very human difficulty of growing up in a world that tries to shape you to its norms, rather than to your own conceptions of yourself.

The worksheets on pages 94–104 may be assigned collectively, perhaps in a packet required for submission at the conclusion of students' study of the play, or individually, providing an opportunity for students to reflect and interact in a traditional jigsaw activity or via oral presentations. Regardless of how you choose to assign or issue these analytical worksheets, I definitely advise that you distribute to all students the completed sample sheet, which models for them not only an appropriate length of response, but also the type of answer, in terms of content, suitable for each reflective question. As with most analytical activities proposed by this book, it is important that students recognize the fact that there is not one right way to complete these worksheets; certainly some responses are potentially more reasonable than others, but students should feel free to interpret and extrapolate these quotations' significances as they individually wish. Thus, you may wish to assess them based on completeness and legitimacy, rather than on "correctness," a criterion that is subjective at best.

Conclusion

The materials that follow include the various quotation worksheets for this chapter. These and the other activities in this chapter will aid your students in preparing for the activities in later chapters, where they will be asked to apply their understanding of the play orally, textually, and, in the next chapter, dramatically . . . in performance!

Chapter Materials

Art? Not Art?

❧ **Purpose/Objective:** Too often, high school students are unable to answer the simple, yet fundamental, question, "Why is this piece of literature considered artistic?" Students often responding unthinkingly with, "It is considered art because we read it in school." By asking students to compare and contrast two pairs of poetic examples, this activity aims to help students develop or refine their own calculi for determining the artistic qualities and merits of various pieces of literature.

❧ **Placement:** This activity should be conducted midway through the students' study of *Romeo and Juliet*, after they have absorbed the balcony scene.

❧ **Materials Required:** Photocopies of the two side-by-side comparative tables that I include in this lesson plan are necessary for this activity. If too many photocopies are required for a given class, then an overhead projection of the tables should suffice.

❧ **Duration:** This activity should occur over approximately 45 minutes of one class period.

❧ **Lesson Plan:**

1. *Anticipatory Set:* At the beginning of the activity, ask students to consider independently this question, then write an honest response to it in their notebooks: "What is the most artistic piece of literature that you have ever read, and why do you consider it artistic?" After allowing them a few minutes to pen their answers, ask that the students pair with one another to discuss their responses, then reconvene as an entire group and ask for student volunteers to share their individual replies with the class.

2. *Communication of Objective:* Inform the class that they will be considering, side by side, a few excerpts of romantic verse, attempting to decipher why not all poems, *per se*, are created equally, but some ultimately gain acclaim for their artistry more than others do. There is no right answer that students are searching for; the ultimate goal is for the pupils to engage in the comparative consideration of different works of art, thereby refining their own critical faculties and calculi.

3. *Consideration of Two Love Poems:* Distribute to students one copy each of Table 5, asking them to compare and contrast the two poems it includes. Students could read both poems silently, or a student volunteer or two could read them aloud. Either way, after students have read both poems, ask them to jot either in their notebooks or below the poems themselves a list of qualities in each that is artistic.

4. *Discussion:* After the students have brainstormed some ideas as to why these two poems are considered literary art, ask them the question, "Is one of them more artistic than the other?" which should engender a dialogue concerning the natures of literary art, criticism, and personal taste. This discussion should grow organically, as certain students comment upon others' ideas along the lines of, "No, I disagree that you can claim that something is more artistic in general because it speaks more clearly to you," or "This poem does not seem to focus as particularly upon specific qualities of its subject, making it less descriptive, and thus less artistic, in my opinion." After a few minutes of discussion, reveal to the class that the poem on the left, penned by "Anonymous," actually was written by me, the author of this book, specifically for the purpose of this activity; I wrote it in approximately 80 seconds, thinking of nobody in particular as I wrote, and attempting as best I could to mimic the tone and atmosphere of an inartistic greeting card. Having revealed this information, reopen the discussion, asking again, "Now does anybody think that these two poems are equally artistic?" Perhaps the discussion will now sway in a new direction, considering the degree to which true art must be authentically communicative or its expression sincere.

5. *Consideration of Two Elizabethan Dramatic Excerpts:* Next, distribute to students one copy each of Table 6, asking them to compare and contrast the two dramatic excerpts that it includes. Again, the students could read both excerpts silently, or a student volunteer or two could read them aloud. After the students have digested both pieces, ask them to consider in their notebooks or below the excerpts themselves the question of which of the two excerpts is, in their critical opinion, more artistic and why.

6. *Discussion:* After this brainstorming, reopen the question, "Is one excerpt more artistic than the other?" which should expand the previous dialogue concerning literary art. Again, this portion of the discussion should grow organically, building upon students' opinions and comments to create a holistic, though probably not homogenized, view of what makes some literature more artistic than other literature.

Closure: Once this discussion has reached a relative lull, ask the students to respond individually in their notebooks to the question that is the ultimate aim of this activity, "In your opinion, what makes literature artistic?" After a few minutes of silent, written reflection, ask that the students pair with one another to discuss their responses, then reconvene as an entire group and ask for volunteers to share their individual replies with the class. It is important at the activity's conclusion to note that there is no singular right answer, but that ultimately the point of any such consideration is to help them get past the very orthodox view that "artistic literature is literature that is read in school."

TABLE 5
Compare and Contrast: Two Love Poems

Through all the years we've been a pair,
You've always stood by my side.
And though I'm sure you're unaware
How easy it's been to decide
To stay the course
And remain true,
The strongest force
In all my life
Has been
And remains you.
 	
        —Anonymous
	My lady's presence makes the roses red,
	Because to see her lips they blush for shame.
	The lily's leaves, for envy, pale became,
	And her white hands in them this envy bred.
	The marigold the leaves abroad doth spread,
	Because the sun's and her power is the same.
	The violet of purple colour came,
	Dyed in the blood she made my heart to shed.
	In brief: all flowers from her their virtue take;
	From her sweet breath their sweet smells do proceed;
	The living heat which her eyebeams doth make
	Warmeth the ground and quickeneth the seed.
	The rain, wherewith she watereth the flowers,
	Falls from mine eyes, which she dissolves in showers.
	
	        —Henry Constable

TABLE 6
Compare and Contrast: Two Examples of Romantic Elizabethan Verse

Faustus:	Romeo:
[*Having magically conjured Helen of Troy*]	[*Below Juliet's balcony*]
Was this the face that launch'd a thousand ships,	But soft, what light through yonder window breaks?
And burnt the topless towers of Ilium?	It is the East, and Juliet is the sun.
Sweet Helen, make me immortal with a kiss.	Arise, fair sun, and kill the envious moon,
[*He kisses her.*]	Who is already sick and pale with grief
Her lips suck forth my soul; see where it flies! –	That thou, her maid, art far more fair than she.
Come, Helen, give me my soul again.	Be not her maid since she is envious.
Here will I dwell, for Heaven be in these lips,	Her vestal livery is but sick and green,
And all is dross that is not Helena.	And none but fools do wear it. Cast it off.
I will be Paris, and for love of thee,	It is my lady. O, it is my love!
Instead of Troy, shall Wittenberg be sack'd;	O, that she knew she were!
And I will combat with weak Menelaus,	She speaks, yet she says nothing. What of that?
And wear thy colours on my plumèd crest;	Her eye discourses; I will answer it.
Yea, I will wound Achilles in the heel,	I am too bold. 'Tis not to me she speaks.
And then return to Helen for a kiss.	Two of the fairest stars in all the heaven,
Oh, thou art fairer than the evening air	Having some business, do entreat her eyes
Clad in the beauty of a thousand stars;	To twinkle in their spheres till they return.
Brighter art thou than flaming Jupiter	What if her eyes were there, they in her head?
When he appear'd to hapless Semele:	The brightness of her cheek would shame those stars
More lovely than the monarch of the sky	As daylight doth a lamp; her eye in heaven
In wanton Arethusa's azur'd arms:	Would through the airy region stream so bright
And none but thou shall be my paramour.	That birds would sing and think it were not night.
—Christopher Marlowe	See how she leans her cheek upon her hand.
Doctor Faustus (5.1.99–118)	O, that I were a glove upon that hand,
	That I might touch that cheek! . . . She speaks.
	O, speak again, bright angel, for thou art
	As glorious to this night, being o'er my head,
	As is a wingèd messenger of heaven
	Unto the white-upturnèd wond'ring eyes
	Of mortals that fall back to gaze on him
	When he bestrides the lazy puffing clouds
	And sails upon the bosom of the air.
	—William Shakespeare
	Romeo and Juliet (2.2.2–35)

Apothecary's Cabinet

- **Purpose/Objective:** This activity aims to help students reinforce or deepen their understandings of particular characters' dispositions, engage in historical research of a societal and/or scientific nature, and utilize creativity in representing visually and orally their research findings/conclusions.

- **Placement:** This activity can effectively be conducted at any point within the class's study of Acts II through IV.

- **Materials Required:** Available access to the Internet and/or to a local or school library. Moreover, students will bring to school several objects from home in order to represent visually their "prescriptions," yet these resources are not ones that the school or classroom teacher should provide.

- **Duration:** This activity takes approximately 2 days: one of in-class research and another of oral and visual presentations. Depending on the difficulty and depth of students' research, though, more days than one might be necessary for satisfactory completion of the research stage.

- **Lesson Plan:**

  1. *Anticipatory Set:* At the beginning of the activity, ask your students to respond in their notebooks to the following hypothetical questions: Imagining yourself as a psychologist or medical doctor, what would you diagnose as Romeo's major malady or "illness" (can be either medical or psychological)? How about Mercutio's? Tybalt's? After students respond to each question, direct them to share their answers in pairs, then ask for volunteers to share their diagnoses with the entire class. In all cases, ask students to support their ideas by referencing either particular lines of dialogue or events in the text, and after each diagnosis, inquire of the rest of the students how the characters might deal with or attempt to remedy the given malady (i.e., what would the class prescribe for each character: a vacation? Medicine? Social activity?) Keep in mind that this anticipatory set has the potential to become very humorous and loud, which might be in keeping with the lighthearted, creative tone of this lesson as a whole.

  2. *Communication of Objective:* Next, tell your students that this activity requires them to investigate what different cultures over time have considered "solid" or state-of-the-art medical practice, then to utilize that research in diagnosing, from a given historical culture's perspective, the ailments or disorders of three characters of their choice from *Romeo and Juliet*, for each of whom a historically accurate remedy should be prescribed. Moreover, each student will be required to bring from home three objects or substances representing the three anachronistic prescriptions.

It is perhaps necessary to demonstrate for your class an example of such a diagnosis-prescription-object combination; a simple example can be made of a package of unsalted pretzels and/or a pocket watch, which could be swung metronome-style to induce mock hypnosis upon Lord Capulet, whose high-strung anxiety and quick temper might be diagnosed today as symptoms of high blood pressure, prescriptions for which could include ample rest, hence the pocket watch, and a lessened intake of salt/sodium, hence the unsalted snack.

3. *Assigning Historical Periods and Cultures:* There are quite literally an unlimited number of eras' and societies' medical and psychological beliefs that students might research for this project. Keep in mind, though, that the most well-documented periods and cultures in history will produce the simplest and shortest bouts of research. Thus, you should accord the cultures and periods assigned or available to your students with the length of time and energy that you wish them to spend in research. In other words, if you want their research to take short amounts of time, then assign them recent and well-documented cultural periods, such as the United States at the turn of the 19th century or England in the mid-1700s, but if you want their research to stretch their abilities and force their utilization of vast resources, then assign such obscure or archaic societies as ancient Babylon or Egypt, or even native tribes found today in the South American rainforest. Obviously, difficult research assignments such as the latter few will require that you extend the number of days (and potentially nights of homework) spent on this project. You can allow students to choose blindly their own cultures to research, assign them randomly, or designate topics of inquiry by other appropriate means.

4. *Research:* Once all of your students have obtained research assignments, each of which should be distinct from their peers' topics of research, proceed to your local or school library, to the computer lab, or to another location where students can get to work. Inform them immediately that during their ultimate oral presentations to the rest of class, they not only will have to diagnose three characters of their choice with maladies or disorders appropriate to their researched time period, but also prescribe remedies that are likewise anachronistically and culturally legitimate, *and* defend their diagnoses and prescriptions by citing actual research that they found concerning their given culture and time, as well as represent their prescriptions visually via household objects! Obviously, although this assignment may seem simple at first glance, the variety of its steps undertaken for three different characters ultimately requires much time spent and creativity utilized by your students. Thus, make sure to plan a reasonable amount of time to be spent on this stage of the activity.

5. *Procedural and Legal Safeguards:* Once students have completed their research and are imagining creative ways to represent their prescriptions visually and/or symbolically with objects, you should make them aware of rules or improprieties regarding certain substances or items that they might choose to bring to school. For example, my high school forbids students to carry even as common a pill as aspirin on campus, much less other prescription drugs, so I would advise my own students that they should represent prescribed medical "pills" perhaps with small candies, such as Skittles, rather than with legitimate capsules. Make sure to investigate and communicate to your students any similar policies *before* they inadvertently break them.

6. *Oral Presentations:* On the appointed day, somehow designate an order (e.g., alphabetical, chronological, by lottery) in which students will present their findings and conclusions to each other, then let the show proceed. Keep in mind that the medical absurdities that some students may present as anachronistically cutting-edge may be quite humorous, which will only enliven the day's activity; it is totally legitimate, for example, that someone who researched Europe during the Middle Ages will prescribe for each of his or her three chosen characters, regardless of those characters' distinctly diagnosed ills, a good old-fashioned leeching. Yech! For grading purposes, it probably is implausible for you to collect three household objects from every student in your class, so you might therefore choose to require instead a short sheet of notes from each presenter, listing for every chosen character a diagnosis and resultant prescription, supported by research findings and citations, plus a description of the symbolic object. Because the name of the game here is creativity, full credit probably should be awarded to all students who complete all of the required steps of this activity, so long as their findings and ideas are historically legitimate.

❧ **Closure:** A fun and creative way to close the activity is to ask students once again to diagnose and prescribe anachronistically, but this time into the future. Firstly, direct students in their notebooks to compose a short paragraph describing what they imagine state-of-the-art medicine might be like 100, 300, or even 1,000 years into the future, their conceptualizations of which they should share with partners and perhaps with the rest of the class. Next, list several characters from *Romeo and Juliet* and ask students to predict what future medical science might diagnose as those characters' personal maladies, plus what kinds of remedies eventually could be prescribed for them. These creative answers, of course, should be shared among students. Although this follow-up activity is lighthearted and has no real basis in fact or research, it reinforces the point that while science and technologies change quickly, as do societal views of the well and the ill, human nature—our thoughts, dispositions, and emotions—really does not change all that much, which is largely the reason why Shakespeare and his characters never cease to be relevant.

Example Quotation, Including Adequate Student Sample Responses

Quotation: "A plague o' both your houses."

This quotation is spoken by _Mercutio_ **in Act** _Three_ **, scene** _One_ **.**

What is the logical importance of this quotation?

This quote is spoken by Mercutio after he has been stabbed. He is about to die, and his death signals the climax of the entire play, as afterwards there is no turning back. Murder has been committed, and both Romeo and Tybalt must somehow pay.

What is the dramatic or emotional importance of this quotation?

This quote really signals the futility (even the stupidity) of the feud between the Capulets and Montagues. It truly has been fought for no real cause, and now not only has it prevented Romeo and Juliet from proclaiming their love publicly, but it also has resulted in the death of an innocent man. When Mercutio screams this at Tybalt and Romeo, he has realized just how pointless the whole fight has always been, and he lets loose his frustration in this vehement curse. The audience, watching the comical, lighthearted Mercutio stumble about wounded onstage, and then finally turn bitter in the moment before his death, has no choice but to feel scorn for the feuding families and terrible sympathy for Mercutio, murdered before his time.

Who is a cultural figure that might quote this line in response to the events of his or her own life?

This person is not really famous, but any civilian who is caught up in a war fought in his or her homeland might utter this bitter line. I imagine, for example, a young Vietnamese or Afghan mother, having just witnessed the murder of her child who was caught in crossfire and killed during a village battle, cradling her child's body in her arms and screaming this line at the soldiers. Just like Mercutio, she and her child are the victims of a fight in which they are not participants, and the "two houses" that she is cursing with plague are the two sides or armies fighting in the war.

Name: _____ Date: _____

Quotation: "He that is strucken blind cannot forget
The precious treasure of his eyesight lost."

This quotation is spoken by _____ **in Act** _____ **, scene** _____ .

What is the logistical importance of this quotation?

_____

_____

_____

_____

_____

_____

_____

_____

_____

What is the dramatic or emotional importance of this quotation?

_____

_____

_____

_____

_____

_____

_____

_____

_____

Who is a cultural figure that might quote these lines in response to the events of his or her life?

_____

_____

_____

_____

_____

_____

_____

_____

Name: _____ Date: _____

Quotation: "What is [love]? A madness most discreet...."

This quotation is spoken by _____ **in Act** _____ **, scene** _____ **.**

What is the logistical importance of this quotation?

_____

_____

_____

_____

_____

_____

_____

What is the dramatic or emotional importance of this quotation?

_____

_____

_____

_____

_____

_____

_____

Who is a cultural figure that might quote these lines in response to the events of his or her life?

_____

_____

_____

_____

_____

_____

_____

_____

Name: _____ Date: _____

Quotation: "That which we call a rose
By any other name would smell as sweet."

This quotation is spoken by _____ **in Act** _____ **, scene** _____ **.**

What is the logistical importance of this quotation?

_____

_____

_____

_____

_____

_____

_____

_____

What is the dramatic or emotional importance of this quotation?

_____

_____

_____

_____

_____

_____

_____

_____

Who is a cultural figure that might quote these lines in response to the events of his or her life?

_____

_____

_____

_____

_____

_____

_____

_____

Name: _____ Date: _____

Quotation: "Love goes toward love as schoolboys from their books;
But love from love, toward school with heavy looks."

This quotation is spoken by _____ **in Act** _____ **, scene** _____ .

What is the logistical importance of this quotation?

_____

_____

_____

_____

_____

_____

_____

_____

_____

What is the dramatic or emotional importance of this quotation?

_____

_____

_____

_____

_____

_____

_____

_____

Who is a cultural figure that might quote these lines in response to the events of his or her life?

_____

_____

_____

_____

_____

_____

_____

_____

Name: _____ Date: _____

Quotation: ". . . naught so vile that on the earth doth live
But to the earth some special good doth give."

This quotation is spoken by _____ **in Act** _____ **, scene** _____ **.**

What is the logistical importance of this quotation?

_____

_____

_____

_____

_____

_____

_____

_____

_____

What is the dramatic or emotional importance of this quotation?

_____

_____

_____

_____

_____

_____

_____

_____

Who is a cultural figure that might quote these lines in response to the events of his or her life?

_____

_____

_____

_____

_____

_____

_____

_____

Name: _____ Date: _____

Quotation: "They stumble that run fast."

This quotation is spoken by _____ in Act _____, scene _____.

What is the logistical importance of this quotation?

_____

_____

_____

_____

_____

_____

_____

What is the dramatic or emotional importance of this quotation?

_____

_____

_____

_____

_____

_____

_____

_____

Who is a cultural figure that might quote these lines in response to the events of his or her life?

_____

_____

_____

_____

_____

_____

_____

_____

Advanced Placement Classroom: Romeo and Juliet © Prufrock Press • This page may be photocopied or reproduced with permission for classroom use.

Name: _____   Date: _____

Quotation: " . . . violent delights have violent ends
                    And in their triumph die,
                    like fire and powder,
                    Which, as they kiss, consume."

This quotation is spoken by _____ **in Act** _____ **, scene** _____ .

What is the logistical importance of this quotation?

_____

_____

_____

_____

_____

_____

_____

_____

What is the dramatic or emotional importance of this quotation?

_____

_____

_____

_____

_____

_____

_____

_____

Who is a cultural figure that might quote these lines in response to the events of his or her life?

_____

_____

_____

_____

_____

_____

_____

_____

Name: _____ Date: _____

Quotation: "Venus smiles not in a house of tears."

This quotation is spoken by _____ **in Act** _____ **, scene** _____ .

What is the logistical importance of this quotation?

_____

_____

_____

_____

_____

_____

_____

_____

What is the dramatic or emotional importance of this quotation?

_____

_____

_____

_____

_____

_____

_____

_____

_____

_____

Who is a cultural figure that might quote these lines in response to the events of his or her life?

_____

_____

_____

_____

_____

_____

_____

_____

_____

Name: _____ Date: _____

Quotation: "She's not well married that lives married long,
                   But she's best married that dies married young."

This quotation is spoken by _____ **in Act** _____, **scene** _____.

What is the logistical importance of this quotation?

_____

_____

_____

_____

_____

_____

_____

_____

What is the dramatic or emotional importance of this quotation?

_____

_____

_____

_____

_____

_____

_____

_____

_____

Who is a cultural figure that might quote these lines in response to the events of his or her life?

_____

_____

_____

_____

_____

_____

_____

_____

_____

Quotation: "O mischief, thou art swift
                    To enter in the thoughts of desperate men!"

This quotation is spoken by _____ **in Act** _____ **, scene** _____ **.**

What is the logistical importance of this quotation?

_____

_____

_____

_____

_____

_____

_____

What is the dramatic or emotional importance of this quotation?

_____

_____

_____

_____

_____

_____

_____

_____

Who is a cultural figure that might quote these lines in response to the events of his or her life?

_____

_____

_____

_____

_____

_____

_____

_____

Performing *Romeo and Juliet*

A thorough understanding of *Romeo and Juliet*—its beautiful dialogue, its characters, its comic relief, its dramatic lulls and crescendos—cannot arise simply from reading the play as one would well-crafted prose. Novels and stories differ from staged dramas in that they are written, for the most part, to be encountered and absorbed alone, to be experienced at least initially by individuals, to exist chiefly in the space between the author's words on the printed page and the images created in a reader's imagination. Plays, on the other hand, are envisioned and crafted by dramatists to be performed, to be enacted both physically and verbally. They exist in the open air, a much more communal narrative experience.

In literature classes, therefore, it always is preferable that students not only read Shakespeare's plays individually, but also study and enact them collectively, pondering together over the meanings of his verse, stumbling cooperatively over those especially hard-to-pronounce words and lines, debating and ultimately concluding how a given character is "supposed" to feel, to speak, to move. This chapter offers ways in which teachers can both initiate such performances by students and induce reflective and creative activities aimed at improving the final quality of their presentations.

Stage Terminology

Before we begin considering preparations for actual performance, it is important to consider several key terms common among dramatists. An understanding of these terms and their importance to the successfulness of a staged production is vital both to the following activities' dramatic authenticity and to students' ultimate ability to write fluently and learnedly about Shakespeare's stagecraft on the AP Literature and Composition Exam. When discussing aspects of Shakespearean theatrical production, I suggest that you use these terms as often and as casually as possible, thereby engendering students' understanding of and comfort with them. The terms include:

- *Blocking:* Blocking is a word used to denote the physical movements of actors on stage. Fight choreography falls under the umbrella of stage blocking, as do elements of actors' body language, routes and speeds of their movements around the stage, directions regarding entrances and exits, poses to be struck, and any other aspects of characters' physical performances. Blocking decisions generally are made by directors in preparatory rehearsals, although experienced or insightful actors often have a hand in their own characters' physicality, as well.

- *Delivery:* Delivery is a word describing how lines of dialogue are to be said or delivered aloud to an audience. Especially in Shakespeare, it often is debatable how given lines of text are best delivered. For example, Mercutio's "Ask for me tomorrow, and you shall find me a grave man," legitimately can be spoken painfully, comically, bitterly, furiously, incredulously, sadly, or in any combination of these ways (3.1.101–102). Debates between actors and directors concerning deliveries of ambiguous lines such as this one often get heated, but delve into subtext, such as characters' motivation and background, that ultimately aids the verity and believability of the eventual performance.

- *Upstage, Downstage, Left, and Right:* To theatrical laymen, terms such as upstage, downstage-left, and even center stage can be thoroughly confusing; most of this puzzlement arises from people's not knowing to whose left is stage left located anyhow, the actors' or the audience's? The simple answer is that these locations on stage always are considered from an actor's point of view. To move stage left, as an actor, is to move to *your* left, to move upstage is to move away from your audience, and to frown at someone located offstage right is to glare into the wings to your right. Figure 12 demonstrates all of these directions.

- *Set:* A theatrical set is the stage's physical layout: how it looks aesthetically, what furniture or decoration is present, and what backgrounds have been painted or adorned. Shakespeare's set directions are even scantier than his stage directions; it is clear that *Romeo and Juliet* requires a bed and a balcony, for example, but directors otherwise are free to stage the drama as they wish. Thus, like almost all of the Bard's plays, this one has been performed in nearly every physical and aesthetic space, from traditional Elizabethan reproductions to otherwise minimalist sets that divert an audience's focus from aesthetics to

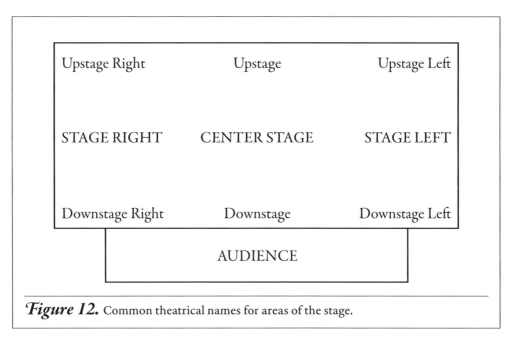

Upstage Right	Upstage	Upstage Left
STAGE RIGHT	CENTER STAGE	STAGE LEFT
Downstage Right	Downstage	Downstage Left

AUDIENCE

Figure 12. Common theatrical names for areas of the stage.

dialogue and drama, and from adaptive sets transporting *Romeo and Juliet* to locations and ages quite distinct from Shakespeare's Veronese original (Baz Luhrmann's 1996 cinematic version is a good example), to black box theaters entirely devoid of recognizable sets.

❧ *Prompt Book:* A prompt book is a copy of the text that has been marked up by its owner (usually a play's director, although actors themselves will have prompt books concerning their own roles in a production), who has noted details concerning actors' blocking and delivery of lines, set decorations, and every other bit of information needed to make a performance come off smoothly. To see a prompt is more useful than to read an explanation of it, so Figure 13 provides an excerpt from a *Romeo and Juliet* prompt book.

Understanding Characters: Questions for Discussion or Written Reflection

Directors and actors of staged plays always need to envision their eventually performed products long before the curtain goes up, of course. Actors especially require thorough, textually grounded understandings of their characters in order to present to their audiences convincing portrayals of these "people" that, until brought to life on the stage, are truly nothing besides ink on pages. There probably is no better way to arrive at such deep understandings of characters than to discuss their attributes with fellow dramatists: their backgrounds, their emotional dispositions, their motivations for acting and speaking as they do at given points during the text, the tones of their voices, and their relationships with other characters and

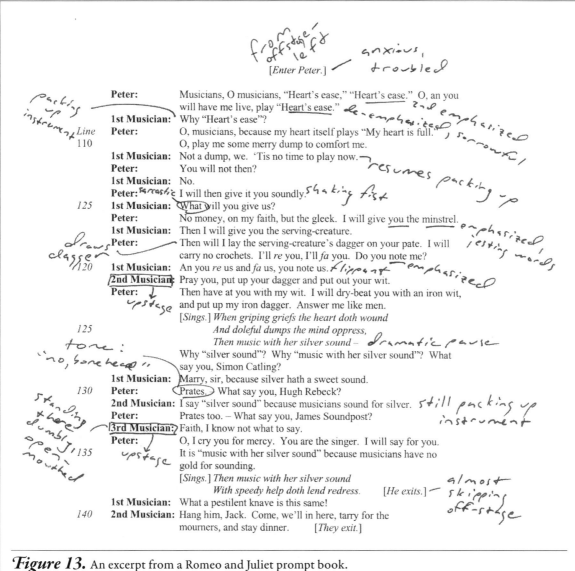

from offstage left
[Enter Peter.] — *anxious, troubled*

packing up instrument

Peter:	Musicians, O musicians, "Heart's ease," "Heart's ease." O, an you will have me live, play "Heart's ease." *de-emphasized, 2nd emphasized*
1st Musician:	Why "Heart's ease"?
Peter:	O, musicians, because my heart itself plays "My heart is full." *, sorrowful* O, play me some merry dump to comfort me.
1st Musician:	Not a dump, we. 'Tis no time to play now. *resumes packing up*
Peter:	You will not then?
1st Musician:	No.
Peter: *sarcastic*	I will then give it you soundly. *shaking fist*
1st Musician:	What will you give us?
Peter:	No money, on my faith, but the gleek. I will give you the minstrel. *emphasized, jesting words*
1st Musician:	Then I will give you the serving-creature.
Peter:	Then will I lay the serving-creature's dagger on your pate. I will carry no crochets. I'll *re* you, I'll *fa* you. Do you note me?
1st Musician:	An you *re* us and *fa* us, you note us. *flippant, emphasized*
2nd Musician:	Pray you, put up your dagger and put out your wit.
Peter:	Then have at you with my wit. I will dry-beat you with an iron wit, and put up my iron dagger. Answer me like men.
	[*Sings.*] *When griping griefs the heart doth wound*
	And doleful dumps the mind oppress,
	Then music with her silver sound — *dramatic pause*
	Why "silver sound"? Why "music with her silver sound"? What say you, Simon Catling?
1st Musician:	Marry, sir, because silver hath a sweet sound.
Peter:	Prates. What say you, Hugh Rebeck?
2nd Musician:	I say "silver sound" because musicians sound for silver. *still packing up instrument*
Peter:	Prates too. – What say you, James Soundpost?
3rd Musician:	Faith, I know not what to say.
Peter:	O, I cry you for mercy. You are the singer. I will say for you. It is "music with her silver sound" because musicians have no gold for sounding.
	[*Sings.*] *Then music with her silver sound*
	With speedy help doth lend redress. [*He exits.*] *almost skipping off-stage*
1st Musician:	What a pestilent knave is this same!
2nd Musician:	Hang him, Jack. Come, we'll in here, tarry for the mourners, and stay dinner. [*They exit.*]

Line 110

125

draws dagger 120

125

tone: "no, bonehead"

130

standing there dumbly, open mouthed 135

140

upstage

upstage

Figure 13. An excerpt from a Romeo and Juliet prompt book.

the reasons therefore. To enact a role realistically is to get inside of that character's skin, and there really is no way to do so without arriving at some understanding of just who that character truly is and why.

To that extent, I have included here several prompts and questions that should help students to dissect some important characters in *Romeo and Juliet* who are not quite the "stars of the show." These questions will not help students to block any scene, nor will they detail the deliveries of particular lines, but, if considered thoughtfully, they will help inquisitive actors to arrive at fundamental understandings, or at least their own opinions, of who these characters essentially are and why, as well as how their roles should or can be performed in a holistic sense.

Some character analysis regarding specific minor characters might include the following:

℘ *Mercutio:* Eminent Shakespearean scholar Harold Bloom (1998) called Mercutio "the most notorious scene stealer in all of Shakespeare" (p. 93). Doubtless, an outstanding performance of his role is one of the most enjoyable and memorable aspects of a good production of *Romeo and Juliet.* Why is it that Mercutio, whose appearance in the play ceases halfway through it, is so wonderfully enjoyable a character to encounter? Consider not only what Mercutio does and says that makes him enjoyable, but also why he may do it (i.e., who he fundamentally is).

℘ *Lady Capulet:* Despite her grief upon perceiving Juliet dead in Act IV, scene v, Lady Capulet remains quite a static character throughout the play, as her character undergoes next to no emotional growth between the text's covers. Thus, she is simpler to apprehend than more dynamic characters in *Romeo and Juliet.* How exactly would you describe Lady Capulet, and what do you think is a typical audience's response to her? What real person (or people) whom you know does Lady Capulet perhaps resemble, and why?

℘ *Friar Lawrence:* As the play progresses, the audience's reaction to and perception of Friar Lawrence changes drastically. Most of his appearances take place during the final two acts, but we first meet the Friar in Act II; from the initial portrayal of him at that point to his final exit in the play's last scene, we are presented with various, often contradictory impressions of Lawrence's character. Considering his myriad actions and speeches, what is your impression of Friar Lawrence? What kind of a man is he truly?

℘ *Lord Capulet:* Lord Capulet perhaps seems quite a paradoxical character. On the one hand, he prevents Tybalt from fighting Romeo at the Capulets' ball, an affair in preparation for which he comes off as quite an amiable, jocund man. On the other hand, he decides impulsively to speed up Juliet's arranged wedding to Paris, and he rages furiously and cruelly when she resists his decision. Overall, is Lord Capulet a sympathetic character in your eyes, or is he unworthy of the audience's sympathy by the end of the play?

Questions such as the ones above can be asked regarding the play's other characters, of course. However, their answers tend to be tremendously complex and multifaceted, and thus tied to particular narrative moments, in cases of focal, main characters such as Romeo and Juliet themselves, or reductive and unsatisfying, based largely on conjecture, in cases of characters so minor that we have very little dialogue upon which to make any inferences about them, such as the examples of Lady Montague or Friar John. Nevertheless, it *always* is valuable to consider characters' essential personalities and the audience reactions that they engender.

You may wish that students consider these questions in informal and independent writing assignments or in discussion, or perhaps a combination thereof, whereby written reflection is used to fuel dialogue among classmates. Regardless of your administration of them, such questions provide students with an opportunity to react to roles in a holistic, interpretive way, thereby improving and easing the eventual decisions that they make regarding these characters' blocking, delivery, and emotions at more particular points of the play.

When it comes down to deciphering individual scenes and moments of the drama, the following questions will prove more valuable in helping students to envision and articulate how they should be played. Again, they may be considered by students individually, but communal debate and discussion probably will fuel a clearer vision and a deeper understanding by all students of how an eventual staging should or might come off. Other questions to ask of students include:

- What is the character thinking at this moment of the play?

- What is the character feeling at this point?

- How are the other characters onstage responding to this character, and why are they responding this way?

- How might the character's body language reflect his or her emotions?

- Can the other characters' thoughts be represented by their body language?

- How much personal space does this or other characters want right now, and why?

- What physical actions might this character take to emphasize clearly the point of his or her lines?

- Could a lack of movement by this character communicate his or her emotions or thoughts even more clearly than would action? Why or why not?

- Tone conveys a person's attitude, so in what tone of voice should these lines be delivered?

- If standing deadly still, how might this character communicate his or her emotions or thoughts clearly just by altering his or her delivery of these lines?

As usual, there really are no singular answers to any of these questions, at least within the boundaries fixed by Shakespeare's content, that is. For example, as he delivers his final soliloquy and drinks poison within the Capulets' crypt, Romeo clearly is neither feeling nor acting upbeat. If students respond to these questions as they read or prepare to stage *Romeo and Juliet*, however, then they will arrive at deep and personal understandings of the play and its characters, as well as picture more clearly just how Shakespeare's action "looks." All of these processes will aid their understanding, mastery, and retention of the play.

Prompt Booking and Performance

Once students are able to discuss fluently these aspects of characterization and stagecraft, you may wish to require that they practice these productive skills in an assessable way. To create a prompt book, even a truncated one, directing and staging but a scene or two from a play, is a tremendously valuable exercise in close reading and deep thinking. Successful prompt booking necessitates that students get into the minds of characters, envision sets and actors' uses of props, and block every character on stage throughout the entirety of the performance. When students can pull all of these aspects of stagecraft together, and are able to explain their choices persuasively, they absolutely have developed not only their close reading skills, but also their interpretive-analytical faculties, both of which they will need for eventual success on the AP Literature Exam.

I recommend that teachers assign hybrid assignments to their gifted and talented students, requiring sections (acts, scenes, or even longer speeches) of *Romeo and Juliet* to be outlined and directed in the style of prompt books, as well as accompanying essays explaining all of the intellectual processes that they undertook and choices that they ultimately made when creating their prompt books. When prompt booking the first scene of Act III, for example, it is one thing for students to state that Tybalt should move smoothly stage-left as he draws his sword just as Mercutio jumps upstage, surrounding himself with friends—backup—from Montague's house, but it is something quite different and cognitively more challenging for students to do the same, plus articulate logically why they chose such blocking maneuvers over other possibilities, especially in light of how the rest of the scene and its fight choreography transpires. You might assign each student, for example, to create a prompt book for an individually chosen 150-line section of the play, as well as produce an essay explaining the decisions of delivery and blocking that he or she made as a hypothetical director, plus a sketch of an envisioned set for the excerpt. Quite an in-depth assessment! Even those students who consistently excel in the reading and interpretation of literature generally will be stretched to produce and articulately defend such a multifaceted product.

As a mechanism for instigating students' close reading and interpretation of text, prompt books are a pedagogical end in themselves, but theatrically they always serve as a means toward an even larger end: eventual performance for an audience. Certainly it is plausible to assign prompt book requirements to your students yet never require their public expositions; however, demanding that students perform speeches, scenes, and acts from *Romeo and Juliet* without having designed preparatory prompt books is potentially disastrous, akin to beginning an impromptu recipe in one's kitchen, totally unaware of the ingredients or time required. If you are going to have your students perform the play or parts of it, then I strongly suggest that you first insist on their production of prompt books.

Lesson Plan 4: Interpretive Group Performances

After learning about prompt books and various stage terminology, students are ready to put what they have learned into action. This activity requires students to work in small groups of five not only to analyze, block, and designate proper line deliveries throughout a scene, but also to perform it for their peers. This lesson plan can be found on pages 116–117.

Comparisons of Various Cinematic Versions

Every teacher knows that students love "movie day." Often, however, the same students that cheer when viewings of films are announced soon fall asleep once the movies begin rolling, at least when those films are Shakespearean adaptations. The stereotypical cinematic version of Shakespeare, as parodied so well by Robin Williams in *Dead Poets Society*, is banal, conceited, and overdramatized, probably including lots of unnecessary hand gestures and some kind of funny accent, too. The key to opening students' minds to Shakespeare on film, in my opinion, is not to bore students (and reinforce that stereotype) by showing them entire 2-hours-plus-long movies, especially those versions shot in black-and-white; there is nothing inherently bad or inadequate about older films, of course, but my experience is that modern teenagers have a natural and immediate aversion to them.

Such stereotypes can be overcome not by subjecting students to overexposure, attempting to force appreciation down their figurative throats, but by showing them selected excerpts of older Shakespearean adaptations juxtaposed with newer versions or alternatives set in adaptive locales. If students watch numerous versions of one Shakespearean scene—the same dramatic moment staged in two or three distinct ways—then they undoubtedly will recognize the great variety of potential interpretations that the Bard allowed his future directors and actors. There's more than one way to skin a cat, especially in Shakespearean theater, and this point can be made clear in no better way than by comparing, contrasting, and dissecting various professionals' visions.

Romeo and Juliet has been filmed more times than any other Shakespearean play except *Hamlet*. Thus, your local library, rental hub, or retail store probably already houses a number of the play's cinematic adaptations, with even more available via the Internet. Previewing whatever versions you acquire is the best and most advisable way to find particular scenes that differ in the hands of various directors and actors, but among the most plausible suspects for such diversity are the Capulets' ball, the interactions of Mercutio and Juliet's Nurse in Act II, scene iv, Juliet's feigned suicide in Act IV, and the ultimate scene in the Capulets' tomb. Juxtaposing Baz Luhrmann's 1996 *Romeo + Juliet*, set in modernized "Verona

Beach," with a more traditional film version, such as Franco Zeffirelli's excellent release from 1968, generally engenders fertile discussion regarding how students' own conceptions of a given scene differ from either director's staging.

Requiring students to focus on particular aspects of stagecraft, such as blocking and vocal delivery, or strictly cinematic touches like camera angles also sharpens their analytical acumen, thereby providing them with more precise fodder for discussion and debate. At the end of this chapter (pages 121–122), I include two worksheets that you may use to help students compare and contrast just such particular elements as they watch different versions of Shakespearean scenes.

Lesson Plan 5: Courtroom Drama

Although literally performing scenes (or the entirety) of *Romeo and Juliet* certainly helps increase student understanding through performance, incorporating other performance tasks only can add to that understanding and maintain student engagement. The large-scale performance activity in this lesson plan allows for teachers to move beyond the play and test students' comprehension and ability to apply that comprehension. In this activity, students will put Friar Lawrence and Juliet's Nurse on trial for their roles in aiding the young lovers. Students will be required to research various legal systems, develop cases based on the play's events and dialogue, and present those cases. This lesson plan can be found on pages 118–120.

Conclusion

This chapter's activities offer various ways to engage your students in dramatic, thoughtful, and otherwise effective performance of Shakespeare's text. The next chapter focuses instead on considered, deliberate discussion of the play: its relevancies, themes, and characters.

Chapter Materials

Interpretive Group Performances

- **Purpose/Objective:** Potentially among the most comic interactions in Shakespeare's early plays is the initial meeting between Mercutio's band of rascals and Juliet's bawdy, yet earnestly goodhearted, Nurse in Act II, scene iv. When Romeo's achingly romantic yearning and youthful impatience are added to the scene, it becomes among the most difficult scenes in the play to pull off on stage, yet potentially one of the most rewarding for the audience if performed well. This activity requires students to work in small groups to analyze, block, and designate proper line deliveries throughout the scene, and perform it for their peers. It is an exercise in close reading, directorial analysis, and actual translation of a scene from text to stage, all of which will acquaint students with the ins and outs of theatrical production, at least on a small scale, as well as prepare them to create their own larger prompt books at a later date.

- **Placement:** This activity should be conducted when Act II, scene iv arises in the students' reading of *Romeo and Juliet*. It likewise should be conducted fairly early in the class's overall experience with prompt books.

- **Materials Required:** One copy of Act II, scene iv, or a portion thereof, for every student in the class.

- **Duration:** This activity requires an initial 60–90 minutes of textual analysis by each group, additional time to rehearse—longer, of course, if you require students to memorize their lines, rather than read them from scripts—and approximately 10 minutes for each group's presentation. The total duration of this activity will largely depend upon the size of your class and the parameters that you set for students' eventual performances.

- **Lesson Plan:**

  1. *Anticipatory Set:* At the beginning of the activity, introduce students, if you have not done so previously, to theatrical terminology such as blocking and delivery. If they are unfamiliar with a prompt book, then discuss it, perhaps offering a few examples of what a completed prompt book might look like and include.

  2. *Communication of Objective:* Inform students that they are to be working in groups of five over the next few days to analyze one scene from *Romeo and Juliet*, to determine collectively the verbal and physical ways in which it is best staged, and to perform it for the rest of the class. Because multiple groups will be assigned the same portion of the text, remind your students that there is never only one "correct" way to interpret and stage any scene from Shakespeare. An additional aim of this activity is to help the class dialogue about differences among groups' stagings, as well as why certain

students chose to interpret and perform portions of the script differently than others.

3. *Work Time:* Three members of each group should plan to play Romeo, Mercutio, and Benvolio, while the remaining pair will enact the roles of the Nurse and Peter. Allowing them between 60 and 90 minutes to work together, inform all of the groups that they are to brainstorm and plan collaboratively, walking through the text line-by-line and action-by-action, discussing various possibilities for blocking and vocal emphases. Whenever an aspect of blocking or vocal delivery is agreed upon, someone in the group should write it down on a copy of the script, which will be transformed into a prompt book. To ensure students' accountability for being productive during this work time, you may wish to inform them that you will be collecting and assessing the prompt books at the end of this period of group work.

4. *Rehearsal:* For homework or even in class the next day, assign students to rehearse the scene as they envisioned it, incorporating every aspect that they included in their prompt book, from blocking to delivery. If you want them to be accountable for memorizing their lines, then a longer period of rehearsal time—potentially between one weekend and one week—is probably fair. On the other hand, if you allow time during class for rehearsal, then you would grant yourself the ability to mingle among groups, keeping an ear out for potential pitfalls and otherwise helping or advising the students as necessary.

5. *Performance:* On a designated day, all groups should enact for their peers their versions of Act II, scene iv, one after another. You may wish to hold students accountable for bringing their own props on the day of performance, or your might supply them yourself. Grading criteria should align with whatever performance parameters you set and communicated to students at the beginning of this activity.

Closure: Once all of the groups have performed, ask the students to organize themselves physically in a way conducive to discussion, such as a large communal circle. Remind them of some of the visible or audible differences among their performances at certain key points—there is bound to be divergence—and ask students why they chose to direct those moments as they did. An in-depth, textually grounded discussion of the scene should develop organically, focusing on everything from characterization to the use of physical space; regardless of the topics upon which the students hit, such discussion should be a valuable way to broach the topic of Shakespeare's enormous interpretability, largely due to his avoidance of concrete set and stage directions. At the end of the discussion, you may want to remind your students one more time that when it comes to theatrical interpretation, there really is not one "right" answer.

Courtroom Drama

🖎 **Purpose/Objective:** This large-scale activity incorporates a number of diverse objectives as students put Juliet's Nurse and Friar Lawrence on trial: it requires students to mine the play for relevant quotations and to formulate a persuasive argument utilizing those quotes; it necessitates that students verbalize their beliefs, claims, and findings publicly; it compels them to work together in small groups, both researching a topic about which they perhaps have no background knowledge and utilizing the fruits of their research in practical ways; and it aims to expose them to the legal profession, potentially illuminating procedures and distinctions in various countries' enactment of law.

🖎 **Placement:** This activity should be conducted when students have concluded their reading of the play.

🖎 **Materials Required:** Available access to the Internet and/or to a local or school library.

🖎 **Duration:** This activity should be spread over at least a week of in-class and out-of-school time, requiring at least 2 days for initial research, both of legal procedures and of *Romeo and Juliet*'s relevancy to students' individual cases, one day to collaborate in designating the ground rules and procedures by which students will present their cases "in court," one day for the students to prepare their respective cases, and at least one day for the actual trials to occur.

🖎 **Lesson Plan:**

1. *Anticipatory Set:* After your students have finished reading *Romeo and Juliet*, ask them to respond individually in their notebooks to these questions: Should Friar Lawrence be held legally accountable for the deaths of Romeo, Juliet, and Paris? Also, how culpable is Juliet's Nurse, and should she be condemned for her role in their deaths? Allow them at least 5 minutes to consider and respond to both questions, then ask for volunteers to share their answers. No harm will be done to the ultimate success of this activity by allowing a small discussion of the topics to develop.

2. *Communication of Objective:* Inform students that the purpose of this activity is to initiate legal proceedings in order answer these questions. Therefore, the class will need not only to research legal procedures, either of the United States or of Italy, but also to act as lawyers in preparing cases, both for prosecution and for defense. To accomplish these goals, students will need to work in legal teams or to assume the personas of Friar Lawrence, the Nurse, and any other characters from the plays that might be called as witnesses.

3. *Assigning Roles and Duties:* There are three distinct segments of this activity, for one of which there should be no dividing of students or their assignments. The first portion requires that students research the legal procedures of a particular country, and every student should be homogeneously involved. The second and third parts of this activity—the preparation for trial and the actual trial itself—necessitate that different students assume distinct roles and responsibilities. Thus, once initial legal research has been accomplished, you should divide up your class so that the following roles are filled: four legal teams of at least three students each should be created, one to prosecute and one to defend Friar Lawrence, and another to prosecute and a fourth to defend Juliet's Nurse; someone needs to act as a judge in both trials, so either one student could serve the function during both trials or two students could be assigned the responsibility and share the duty; one student needs to enact Friar Lawrence while he is on trial; and someone else is needed to play the part of Juliet's Nurse during her trial. If the size of your class exceeds this number of roles, then you could assign to students additional positions as critical witnesses during either or both of the trials, such as Friar John, Peter, and Lady Capulet.

4. *Legal Research:* Both characters are charged as accessories to murder, so you need to decide as a class according to what country's laws and procedures you wish to try Lawrence and the Nurse. The students may wish to research and follow the American legal system, but it also is sensible to try these two characters according to the procedures of their homeland, Italy. You may wish to try the characters according to differing legal procedures, perhaps utilizing the American system during Friar Lawrence's trial but the Italian system for the Nurse's. Regardless of which of these two—or other—options is chosen, at least one day should be spent in a library or on the Internet, researching the legal procedures and large-scale concepts of that country(ies). You may prefer that students conduct individual research, or you may allow them to work in pairs or small groups; eventually, however, the entire class should reconvene in order to synthesize all of the students' potentially disparate findings into a cohesive plan for the trial itself. Decide collectively on what procedures will be followed and in what order, what time limits (if any) will be imposed upon the legal teams, how many witnesses each team is allowed to call, and who will decide Lawrence's and the Nurse's ultimate fate, the judge or a jury of nonparticipants. Once these ground rules are laid, students probably will not reconvene as a class until the day(s) of the trials themselves.

5. *Textual Research:* The next phase of research requires students to mine *Romeo and Juliet* itself for relevant quotations and moments from the play that might help them to present their cases or enact their roles more con-

vincingly. If a prosecuting attorney can show with a solid piece of textual evidence, for example, that Juliet's Nurse *knowingly* went behind the backs of Lord and Lady Capulet in arranging the location and time of the young lovers' nuptials, then her guilt is much less conjecturable. Students assigned to portray individual characters during the trial should likewise go through the drama, reviewing their respective roles, lines, and interactions with the accused. You may or may not wish to allow members of the legal teams to speak with potential witnesses. In the United States, lawyers communicate with the witnesses whom they potentially shall call during trials, so allowing such dialogue in your classroom would closely replicate this candor; on the other hand, making the legal teams present their cases and call witnesses without any foreknowledge of what the characters might say certainly adds an element of intrigue and suspense to the proceedings.

6. *Final Preparations and Extensions:* This activity's last step before the trials actually get underway requires that the legal teams synthesize all of their findings into cogent, well-organized, persuasive cases to be presented before the judge and possible jury members. These cases should, of course, accord with the legal procedures and requirements of the country according to the law of which the trials are to be conducted. Keep in mind that during this stage of the activity, students assigned to assume the roles of characters from the play rather than lawyers, as well as the judicial figure(s), probably will have little to do. A simple extension project that you may wish to assign these students could incorporate further research of the same or another legal system, the basis of general legal constructs such as statutes and precedents, or even actual cases from the past wherein Shakespeare somehow played a critical role (in 1987, for example, three Justices of the Supreme Court of the United States actually conducted a mock trial regarding the Shakespearean authorship debate, on which they unanimously voted in the Bard's favor).

7. *The Trial:* Finally, it's showtime! Your role on the day(s) of the trials should be to maintain the students' orderly following of procedure and a relatively appropriate level of legal decorum. Because the entire class decided together on the procedures to be followed, the trials largely should run themselves, allowing you perhaps to sit back and enjoy the show.

Closure: Following their hearings of each case, United States Supreme Court Justices write and release concurring or dissenting opinions (i.e., statements as to why they do or do not individually agree with the trial's outcome). Assigning your students to do likewise allows them the opportunity to meld all of their thoughts into a coherent written statement of personal opinion, bringing closure to the proceedings on both a collective and an individual basis.

Name: _____ Date: _____

Romeo and Juliet on Film
Compare and Contrast

Film #1	Film #2
Director:	Director:
Year Released:	Year Released:

Costuming and Props	

Sets (i.e., Locations of Scenes)	

Camera Work (On Whom Does the Camera Focus, and From What Angles?)	

Romeo and Juliet on Film
Compare and Contrast

Film #1	Film #2
Director:	Director:
Year Released:	Year Released:

Physical Actions (i.e., Blocking)	

Actors' Deliveries of Lines	

Talking About
Romeo and Juliet

When I underwent the process to earn my National Board Certification in English Language Arts, I had to produce four portfolio entries documenting my abilities in distinct areas of classroom and school leadership. I was asked to produce only one entry concerning the ways in which I help individual students to develop as both readers and writers, but the National Board required that *two* of my four entries regard my guidance of students' verbal interactions: for one of these I led a class discussion and for the other I helped small groups of students to collaborate orally. The National Council of Teachers of English incorporates dialoguing about literature in its 12 core standards; the College Board does likewise in its expectations of AP Literature and Composition teachers. I mention these facts to illustrate the point that some of the biggest authorities in English education today consider the collective, collaborative discussion of literature, involving real-time interactions among students and teachers, at least as important as—if not *more* critical than—the solitary processes of reading and writing about that literature.

Anyone who has ever been involved in a truly engaging, insightful college seminar discussion probably agrees. Listening actively and openly to peers' perspectives and bouncing them off our own helps to shape and ultimately solidify our opinions. Classroom discussions of themes, characters, motivations, and symbolism are not pedagogical peripheries; I personally believe that they are the collective core of any effective study of literature. After all, who among us English teachers doesn't enjoy a really profound conversation or a good debate? In our academic discipline, it quite often is true that many heads are better than one.

This chapter focuses on ways to implement and assess, plus individual topics to spark, such dialogue. It centers on two distinct types of classroom interactions:

cooperative seminar-style discussions and competitive debates. For each of these types I provide suggested procedures to follow, questions to consider, and rubrics by which to assess students' interactions.

Socratic Seminar

Regarding classroom instruction, the phrase "Socratic seminar" and the Greek word *paideia* often are used synonymously. Some educators choose to distinguish between the two, but both practices are really very similar, not only in their historical underpinnings and recent popularization at the hands of Mortimer Adler, Director of Chicago's Institute for Philosophical Research, but also in their diminishment of the teacher's instructional role from the traditional, cliché "sage on the stage" to either a fellow participant with students or simply an observer and assessor of their dialogue. When questions are asked, according to either model, the point is not simply to find the "right" answer, especially because it may not exist for such deep, thematic, theoretical questions as, "What does *Romeo and Juliet* truly teach us about the natures of familial relationships?" The point of any seminar dialogue is to interact, to bounce ideas off one another, to search collaboratively for meaning—even if that meaning only matters to individual students—and to develop both communicative and interpretive-analytical skills. In other words, it's not the destination that matters so much as the journey to it; perhaps even Socrates himself would agree.

The most common conundrums facing teachers who wish to implement seminar discussions in their classes, though, involve less romantic, more pragmatic classroom issues: How do I ensure that my students will participate? How do I prevent them from settling for the simplest, quickest answer? What do I do about the shy kids who won't speak up? How do I assign grades?

A clear mechanism for assessing students' dialogic responses is necessary and should be communicated to if not physically given to participants beforehand. Table 7 includes a sheet of grading criteria; it is the one that I distribute to my own students, AP and otherwise, prior to seminars.

Modeling also is an important preparatory component of successful seminars. When I first distribute to my students this sheet of grading criteria, I describe to them what good and bad seminar discussions "look like," expanding upon the points bulleted at the top of the page. I then give them plenty of quiet time to peruse the entire sheet, after which I ask them to use the criteria to assess three sample answers to a question that I provide: one mediocre (1 point), one outstanding (3 points), and one silly or immaterial (minus 2 points). And, yes, I tell them when they inevitably ask, I really shall take points away from your score for random and irrelevant comments. It takes between 5 and 10 minutes even

TABLE 7
Rubric and Guidelines for Socratic Seminar

Some general rules of thumb:

- The less the teacher has to talk, the better.

- A *good* seminar looks like 20 people having a fun discussion on a literary topic, as if trying to solve one of the book's "puzzles" together.

- A *bad* seminar resembles the Teacher-as-Dentist idea—asking questions should not be like pulling teeth!

How Each Answer Will Be Graded:		
Potential Score	*Where Your Response Comes From*	*What Your Response Might Contain*
√ ++ (3 pts.)	You reply to other people's responses to the original question, either supporting an argument in agreement or refuting one in polite disagreement.	Your response ties together: - aspects of the discussion to this point, - passages from the text itself, and/or - relevant connections to extraneous studies or observations.
√ + (2 pts.)	You reply to other people's responses to the original question, either supporting an argument in agreement or refuting one in polite disagreement.	Your response is supported either by: - a passage or two from the text itself, or - relevant connections to outside studies or observations.
√ (1 pt.)	Your response is either your individual answer to the initially asked question or a response to another person's answer to the question.	Your response also *may* be supported either by: - textual passages or - relevant connections to outside resources.
√ - (minus 1 pt.)	Your response is solely your individual answer to the initially asked question.	Regardless of the content of your response, it is a repetition of something already said in the discussion.
√ - - (minus 2 pts.)	It is hard to tell, actually.	Nothing of value; you are talking just to hear yourself.

to begin our first discussion, but such modeling of my expectations ensures that everyone begins on the right foot; I usually inform the class, too, of my numerical assessments of the first three or four comments made during our initial discussion, explicitly tying their points' values to the grading criteria.

The individual assessments themselves are generally very simple. Having asked students to rearrange their desks and chairs into a circle, I sit among them with a roster of their names, tallying checks as the discussion proceeds, interjecting my own thoughts and steering the dialogue when appropriate or necessary. Figure 14 is a sample checklist from one of my AP classes' seminar discussions.

I always determine the total point value of any seminar discussion at its conclusion, basing my decision upon the length of time that it consumed and how insightfully high-scoring students' comments were. The discussion exhibited by this checklist lasted approximately 70 minutes, and I determined based on the quality of students' responses that it should be worth 8 total points. Making such determinations perhaps may be difficult at first, but the more seminars you lead, the more skillful you will become at gauging their relative levels of success.

This checklist reveals some additional issues requiring consideration, too. During the discussion that it records, 11 of the 28 students involved did not contribute at all, and only 6 participants earned their full score. It simply is the nature of the scholastic beast that there inevitably are going to be students who do not speak up, for any variety of reasons, during a particular discussion. I inform my own students prior to their first seminar that I recognize and accept this fact. "If you know right now that you are simply the type of student that will be more liable to sit and listen during this discussion than to speak up regularly," I tell them, "then I advise that you take notes on the flow of the conversation as it is occurring." I explain to my students that I will allow them to take their notes home that night and write what they would have said had they participated more in the discussion; I then grade their written responses using the same criteria that I use to grade commentary during the seminar itself. Numerous students take advantage of this policy following every graded discussion, especially because I also allow those who contributed somewhat, but not enough to garner their full share of points, to supplement their verbal totals with additional points earned for written responses. This policy inevitably leads to additional homework for my students following any seminar, but it also eliminates the inequity that would otherwise result among extroverted and introverted pupils' grades.

Also, it probably is inevitable in classes composed of predominantly gifted and talented students that certain of them will lead conversations and contribute inordinately more than other members of their group. Such verbal inequity is foreseeable, and I personally only consider it a problem when these outspoken persons actually dominate a conversation so much that other students are prevented from speaking their mind, and thus garnering their reasonable share of points. To

Kris	Erik
Melissa – √, √+	Kelsey #3 – √, √+
Justin	Charlie – √+, √++, √, √, √
Kelsey #1 – √+, √+	Garrett
Juliet	Brittany
Corinne – √+, √++, √, √+, √+	Lily
Johannes	Ashlee – √++, √, √+, √++
Pete – √, √, √+	Kyle – √, √+, √++
Kelsey #2 – √++, √	Ada – √+, √+, √, √, √+, √+
Virginia – √+, √++, √+, √+	Amanda
Darian	Hannah – √, √+, √++, √
Val	Graham – √, √, √+
Cathryn – √	Leah – √+, √++, √
Andrew – √+, √+, √+, √+	Jack – √+, √

Figure 14. Sample assessment checklist from an AP class' Socratic seminar discussion.

inoculate my classes against this unfairness, I inform my students—again, before we hold even our first seminar discussion—that I actually shall begin to deduct points from students who exhibit this overly dominant behavior. In certain classes, I even have taken to using soccer referees' yellow and red cards to signal to students their statuses in this regard; flashing them a yellow card communicates that they are probably nearing their full score of points, but a red card indicates to them that they are speaking too often and that if they do not let peers get more words in edgewise, then I shall soon begin taking points away.

Generally, there are two types of topics that students address during seminar discussions of any literary work: questions considering particular and locatable parts of the text, such as symbolism, diction, and style, and questions concerning deeper, more thematic, "big picture" issues. The practical aspects of initiating and assessing seminar discussions should not vary for either type, but the contents of these two types of discussions certainly do. Tightly focused, textually centered discussions utilize a great number of supportive quotations from the text, and they rely largely on close readings of particular points of the play in order to arrive at conclusions; on the other hand, more philosophical and/or thematic discussions refer less frequently to particular moments of dialogue and instead consider the narrative as a whole, examining the larger issues that Shakespeare imparts over the course of five acts. I here offer a number of questions of each type, to each of which, as usual, there is no single "right" answer that requires illumination.

Textually Based Questions

- Juliet's language changes dramatically upon meeting Romeo at her family's ball. Compare her diction both before and after this critical event. What do the differences in her language imply about her as a character, her feelings for Romeo, and her outlook on her own life?

- Character foils are opposites of one another, usually in very specific ways; such personal opposition serves to illuminate and accentuate the individual characteristics that each foil possesses. Some critics interpret Romeo and the Nurse as foils for one another. In what ways can you see a characteristic contrast between their personalities, and what do these differences say about each one's integrity?

- Mercutio is named after the Roman god Mercury, who was, among other embodiments, the god of impudent thievery. In consideration both of his character and of his importance in the play's narrative, why is this detail telling (i.e., in what ways is Mercutio's name appropriate)?

- Although only one half of the play's eponymous duo, Juliet often has been interpreted as the strongest, and certainly the most courageous, character in the play. Importantly, this portrayal of a strong, young female character was quite contrary to the traditional Elizabethan portrayal of women as "the weaker sex." Kudos to Shakespeare for this untraditional characterization, certainly, but what elements of the play actually imply this strength and courage (i.e., where do we see these traits in her character, and what circumstances or conditions engender their development in the plot)?

Beyond the initial Prologue's description of the play as a story of "a pair of star-crossed lovers," there are many coincidences and other freak conditions in the plot that imply, somehow, that perhaps Romeo and Juliet's doom truly is fated by the stars, and thus unavoidable (6). What are some of these incidents that occur?

Philosophical and Thematic Questions

In Shakespeare's most prominent source for the story of Romeo and Juliet, the character Tybalt does not even appear, but simply is mentioned as the victim of a deadly street fight. In the Bard's version, however, Tybalt plays a much more important and well-characterized role. His belligerence is easy to apprehend, but do you think that he, as a character, is crucial to the occurrence of the tragedy? Would Romeo and Juliet meet their disastrous end even without Tybalt's contribution to the families' feud and the plot's progression?

As many critics have remarked, there are various types of love portrayed in this play: the type that Romeo describes initially as his love for Rosaline; the kind typified by Lord and Lady Capulet, as well as by Paris; the more cynical and unromantic form of love characterized by Mercutio and Juliet's Nurse; and the type of love that seems to overtake and bind Romeo and Juliet themselves. How are these four types of love different than one another, and what inferences can you draw about the characters that respectively subscribe to these four distinct conceptions of love?

Beginning with the lovers' initial dialogue at the Capulets' ball, there are many instances throughout the play when love is described in terms of or as somehow dependent upon religion. What examples of this connection can you find? Do you think that such a suggestion on Shakespeare's part is legitimate, or is human love essentially different than all aspects of religion?

There truly is no traditional villain, as per Shakespeare's Iago or Edmund, in this play. As Northrop Frye (1986) commented, "Tybalt comes closest, but Tybalt is a villain only by virtue of his position in the plot" (p. 28). What impact do you think that the absence of true villainy has upon the thematic meaning of the play? Upon a reader's or observer's interpretation of the play's ending? Upon the effectiveness of the story simply as a piece of entertaining theater?

The audience is, of course, never told what the origin of the feud between the Montagues and Capulets was. Do you think that such an omission of information matters to Shakespeare's effective portrayal of his themes? Does it matter to you as a reader?

Lesson Plan 6: The Play as a Consideration of Government and Law

Once your students have some experience with Socratic seminars and with discussing the play in general, you might be ready to implement the lesson plan on pages 138–140. This lesson uses a Socratic seminar discussion to have students consider the role of government in the actions of its people: in this case, the role of the Veronese government in the deaths of Romeo and Juliet.

Debate

While Socratic seminar discussions are cooperative, debates between groups of students pitted on opposite sides of a subjective issue are competitive. There are many ways to structure such debates, as well as many questions to consider during them, yet I here propose two similar arrangements modified from procedures common among high school debaters nationwide. Thus, some of your students not only may be familiar with these methods of interteam debate, but also proficient at them.

The questions to be debated during any competitive round should be answerable with either "yes" or "no" answers. Students' creativity is required and rewarded in such debates not in their simple response to the question itself, but rather in the methods and textual support that they utilize in scaffolding that answer. Each debate therefore is conducted between two teams, one of which affirms the question (answers "yes") and the other of which denies it (answers "no"); per tradition, I refer to these groups as the Affirmative and Negative teams, respectively. Moreover, each team is composed of two distinct participants, the first and the second speakers.

Each speaker—the 1st and 2nd Affirmative speakers, and the 1st and 2nd Negative speakers—are required to present either one or two speeches during the debate. If each speaker delivers two speeches, then they are distinguished as Constructive speeches, the purpose of which is to build a case, and Rebuttal speeches, the purpose of which is to defend one's own case from opposing argumentation (i.e., to rebut the other team's reasoning). A team's initial Constructive speeches should be prepared prior to the debate round and include much textual support for the case being made, all taken from the play itself. Rebuttal speeches, and to some extent 2nd Constructive speeches, are prepared impromptu, based largely on the direction in which the teams' argumentation proceeds. Table 8 is an outline of the times that should be allowed for each speech, as well as each speaker's individual responsibilities.

TABLE 8
Order of Speeches, Two per Debater

Name of Speech	Time	Purpose of Speech	Preparation
1st Affirmative Constructive	5 min.	To present the affirmative team's initial case affirming (answering "yes" to) the question.	This speech should be prepared before the debate and include a variety of quotations from the text.
1st Negative Constructive	5 min.	To present the negative team's initial statement denying (answering "no" to) the question.	This speech should be prepared before the debate and include a variety of quotations from the text.
2nd Affirmative Constructive	5 min.	To further build the affirmative team's affirmation of the question, plus to respond to aspects of the negative team's first constructive speech.	Portions of this speech may be prepared before the debate, but parts of it will be impromptu responses to the opposing teams' arguments.
2nd Negative Constructive	5 min.	To further build the negative team's denial of the question, plus to respond to aspects of the affirmative team's constructive arguments.	Portions of this speech may be prepared before the debate, but parts of it will be impromptu responses to the opposing teams' arguments.
1st Affirmative Rebuttal	2 min.	To rebut any arguments against the affirmative team's case made by the negative team.	This speech will be prepared impromptu.
1st Negative Rebuttal	2 min.	To rebut any arguments against the negative team's case made by the affirmative team.	This speech will be prepared impromptu.
2nd Affirmative Rebuttal	2 min.	To reinforce the affirmative team's case affirming the question, plus to contribute any final remarks upon the negative team's opposing case.	This speech will be prepared impromptu.
2nd Negative Rebuttal	2 min.	To reinforce the negative team's case denying the question, plus to contribute any final remarks upon the affirmative team's opposing case.	This speech will be prepared impromptu.

TABLE 9
Order of Speeches, One per Debater

Name of Speech	*Time*	*Purpose of Speech*	*Preparation*
1st Affirmative	6 min.	To present the affirmative team's initial case affirming (answering "yes" to) the question.	This speech should be prepared before the debate and include a variety of quotations from the text.
1st Negative	6 min.	To present the negative team's initial statement denying (answering "no" to) the question.	This speech should be prepared before the debate and include a variety of quotations from the text.
2nd Affirmative	6 min.	To rebut the negative team's case denying the question, plus to reinforce the affirmative team's case affirming the question.	This speech should be prepared impromptu.
2nd Negative	6 min.	To rebut the affirmative team's case affirming the question, plus to reinforce the negative team's case denying the question.	This speech should be prepared impromptu.

The details of each speech are occasioned by the question itself that is being debated, of course. You may choose to assign questions—and thus match pairs of teams—in advance of the debate, perhaps allowing students to prepare arguments for homework, or you may wish to reveal such match-ups immediately prior to a round, thereby allowing both teams a truncated amount of time to mine the play for supportive evidence, compose a cogent argument and speech, and anticipate their opponents' dissimilar argument. I caution you that while the latter procedure certainly adds to the excitement of any debate round, it is really only feasible with teams of students who know the play very well and can therefore navigate its intricacies, searching for textual details quickly.

The second arrangement for a debate round allows each debater to speak only once, albeit for a slightly extended length of time. Because the outcome of this second type of debate hinges so clearly on the delivery of the second Affirmative and Negative speeches, it is critical—perhaps unlike the requirements of the first organization, which allows every speaker two times at bat, so to speak—that the second speakers for each team be very quick-thinking, loquaciously persuasive speakers. Table 9 is an outline of this second format for debates.

Regardless of which arrangement you choose to utilize in your classroom, note that each team engaged in any round should be allowed 4–5 minutes of preparatory time to use as they see fit. During this time, they should be allowed to mine the play for evidence, prepare argumentation, outline their upcoming speeches, discuss strategy, and the like, and although the opposing team and the judges of any round will have little to do but sit there during this preparatory time (well, the opposing team actually would be wise to prepare themselves simultaneously, too), your allowance of it will prove invaluable in raising the ultimate quality of the debate itself. After all, even a moment or two to gather one's thoughts immensely aids his or her communication and cogency of logic.

Perhaps the most enjoyable role to be played during any debate round is that of the judge. Because each round requires only four total speechmakers, I advise you to allow the remainder of your class to judge the participating teams' performances. Roman-style verdicts via thumbs placed up or down may be simple to orchestrate, but focusing your student judges' attention on less holistic details of a round absolutely will augment their judicial skill and the legitimacy of the outcome, plus provide valuable feedback to the debaters and you. Figure 15 includes a ballot for you to use in judging these rounds; if distributed to every observing student in your class prior to each debate, then a sum total or average of the many judges' points might be used to determine the winning side.

All portions of this ballot should be completed by the judges, and you may wish to photocopy the lot of them to pass on to the participants of each debate. All of us, of course, love getting feedback from our peers! Any teacher of the gifted, too, will admit that students' intellectual competitiveness can sometimes devolve into unsportsmanlike or otherwise immature behavior. You may or may not wish to include sportsmanship as a component of the decision-making process in your class's debate rounds, but I provide an additional ballot (see Figure 16) considering just this element. If you do include it alongside the other three criteria for judgment, then the total points possible during any round, of course, will rise from 15 to 20.

Finally, I include a number of questions to be debated. Because four students are involved in any debate round, these five questions account for the involvement of every member of a class of 20 students.

Questions for Debate

- Based on evidence from Acts I to III, can we claim that Romeo every truly loved Rosaline? Make sure that a major part of your argument includes a realistic definition and supportable examples of love.

- When slain in Act III, Mercutio famously condemns both Tybalt and Romeo, cursing both of their warring households with a plague. Is he justified in blam-

Date _____ Judge _____

Topic _____

Affirmative Team _____

Negative Team _____

Before allotting to students any points or ranks, or determining the winning team, fill out the following table. Assess the four debaters separately in each category. Do not assign more points in any category than the maximum possible. Then, rank each debater in order of performance (1 for the most successful, 2 for the next highest performer, etc.).

1st Affirmative	2nd Affirmative		1st Negative	2nd Negative
Points:	Points:	Delivery (Pace, Clarity, Tone, Sportsmanship) **5 pts. Maximum**	Points:	Points:
Reasons Why:	Reasons Why:		Reasons Why:	Reasons Why:
Points:	Points:	Persuasiveness (Organization, Argumentation) **5 pts. Maximum**	Points:	Points:
Reasons Why:	Reasons Why:		Reasons Why:	Reasons Why:
Points:	Points:	Textual Support (Quotations, Logical Analysis) **5 pts. Maximum**	Points:	Points:
Reasons Why:	Reasons Why:		Reasons Why:	Reasons Why:

1st Aff. _____   1st Neg. _____

Total Points _____ Rank _____   Total Points _____ Rank _____

2nd Aff. _____   2nd Neg. _____

Total Points _____ Rank _____   Total Points _____ Rank _____

Total Score, Affirmative Team _____   Total Score, Negative Team _____

In my opinion, the better debating was done by the _____, for these reasons:
                                                    (Affirmative or Negative)

Signature of Judge _____

Figure 15. Interteam debate ballot.

Date _____   Judge _____

Topic _____

Affirmative Team _____

Negative Team _____

Please score the four debaters in terms of their portrayal of ethical, sportsmanlike behavior. Consider their delivered speeches, as well as their body language, tones of voice, and general attitudes during the debate.

Sportsmanship Rating	1st Affirmative Debater	1st Negative Debater	2nd Affirmative Debater	2nd Negative Debater
5 Outgoing, friendly, civil, and fair throughout the debate				
4 Civil and fair throughout the debate				
3 Civil and fair throughout most of the debate, but bordering on unfriendliness at times				
2 Somewhat civil during part of the debate, but rather unfriendly or combative at certain times				
1 Unfriendly or combative throughout most of the debate, bordering on offensive disrespect				

Figure 16. Interteam debate sportsmanship ballot.

ing the Capulets and Montagues for his own death, or does he contribute to it as much as anyone else does?

- At the conclusion of the play, Prince Escalus admits partial blame for the lovers' untimely deaths, expressing contrition for previous ignorance of the families' discord. Is he correct in assuming that the government of Verona is to a degree responsible for the tragedy (i.e., is there more that he could have done to prevent the plot's tragic denouement)?

- Other than their passionate love for one another, almost every condition or character in the play is set or eventually turns against Romeo and Juliet's union: their families, their trusted friends and allies, the Veronese government, the all-too-quick passage of time itself, and the fated destiny set forth by the stars. Considering this fact, can we consider the two lovers as heroes? Make sure that a major part of your argument includes a realistic definition and supportable examples of what a hero is or does.

- *Romeo and Juliet* certainly has the reputation as Shakespeare's, if not the English-speaking world's, most romantic play. In fact, some critics and theatergoers may go so far as to label this drama the most romantic piece of literature ever written in any genre, a flawless expression of the trials and yearnings of young love. Is such an estimation overblown, or is *Romeo and Juliet* quite literally *the* perfect expression of desirous love and passionate romance?

Lesson Plan 7: Art Museum Field Trip

This lesson aims to get your students out of the classroom and into art . . . literally. Its field trip can be completed physically or virtually via the Internet, and it will help your class to locate and verbalize intertextual connections between *Romeo and Juliet* and apparently unrelated works of visual art. The complete lesson plan for this trip and its subsequent presentations is included on pages 141–143.

Conclusion

The techniques and activities outlined in this chapter all are designed to augment your students' deep understanding of *Romeo and Juliet* by getting them talking about the play. In the next chapter, I propose various methods by which you can help them to illustrate their understanding textually, from traditional analytical essays to original (not necessarily linguistic) creative-interpretive projects. I also include in Chapter 8 a variety of original assignment sheets, instruments, and grading rubrics.

Chapter Materials

LESSON

The Play as a Consideration of Government and Law

❧ **Purpose/Objective:** This activity is a Socratic seminar discussion concerning the degree to which Prince Escalus, and by association the Veronese government that he represents, is responsible for the deaths of Romeo and Juliet. Through this discussion, students not only will read closely many portions of the play, considering and developing strong opinions and understandings of the Prince's actions and inactions in response to the Montagues and Capulets' ongoing feud, but also consider a number of corresponding philosophical and governmental topics related to the discussion, thereby synthesizing their understanding of the play's events with their personal political beliefs regarding the role and limits of government in civilian life.

❧ **Placement:** This activity should be conducted near the end of the students' study of *Romeo and Juliet*, certainly after they have finished reading the play, as its success requires students' consideration of the deaths of the lovers and Prince Escalus's spoken response to it in Act V, scene iii.

❧ **Materials Required:** Each student should have a copy of the play for reference and copies of the Socratic seminar grading rubric.

❧ **Duration:** The length of this discussion will vary depending upon the involvement and success of the students involved, but 60 minutes probably is an adequate amount of time.

❧ **Lesson Plan:**

1. *Anticipatory Set*: Prior to engagement in the discussion, ask students to answer, either in their notebooks or on a separate sheet of paper, this question: "Do you believe that the United States Government exerts too much control, too little control, or just the right amount of control in protecting the safety and lives of its citizens?" Allow the students about 4 minutes to answer this question, then ask them to pair with partners and briefly discuss their responses, after which a few answers and examples from volunteers might be shared with the entire class.

2. *Communication of Objective:* Following consideration of this issue, inform the class that today's discussion will concern a very similar issue within the world of the play. It is important, also, to note the degree to which the question of the state's guilt in the lovers' deaths is tied to other related issues, such as the question just posed concerning the U. S. Government. Tell the students that in discussing this issue, you hope that they also will formulate, modify, or strengthen their own ideas not only about the world

138   *Romeo and Juliet*

of *Romeo and Juliet*, but also about the role and duty of government in our modern world.

3. *Seminar Discussion:*

   a. Ask the students to form a large circle with their chairs and desks, at which they each should have copies of the play to which to refer. If the class is not familiar with the grading criteria for Socratic seminars, then distribute copies of it to the students, taking 5–10 minutes to explain it.

   b. Next, open the discussion to students by stating the initial question, either by reading it aloud or by writing it on the board:

      i. Question: At the conclusion of the play, Prince Escalus, who represents social and civic order, admits partial blame for Romeo and Juliet's untimely deaths, expressing guilt for "winking at [the families'] discords" (5.3.304). Is he correct in assuming that the state is responsible for the tragedy?

   c. As the discussion proceeds, it naturally should venture into the realistic—rather than literary—arena of modern politics, but if not, then extend the discussion by asking this second question:

      ii. Question: What does *Romeo and Juliet*, and thus Shakespeare, apparently conclude about the role of government in civilians' private lives, especially when it comes to maintaining the peace?

   d. You should score each student's individual responses and involvement in the discussion, marking checks, pluses, and minuses next to their names as they make comments, according to the grading criteria. It is an educational fact that some students simply are more verbally outgoing than others; thus, as a concession to those pupils who are less liable to participate fully in the discussion, you might wish to allow students to supplement the points that they garner in class by writing the comments that they would have made during the discussion had they spoken. In this way, you not only allow the students flexibility to be themselves and feel comfortable with their own personalities, but also provide a safety net of sorts for large classes in which not everyone is going to have the chance to speak enough to earn full credit during the seminar.

   e. As the Socratic seminar grading rubric indicates, the less the teacher has to talk in a seminar, the better, because it means that the students are doing more of the intellectual work. It is sometimes necessary for the teacher to interject points into the discussion as a means of moving it along productively; as such, please note that the following scenes are especially relevant to the discussion of this question:

iii. Act I, scene i, in which the Prince describes the feud between the Montagues and Capulets, plus threatens death to any further transgressors of the peace.

      iv. Act III, scene i, in which Prince Escalus exiles Romeo from Verona for Tybalt's murder, stating his belief that in observing the law, "Mercy but murders, pardoning those that kill" (207).

      v. Act V, scene iii, in which the Prince acknowledges the resolution of the two families' feud and accepts partial culpability for the lovers' deaths, admitting to "winking at [the families'] discords" in the past (304).

    f. Inform the class near the beginning of the seminar, probably once students begin to venture beyond the limited scope of the play, that extraneous examples furthering the discussion are allowed and welcome, including references to historical civics, modern politics, and world affairs, as well as other works of literature. Allow the discussion to continue until its potential for further investigation of the issue seems exhausted. The maximum number of points (full score) that students should be allowed to earn will vary, certainly, based both on the number of students in the class and the length of each individual discussion; as a rule of thumb, 20 students involved in an effective, well-supported Socratic seminar for 60 minutes should aspire to reach a ceiling of 6 or 7 points each; the more students involved or the less time spent discussing, of course, the lower that ceiling should be. When the more vocal members of the class reach the maximum number of points, then you may wish to inform them that they have reached their limit, thereby inspiring them to allow opportunities for some of their less outgoing peers to contribute. Finally, at the end of the discussion and/or class period, inform individual students of how many points they fell short of a full score, and remind them that they may obtain these additional points via supplemental written responses for homework; these written responses should be graded individually using the same Socratic seminar rubric, then added to students' in-class scores for engaging in dialogue.

Closure: At the discussion's conclusion, ask students to respond in their notebooks once again to the same question with which this activity began: "Do you believe that the United States Government exerts too much control, too little control, or just the right amount of control in protecting the safety and lives of its citizens?" After approximately 4 minutes, ask the class if anyone would like to share his or her answer, as well as whether the discussion actually aided anyone in concretizing or altering the opinion that he or she previously held.

Art Museum Field Trip

- **Purpose/Objective:** This activity exposes students to a great variety of visual art—potentially paintings, sculptures, photographs, etc.—in order to accomplish two learning goals: (1) to reinforce their understandings of the major themes, motifs, and characters found in *Romeo and Juliet*, and (2) to discover and verbally articulate intertextuality between Shakespeare's play and other nonlinguistic works of art.
- **Placement:** This activity should be conducted when students have concluded at least Act IV, if not the entirety, of the play.
- **Materials Required:** Access to a museum of visual art is required; this access may be either physical, in which case a field trip to the museum is necessary, or virtual, requiring that each student in your class have Internet access. Moreover, an overhead projector or document camera-projector is necessary, and the quality of students' ultimate presentations will improve with presenters' access to digital cameras and a color printer. Please note that the two paintings and two museums identified below are listed in the Internet Resources section of this book, found on pp. 205–206.
- **Duration:** This activity should be spread over at least 2 days, during the first of which students will investigate a museum's collection of art in order to discern and "capture" examples of intertextuality, and during the second of which (or more, depending upon your class's size) students will present orally to one another their chosen works and interpretations.
- **Lesson Plan:**

  1. *Anticipatory Set:* On either the day before or the day of the museum field trip (be it virtual or physical), present to your class one or two works of art, *not* related explicitly to Shakespeare, that represent some major themes or motifs from *Romeo and Juliet*. You might utilize an overhead projector, a document camera-projector, or even physical prints of your chosen works of art. Some recommendations include Andrew Wyeth's *Christina's World*, which might be interpreted as representative of the loneliness and frustration inherent in a physical inability to go home (i.e., Romeo's banishment), and Edgar Degas's *The Bellelli Family*, in which the overwhelming pressure on youth to conform to parents' wishes or mold is as visible as in any of Juliet's interactions with Lord and Lady Capulet. As you present these works, ask students to interpret their relevancies to a major theme, motif, or character in *Romeo and Juliet*, then vocalize their understandings of those commonalities, first with each other, and then to the rest of the class. It is important, even as you kick off this 2-day activity, that you empha-

size to your students the fact that there is no interpretive "right" answer, no more in this anticipatory set than in the actual museum investigation and subsequent oral presentations; thus, all of their ideas and opinions are valid. After you have discussed in this way several works of art, if your students are unaware of the word *intertextuality* and its meaning, then explain that finding thematic or other similarities between works of art, as they have just done, is to discover their intertextuality, a word composed of the root "text" and the prefix "inter-," meaning "between."

2. *Communication of Objective:* Inform students that the purpose of this activity is to discover and present examples of intertextuality between *Romeo and Juliet* and ostensibly unrelated works of visual art. To accomplish these goals, your class will tour or peruse an art museum's collection, digitally "capture" visual artworks that represent themes, motifs, or characteristics of the play, and ultimately discuss in class these chosen works and their similarities to the play.

3. *Field Trip:* Although an actual off-campus field trip to a local art museum is perhaps ideal for this activity, it also is more difficult to coordinate than an online virtual tour of a museum's collection. Regarding the latter, many excellent and eminent museums of art organize and display their collected works on the Web, such as New York's Metropolitan Museum of Art and Paris's Louvre. Regardless of which type of field trip your class undertakes, as students tour or peruse the artistic collection they should attempt to "capture" two works of art each in order to complete this activity: one of which represents intertextually one of *Romeo and Juliet*'s major themes, and the second of which somehow renders one of the play's major characters, albeit in a form potentially quite distinct from Shakespeare's. When a student happens upon a work which he or she feels meets either of these criteria, he or she should "capture" it in two ways: (1) by snapping a digital photograph of the work (if the museum's policy allows it) or otherwise saving a computerized image of it, and (2) by completing a simple Venn diagram detailing that work's similarities to *Romeo and Juliet*. Figure 17 is a sample Venn diagram, completed for Andrew Wyeth's *Christina's World*.

4. *Preparing for Presentations:* Because students are allowed in this activity to choose whatever artistic representations of intertextuality they wish, the results that they all present to their peers will be totally differentiated, both visually and interpretively. Immediately following the field trip, direct students to conflate their "captured" works of art into a central folio by whatever means is simplest and most appropriate for the class as a whole, such as downloading all of their digital images or photographs into one computerized folder. The images should then be organized according to the order in which your students are going to present their choices

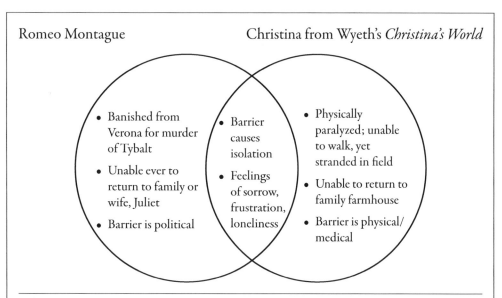

Romeo Montague

Christina from Wyeth's *Christina's World*

- Banished from Verona for murder of Tybalt
- Unable ever to return to family or wife, Juliet
- Barrier is political

- Barrier causes isolation
- Feelings of sorrow, frustration, loneliness

- Physically paralyzed; unable to walk, yet stranded in field
- Unable to return to family farmhouse
- Barrier is physical/ medical

Figure 17. Venn diagram outlining intertextuality between *Romeo and Juliet* and Andrew Wyeth's painting *Christina's World*.

orally to each other. You can determine this presentation order in many ways: alphabetically, through an allowance of students' preferences, by a drawn-straw lottery, etc.

5. *Presentations:* On the assigned day(s), in whatever predetermined order is set, students should each present to their peers the two works of art that they chose as intertextually representative of Shakespeare's themes and characters. During students' oral presentations, their "captured" images should be displayed to the rest of the class—either projected or distributed on printed handouts—and the student audience should be allowed in each case to comment politely or expand upon the presenter's chosen works and interpretive ideas. You may suggest that presenters refer to, or even distribute copies of, their Venn diagrams, which concisely outline the intertextual details upon which they focused. Again, it is important during this final stage of the activity to emphasize to your class the fact that no singular "right" answer exists regarding any of the chosen works of art, and thus that no interpretation is any less valid than others.

Closure: Following all of the presentations, you may wish to have students write responses to (i.e., written "captures" of) the works of art presented by their classmates that they feel were the most poignant, successful, or otherwise memorable. These written responses might then be shared verbally in pairs or with the entire class. An alternate follow-up activity, more differentiated in nature but also more time-consuming and complex, is the assignment to students of individual creative-interpretive projects, as described on pages 163–166 of Chapter 8.

Writing About
Romeo and Juliet

Writing, of course, is the bread and butter of academic scholarship. It is the chief method by which scholars gain knowledge, record knowledge, and communicate knowledge, not that anyone needs to inform English teachers of this fact. Beyond our studies of literature and composition, though, no matter what academic disciplines students gravitate toward in college, they will be evaluated in large part based on their abilities to write well. As such, it simply is a professional responsibility to train our students how to write effectively in a variety of styles and formats.

This chapter presents a multiplicity of writing assignments and assessment instruments, from which I hope that you will cull as suits your educational purposes. In fact, there are five dissimilar genres of writing activities included here, two of which I have modeled to mirror the types of writing that students are asked to produce on the SAT and the AP English Literature and Composition Examination. The SAT requires test-takers to write judgmentally and argumentatively on a debatable topic; these essays are timed to 25 minutes each. The AP English Literature Exam, by contrast, asks students to analyze pieces of literature that they perhaps have never before encountered, scrutinizing their styles, structures, and literary devices within a span of 40 minutes; while essays found on the SAT are argumentative in nature, these AP essays are expository.

Most undergraduate essays, at least in English courses, replicate this latter analytical function, although they usually are much longer and more complex exegeses of larger works of literature. Research-fueled writing, on the other hand, generally presents one's findings more so than engages in and offers scholarly criticism of anything; oftentimes, students' presentations of their research does not even take the form of printed text, as many professors eschew academic traditionalism in favor of arguably more engaging in-class oral presentations. Finally, assignments requiring pupils to digest, reframe, and reproduce in original ways certain thematic aspects of literary works are totally creative in nature, utilizing students' abilities to synthesize real-world issues with fictional literature. All five of these distinct methodologies and compositional styles are represented in this chapter.

25-Minute Argumentative SAT-Style Essays

The writing section of the SAT, introduced and implemented soon after the turn of the millennium, presents students with an issue that is highly debatable, although perhaps not controversially so. Essay questions generally ask students how they feel about a certain issue, which often is presented as a dichotomy (e.g., do you agree with this statement or not?) and test-takers are allowed 25 minutes in which to compose a well-organized, strongly supported answer to the question with which they are presented. The College Board itself makes available many sample SAT questions and a grading rubric for them, as well as anchor papers used to gauge one's proficient assessment of students' answers.

It is itself a highly debatable issue whether standardized test preparation is a legitimately expected part of a professional educator's job. There is value, of course, in training students for success on this examination that holds much sway over the collegiate choices that will be available to them after high school, but "teaching to the test" as an instructional approach or area suffers from a poor reputation among teachers who consider aptitude tests totally extraneous to their particular curricula. Nevertheless, the style of tightly focused argumentative writing that students are asked to produce for the SAT is both a valuable and a potentially underemphasized one, especially among teachers of the gifted who perhaps engage their students more commonly, if not exclusively, in analytical writing more reminiscent of literary criticism and scholarship.

The argumentative essay is a different beast altogether than the literary exegesis and the common book report. Persuasive, effective argumentation, especially with a time limit as demanding as the SAT's, requires students to think and organize themselves quickly and proficiently, culling supportive details from appropriate sources that may or may not involve literature but that always uphold their given position. To write a good SAT-style essay in 25 minutes is a difficult task, and the personal time management that is so necessary for success is itself an excellent skill to be mastered through repeated practice.

As such, I here offer a number of questions designed to engage students' judgmental and argumentative faculties. If you are interested in mimicking the demanding conditions of the actual SAT in your classroom, then limit your students' composition time to 25 minutes. It also is a useful activity, prior to administering any such writing assignment, to consider with students sample questions and responses, such as anchor papers, deciphering together what does and does not make a successful argumentative essay.

Sample Questions

- In Sonnet 116, one of William Shakespeare's (1609/1997b) most famous sonnets, he writes, "Let me not to the marriage of true minds / admit impediments. Love is not love / Which alters when it alteration finds, / Or bends with the remover to remove: / Oh, no! it is an ever-fixéd mark, / That looks on tempests and is never shaken . . ." (1–6). Consider *Romeo and Juliet*; do you agree with Shakespeare that true love is "an ever-fixéd mark" that never changes? Organize and compose an essay in which you consider this issue. Support your argument with examples academic or otherwise.

- The Prologue to *Romeo and Juliet* mentions immediately that the drama is set "In fair Verona, where we lay our scene" (2). Obviously, Shakespeare considered the audience's recognition of the play's geographic setting important. In your opinion, could the story take place anywhere and be just as effective? Organize and compose an essay in which you consider this issue. Support your argument with examples academic or otherwise.

- One way in which Romeo, Juliet, and the couple's love for each other have all been described is "idealistic." Some critics have gone so far as to theorize that the lovers' romantic idealism is actually what causes their downfall and the play's ultimate tragedy. Do you agree with this opinion? Organize and compose an essay in which you consider this issue. Support your argument with examples academic or otherwise.

- Although appearing in only three scenes, County Paris serves a crucial role in advancing the plot of *Romeo and Juliet* toward its denouement. Opinions of literary critics, readers, and theatergoers alike are constantly divided when it comes to Paris and what to make of him; is he a villainous character, worthy of the audience's abhorrence, or is he simply an unwilling tool in the Fates' winding of the lovers' unstoppable fortune? Organize and compose an essay in which you consider this issue. Support your argument with examples academic or otherwise.

- Prince Escalus, and by extension Shakespeare, concludes *Romeo and Juliet* by stating firmly, "never was a story of more woe / Than this of Juliet and her Romeo" (5.3.320–321). Certainly this drama has over the years engendered its share of tears and heartache, but do you agree with this definitive statement regarding its woeful supremacy? Organize and compose an essay in which you consider this issue. Support your argument with examples academic or otherwise.

 Upon seeing Juliet for the first time, Romeo says of his immediate beloved, "Beauty too rich for use, for earth too dear" (1.5.54). Some critics have interpreted in this line a foreshadowing of the eventual downfall of the two characters' love affair, as its larger implication is that anything perfect, celestial, and therefore unearthly cannot possibly exist in a mortal, imperfect, earthy world. Do you agree? Is a truly perfect love attainable for earthbound human beings? Organize and compose an essay in which you consider this issue. Support your argument with examples academic or otherwise.

Grading Rubric

Students' engagement in any writing process is not optimized, of course, without a subsequently prompt provision to them of useful feedback. Figure 18 is an original grading rubric designed to mirror the expectations of the College Board on the writing portion of the SAT. Like any essay actually prepared for the SAT, your students' products are gauged via this rubric on a 6-point scale.

You may wish to employ a process of peer-assessment among your students, whereby they evaluate each others' argumentative essays using this rubric. I caution you, however, that such peer-assessment generally is quite invalid if the students are not trained beforehand on how the rubric "works" and what differently graded essays "look like"; thus, the process of considering scored anchor papers with your students is tremendously valuable in ensuring that they all are on the same evaluative page, so to speak. Moreover, it is advisable to implement peer-assessment on an identity-blind basis, whereby students' essay products are photocopied and distributed for this evaluation, minus the authors' names.

40-Minute Analytical AP-Style Essays

The AP English Literature and Composition Examination requires students to compose three essays, in addition to answering a battery of multiple-choice questions. In contrast to the argumentative compositions found on the SAT, these three essays are analytical; to write them effectively, students must be exegetes, mining various texts—one excerpt of poetry, another of prose, and a work of choice—for symbolism, aspects of syntax and other style, elements of formal structure, and the like. Rather than the defense of a judgmental position, insight into and explanation of an author's purposes and methods is the name of the game

	Grade of 6	*Grade of 5*	*Grade of 4*	*Grade of 3*	*Grade of 2*	*Grade of 1*
Overall Impression	An exceptional composition, indicating obvious and even mastery	A successful composition, indicating reasonably even mastery	A capable composition, indicating sufficient mastery	An inadequate composition, indicating emergent mastery	A highly inadequate composition, indicating slight mastery	An essentially deficient composition, indicating little or no mastery
Essayist's Point of View	Sharply discerning point of view	Able and perceptive point of view	Lucid point of view	Apparent point of view	Unclear point of view	No viable point of view
Support for Position/ Argument	Obviously suitable examples, reasons, and evidence are used	Suitable examples, reasons, and evidence are used	Sufficient examples, reasons, and evidence are used	Insufficient examples, reasons, and evidence are used	Poorly chosen examples, reasons, and evidence are used	Few or no examples, reasons, and evidence are used
Organization and Focus	Excellent organization and focus	Solid organization and focus	Coherent organization and acceptable focus	Limited organization and focus	Poor organization and focus	Disorganized and unfocused
Progression of Ideas	Skillful progression of ideas	Articulate progression of ideas	Reasonable progression of ideas	Some faults are present in the progression of ideas	Highly faulty progression of ideas	Disorderly or unintelligible progression of ideas
Use of Vocabulary	An apparently practiced and exact use of varied vocabulary	Appropriately varied vocabulary	Acceptable but inconsistent use of varied vocabulary	Pedestrian and somewhat incorrect use of vocabulary	Inadequate and often incorrect use of vocabulary	Elementary errors in vocabulary
Sentence Structure	A significant and expressive range of sentence structures	A range of sentence structures	A limited range of sentence structures	No range of sentence structures	Widespread difficulties in sentence structure	Extreme errors in sentence structure
Grammar, Usage, and Mechanics	Free of all major and minor errors	Nearly free of errors	A number of errors exist	Frequent errors exist	Major errors confuse the essayist's point in places	Widespread, serious errors greatly interfere with the essayist's point

Figure 18. Grading rubric for 25-minute SAT-style essays.

here, and a strong background in literary devices and compositional techniques is essential preparation.

These essays must be no less organized than the SAT-style position papers, but they should be more focused, intricate, and supported by precise textual details, especially because students are allowed nearly twice as long to write each of them as they are to defend their theses for the SAT: 40 minutes as opposed to 25, respectively. As they do with the SAT, the College Board consistently releases AP essay topics and examples of students' responses to them, culled directly from the Literature and Composition Exam; the perusal with one's students of legitimately scored anchor papers is thus excellent preparation for their engagement in the writing process.

Teachers can assume that the literary excerpts given to students on the AP Literature and Composition Examination will be ones with which they are not familiar; it is rare, albeit possible, that the College Board asks test-takers to analyze such common works as Blake's "The Tyger" or *Hamlet*. Thus, students preparing to take the exam must hone their analytical, compositional, *and* time management skills, utilizing all three proficiently and without pause during a 2-hour block of time in which they compose three different exegeses on anything from a poet's syntactical patterns to the holistic structure of a prose piece, or from the symbolism extant in a figurative excerpt to the didactic moral of a work read independently and long ago. Although different than the composition of an effective argumentative essay, this process is no less difficult, and constant practice and directive feedback are the keys to students' improvement and eventual success.

I therefore have included five sample AP-style essay prompts in this chapter's materials section (see pp. 170–174) concerning portions of *Romeo and Juliet*. Students who compose essays on all five of these excerpts will benefit from a myriad of analytical focuses: the prompt concerning Act I asks students to analyze diction, syntax, pacing, and tone; the prompt for Act II requires comparison and contrast of characters' points of view and suggests students' consideration of imagery and figurative language; Act III's prompt regards characterization, both direct and indirect, and students are asked to consider meter and irony, among other devices; the prompt concerning Act IV focuses upon linguistic imagery as a mechanism for conveying emotional intensity; and Act V's prompt returns to the particular issue of dialogic pacing, conveyed in large part by Shakespeare's usage of punctuation. Thus, this collection of in-class writing assignments, if administered wholly, necessitates students' consideration of a great variety of literary devices, techniques, and purposes, all of which are legitimate and reasonable topics and focuses for which to prepare as they work toward the actual AP Literature and Composition Examination.

Grading Rubric

As with argumentative SAT-style essays, students' performance in writing timed analytical essays is improved markedly the prompter and more useful their feedback is. The grading rubric in Figure 19, which is designed to mirror the College Board's expectations for success on the AP Literature and Composition Exam, should help your expedient delivery of focused feedback. It serves as a mechanism for assessing students on a 9-point scale, as per the AP exam's instrument, and considers a wide range of compositional factors.

Peer-assessment among students is potentially as helpful an endeavor in their preparation for the AP exam as for the SAT. Again, please note that the legitimacy and helpfulness of such peer-assessment is lessened if student-graders are not trained beforehand on proper usage of the rubric and comparative analysis of dissimilarly scored anchor papers. This preassessment process utilizing anchor papers is valuable in ensuring that all students in a course understand not only the rubric's criteria, but also how to differentiate among various written responses. Again, I advise you to implement peer-assessment on an identity-blind basis, omitting students' names from any responses that are distributed for peer-assessment.

Extended "College-Length" Analytical Essays

Say the phrase "English paper" and most high school and college students—probably most graduate students, too—quite possibly imagine the same thing: a long exposition of the didactic moral, themes, symbolism, or structure of a given work of literature, probably stretching between 6–10 pages and including quotations, citations, and a detailed list of references or works cited at the back. Certainly such products are common in English courses nationwide, especially at undergraduate and graduate levels of literary study, where they make up the foundation, if not the entirety, of students' corpuses of written work.

Because the College Board assumes that teachers of AP courses, to the best of their abilities, replicate college-level instruction, we would be remiss to ignore such long exegeses completely in favor of shorter, timed, in-class prompts aimed solely at higher scores on the AP test. Students' performances on the exam ultimately will determine their potential reception of undergraduate credit, yes, but it is just as important that once they actually reach college they are familiar with the procedure and experience of writing 8-page papers. Additionally, the more background students have composing in a variety of styles and for a variety of purposes, the more fluent and successful writers they resultantly will become.

Despite teachers' best intentions, however, it is no secret that high-achieving, academically competitive students can be prone to plagiaristic urges regarding

Score of 9	Score of 8	Score of 7
• Rhetorical and stylistic devices analyzed correctly with precision *or* • Persuasive argument is cogent, convincing, and well supported	• Rhetorical and stylistic devices analyzed well *or* • Persuasive argument is cogent and convincing, but only somewhat supported	• Rhetorical and stylistic devices analyzed competently *or* • Persuasive argument is cogent, but a lack of development or support is somewhat unconvincing
• Frequent, succinct, and appropriate references to the text, either directly or indirectly	• Some appropriate references to the text, either directly or indirectly	• A few appropriate references to the text, either directly or indirectly
• Point of view is clearly articulated and reinforced extremely well	• Point of view is clearly articulated and reinforced appropriately	• Point of view is clearly articulated, but reinforced only somewhat
• Extremely well-written; any existent errors are inconsequential	• Well-written; very few and only minor errors are made	• Some errors exist, but they do not interfere with the writer's clear expression of ideas

Score of 6	Score of 5	Score of 4
• Rhetorical and stylistic devices analyzed somewhat haphazardly *or* • Underdeveloped and undersupported persuasive argument is only slightly convincing	• Relevant rhetorical and stylistic devices are analyzed very little *or* • Persuasive argument is underdeveloped and undersupported, and thus unconvincing	• Only secondary rhetorical and stylistic devices are analyzed *or* • Persuasive argument is superficial, perhaps missing the point of the question/prompt
• A few references to the text, directly or indirectly, are only somewhat relevant	• The writer refers to the text, directly or indirectly, very little and only somewhat relevantly	• Almost no relevant references to the text are made, either directly or indirectly
• Point of view is vaguely articulated and reinforced only somewhat	• Point of view is vaguely articulated and reinforced hardly at all	• Point of view is developed incoherently and only somewhat clearly
• Errors exist, very few of which are serious enough to interfere with the writer's clear expression	• Errors in diction, syntax, or grammar do interfere with the writer's clear expression of ideas	• Immature errors exist, demonstrating the writer's lack of control over diction and syntax

Score of 3	Score of 2	Score of 1
• Secondary rhetorical and stylistic devices are incorrectly analyzed *or* • Persuasive argument is seriously flawed, as well as mostly off the topic of the question/prompt	• Any attempted analysis of rhetorical or stylistic devices is extremely simplistic *or* • Persuasive argument is seriously flawed, irrelevant, and unorganized	• No attempt is made to analyze rhetorical or stylistic devices *or* • Irrelevant persuasive argument is excessively flawed and extremely unorganized
• No direct references to the text are made, and indirect references are mostly irrelevant	• No relevant references to the text are made, either directly or indirectly	• No references to the text are made at all, either directly or indirectly
• The writer's point of view is unclear and disjointed	• The writer's point of view is expressed quite unclearly	• The writer's point of view is incomprehensible
• Very immature errors exist, demonstrating the writer's lack of control over standard English syntax and grammar	• Overly simplistic errors demonstrate the writer's lack of control over basic English diction, syntax, and grammar	• Overwhelming errors indicate the writer's extreme lack of control over basic English diction, syntax, and grammar

Scores of 0 are given for blank papers, simple paraphrases of prompts, or essays not on assigned topics.

Figure 19. Grading rubric for AP-style 40-minute essays.

such long essays, especially with the senior year's raised stakes of potential college admissions compounded with normal scholastic pressures. The advent of the Internet has increased exponentially students' abilities and opportunities to plagiarize work, as well; one simple Web site search, plus an electronic copy and paste or two, can save student writers hours of late-night stress. Proactively, in assigning to my AP classes long analytical papers, I attempt to preempt my students' potential plagiarism by formatting the essay assignments in particular ways that discourage dishonesty.

Firstly, rather than ask open-ended interpretive questions of students or request their submission of a vaguely defined paper on a topic of their choice, I distribute to them a list of potential essay theses. I allow them to choose whichever thesis they wish to defend, then instruct them to include that actual thesis—word for word—in their paper, probably within their introductory paragraph. This mandate greatly lessens their potential discovery of a useable essay elsewhere, for the likelihood of other persons having not only written, but also published a legitimate high school essay on that precise topic is remote. Moreover, I reward them with extra credit points for using in their essays a multitude of vocabulary words—I generally choose words that are commonly found in works of literary criticism—that we have previously learned in class; in this way, submitted essays are dotted with contextualized words that not only reinforce for students their denotations, but also act as indicators of students' actual composition of a given essay; after all, random persons who publish essays on the Internet have not learned my classes' vocabulary words, and thus are unlikely to include them with frequency in their exegeses.

Below is a list of potential theses concerning *Romeo and Juliet*. In addition to allowing your students to choose from among them, I recommend that you suggest or require essay lengths not in terms of their numbers of total pages, but in terms of their total word counts; writers can alter the amount of text that fits on computerized pages by changing font and margin sizes, but the same effect is impossible to achieve if they need to produce a set number of words. In estimating the sizes of essays that you hope to receive, consider the fact that an average page typed in a standard size and style of font, bounded by one-inch margins, contains approximately 250 to 300 words.

Sample Essay Theses

- In the play's first scene, Romeo remarks that "sad hours seem long," a statement implying the slow passage of time that marks his Veronese life and unsuccessful pursuit of Rosaline (1.1.166). From the second scene onward, however, time seems to move progressively quicker as the play's action mounts; the frequency of characters' mentions of time's passage likewise increases, demonstrating a positive correlation between time's implicit acceleration and Shakespeare's attention to it in his dialogue.

🍂 Juxtaposition is one of the literary devices that Shakespeare uses most commonly in *Romeo and Juliet*. Importantly, the juxtaposition of images and examples of "light" and "dark" occurs in numerous places throughout the text; Shakespeare, in fact, uses various forms of this juxtaposition not only to comment symbolically on the story, but also to signify the causes of the familial feud, the lovers' relationship, and the drama's tragic denouement.

🍂 There are five pairs of lovers that a reader encounters throughout *Romeo and Juliet*: Lord and Lady Capulet, Lord and Lady Montague, Romeo and Juliet, Romeo and Rosaline, and Juliet's Nurse and her late husband. Some critics have interpreted the play as Shakespeare's didactic statement of belief that love between human beings eventually and inevitably fades or dies altogether; one's consideration of each of these five pairs of lovers supports this interpretation of the tragedy.

🍂 Among the words most frequently used by Shakespeare in *Romeo and Juliet* are "fair" (43 occurrences) and "sweet" (36 occurrences). Ironically, the Bard uses these words quite dichotomously throughout the play, sometimes in positive senses, but sometimes with negative connotations; in this way, through his repeated yet varied usage of these two words, Shakespeare implies through *Romeo and Juliet* the dichotomy that is itself the experience of human love.

🍂 Throughout *Romeo and Juliet*, references to youth and advanced age abound, although rarely in consistent ways. At times, Shakespeare's characters imply youth's desirability in contrast to the disadvantage of old age, yet moments later they suggest quite the opposite, that age and experience are to be sought and respected, while youthfulness is but folly and waste; through this dialogic clash between the temporal states of man, Shakespeare implies symbolically the difficulty of human existence, regardless of one's age.

Grading Rubric

I grade my students' college-length analytical essays using the following instrument (see Figure 20), which focuses attention and evaluation on particular criteria of composition, like any rubric does, yet is flexible enough to allow some measure of the holistic assessment that is common among many undergraduate professors of literature. Because I reward my AP students with extra credit for their usage of contextualized, critical vocabulary words in their essays, I generally determine an initial score for each essay using this rubric, then add to that score with the use of each vocabulary word, perhaps allotting one fourth or one half of a point for each word.

– A + (90–100 points)	– B + (80–90 points)	– C + (70–80 points)	– D + (60–70 points)	– F + (below 60 points)
Essays earning grades of "A" are outstanding in their clear and consistent mastery of analytical skills, demonstrating their writers' exceptional control of effective writing techniques, sustaining extremely insightful and in-depth analysis of complex ideas, and developing and supporting their main points with logically compelling scrutiny and highly persuasive examples. Such essays are clear, interesting, and correct, including strong and highly effective introductory and conclusive paragraphs, as well as appropriate transitions both within paragraphs and across the entire piece. They are sharply focused and well-organized essays, demonstrating coherent unity and a smooth analytical progression, as well as referring frequently and carefully to the text, both directly and indirectly. These essays display excellent use of language, highlighted by effective sentence variety and precisely apt vocabulary; they demonstrate their authors' superior facility with sentence structure, grammar, usage, and mechanics, including few, if any, errors.	Essays earning grades of "B" are effective in their clear and reasonably consistent mastery of analytical skills, demonstrating their writers' considerable control of effective writing techniques, sustaining generally insightful analysis of complex ideas, and developing and supporting their main points with logically sound scrutiny and well-chosen, appropriate examples. Such essays are clear, interesting, and mostly correct, including skillful and effective introductory and conclusive paragraphs, as well as transitions that generally are appropriate and relatively widespread throughout the piece. They are clearly focused and well-organized essays, demonstrating good overall coherence and an apparent analytical progression, as well as referring frequently to the text, both directly and indirectly. These essays display fluent use of language, highlighted by generally effective sentence variety and appropriate vocabulary; they demonstrate their authors' good control of sentence structure, grammar, usage, and mechanics, including occasional, though not overly numerous, errors.	Essays earning grades of "C" are competent in their fairly clear and developing mastery of analytical skills, demonstrating their writers' adequate control of effective writing techniques, sustaining relevant analysis of important ideas, and supporting their main points with acceptable inquiry and sufficient examples. Such essays are reasonably clear and mostly correct, including satisfactory introductory and conclusive paragraphs, as well as occasional usages of appropriate transitions. They are passably focused and organized, demonstrating reasonable coherence and a sufficient analytical progression, as well as referring commonly to the text, either directly or indirectly. These essays display adequate use of language to convey meaning, including some sentence variety and generally appropriate vocabulary; they demonstrate their authors' satisfactory control of sentence structure, grammar, usage, and mechanics, including frequent errors, very few of which are simplistic in nature.	Essays earning grades of "D" are inadequate, revealing limited mastery of analytical skills, demonstrating their writers' inconsistent control of effective writing techniques, sustaining weak analysis of important ideas, and addressing relatively unsupported main points with brittle inquiry and insufficient examples. Such essays are superficial, though mostly correct, and include cursory introductory and conclusive paragraphs, as well as few, if any, appropriate transitions. They are disjointedly focused and organized, demonstrating the writer's overall inability to compose coherently and logically, as well as referring vaguely and indirectly to the text. These essays display weak use of language to convey meaning, including little sentence variety and commonly awkward vocabulary; they demonstrate their authors' unsatisfactory control of sentence structure, grammar, usage, and mechanics, including widespread errors, some of which are simplistic in nature.	Essays earning grades of "F" are seriously flawed or limited, revealing very little mastery of analytical skills, demonstrating their writers' lack of control of effective writing techniques, sustaining seriously flawed analysis of important ideas, and addressing main points without support or examples. Such essays are simple and in many ways incorrect, including little or no introductory and conclusive paragraphs, as well as very few appropriate transitions. They are disorganized and/or unfocused, demonstrating the writer's fundamental inability to compose coherently and logically, as well as exhibiting an almost total neglect of reference to the text. These essays display deficient use of language to convey meaning, including almost no sentence variety and highly awkward vocabulary in many places; they demonstrate their authors' inadequate control of sentence structure, grammar, usage, and mechanics, including pervasive errors, many of which are simplistic in nature.

Total Points (Out of 100):

Figure 20. Scoring rubric for extended analytical essays.

Submissions and Returns

One of my educational beliefs is that the more ways in which I can transform summative assessment into formative assessment, thereby helping my students to learn even as they are being assessed, the better, as they ultimately will improve their skills and augment their learning to a related degree. To this end, in my own AP classes I vary in particular ways two procedures that are inherent to the practice of assigning and evaluating long essays: my collection of students' papers and my subsequent redistribution of them to their authors.

On days on which exegeses are due from students, many teachers anticlimactically cap the compositional process simply by collecting students' papers, then moving on to other activities altogether, leaving the essays themselves forgotten or ignored by students until they eventually are returned with grades and feedback. I personally feel that students who work so hard to produce these essays should be provided a sense of closure or culmination greater than that allowed by a simple passing of papers to the front of the classroom; I want my students to feel proud of their work and to share it with their classmates, as well as to benefit from that sharing in numerical terms, rewarded on their essays' ultimate grades.

As such, I allow my AP students when submitting essays not only to read each others' work as a form of peer editing, but also to modify their own as they garner ideas for improvement from their classmates' products. Some teachers utilize the peer editing process as an evaluative, rather than a productive, tool, whereby students simply find and correct mistakes in their classmates' essays. Their incentive for performing well or concentrating hard as they do so is low; after all, especially after a presumably late night spent writing, to nitpick grammatical and stylistic errors from a friend's essay is hardly engaging, especially when there is no immediate personal benefit to a student editor.

Figure 21 contains instructions to students on how otherwise to engage in "peer editing" as they improve and submit their own essays. My usage of the technique outlined by these instructions has been positive and productive, raising students' motivation to read each others' works and allowing them one last opportunity to amend their own before it is evaluated. I invite you to distribute these directions to your own students or to reproduce it on an overhead transparency the next time that they submit college-length essays.

It is human nature in any class, when receiving back from a teacher one's evaluated essay, to look immediately at the score received, then probably to file the essay away, reading few if any of the teacher's comments scattered throughout it. If a writer is happy with the grade received, then why bother reading the comments? On the other hand, if a writer is disappointed or upset by the grade, then he or she may be too disgusted to peruse the reasons for that perceived "failure" to achieve.

1. Carefully checking that all of your pages are in the correct order, please staple your essay, then place and leave it atop your desk.

2. Please stand up, move about the classroom, and choose an essay to read; do so carefully, thoroughly, and silently. When you are finished reading that essay, please return it to the author's desk and choose another to read similarly.

3. I am going to collect the essays "permanently" in 30 minutes. You have that amount of time not only to read as many peers' essays as possible, but also to edit your own in any way that you wish. If you want to add or amend anything to/in your essay, then please do so in pen. I shall read and grade any such additions or amendments as if they were included, typed, as original portions of your essay. Keep in mind, please, that while you may add anything to your essay at all, from quotations to additional explanatory sentences, from extra transitions to formatting minutiae, I am going to grade all such insertions exactly as I would any other portion of your typed analysis (i.e., watch your grammar, punctuation, spelling, etc.).

4. Make sure, through the usage of arrows and other symbols, that I can tell easily where each insertion is supposed to go in your text. If you do not wish to make any changes to your essay, of course, then you need not. You have 30 minutes.

Figure 21. Procedural directions for essay submissions.

Either way, the efforts of teachers who spend so much time and take so much care in commenting upon students' essays largely are wasted.

The above statements are generalizations, of course, but as one of those teachers who edits and comments upon students' exegeses extensively—it usually take me approximately one hour to assess fully one undergraduate-length essay submitted in my AP classes—I want to ensure as best as I am able that students actually peruse the notes and markings that I make. I therefore utilize two procedures to encourage my students to read my feedback on their essays, the first of which is that I do not give them their received grades when I first redistribute to them their marked-up papers. Rather than staple my rubric and final grade to each pupil's essay, I hold them back when I pass back papers; students' immediate and natural impulse to look at the numerical grade is thus preempted, and they instead look through the annotated pages of the essay, searching for clues as to how it was evaluated. I later (perhaps the next day) distribute to them their respective rubrics, once they have had time to consider and digest my commentary upon their work.

Secondly, because I spend much of that time spent assessing papers in the correction of students' grammatical errors, I choose to reward them for following in my editorial footsteps. If students are able to identify and correct a few errors that they made repeatedly in a given essay, then I augment their score on that essay after the fact. Figure 22, which I distribute to my students for this purpose, outlines the procedure by which I encourage such perusal and improvement; I invite you to make use of it likewise in your own classes.

Research Projects and Essays

Students' engagement in and presentation of original research is another valuable experience that prepares them for undergraduate work, in English or otherwise. Especially in social science courses, most professors expect freshmen matriculating nationwide to be familiar with the procedures for undertaking and completing research on assigned topics, as well as to be proficient at synthesizing and presenting their findings clearly and assiduously. Shakespeare's life and times, containing periods of both mystery and clarity, regarding which few and extensive records were kept, respectively, offers students a wonderfully wide and fertile plain of potential research to investigate.

As with college-length analytical essays, I generally stay away from assigning research papers containing set numbers of pages, because alterations to students' font and margin sizes so easily and profoundly impacts the amount of text that will fit on a given page of an essay. If you wish to assign your students to compose traditional research essays, then the same rubric that I offer for your assessment of college-level exegeses can be used in this evaluative capacity. Keep in mind, however, that research essays are far more documentary than they are interpretive, so the rubric's emphasis on persuasion and analysis should be discounted as irrelevant in regard to research papers.

I personally prefer to eschew traditional research essays in favor of more engaging, creative in-class presentations of students' findings. Allowing pupils opportunities to express themselves in a variety of ways is always good practice, I feel, not only because it accesses so many different expressive talents that students may already possess, but also because it helps them to develop proficiencies in academic areas in which they may be relatively deficient; in other words, it's simply good practice for a kid who is used to writing outstanding essays to compose a visual and oral presentation instead, helping that student to develop faculties that are perhaps too seldom accessed in school.

Thus, I offer below a number of potential research topics designed with such presentations in mind. They can, of course, be altered slightly in order to suit more traditional essay products.

Do You Want Two Points Added Immediately to the Total Score of Your Essay?

1. Find two grammatical errors that you commit very commonly in your essay (you must commit each error a minimum of three times for it to qualify as "very common").

2. Complete (typed or handwritten) and submit to me the following four sentences by tomorrow:

One of my most common errors is [name or precise explanation of error], which can be found [first location of error, including a complete description of it], as well as [second location of error, including a complete description of it], and [third location of error, including a complete description of it].

I plan to avoid making this error on my next essay by [explanation of tactic].

Another of my most common errors is [name or explanation of error], which can be found [first location of error, including a complete description of it], as well as [second location of error, including a complete description of it], and [third location of error, including a complete description of it].

I plan to avoid making this error on my next essay by [explanation of tactic].

(There is no need to underline all of your insertions when you type these sentences; it is simply done so here for editorial purposes.)

Figure 22. Extra credit information.

Sample Research Projects

- Scholars traditionally have had difficulty determining exactly when Shakespeare wrote *Romeo and Juliet*, especially in relation to his other early works. Ultimately, we are aided most in this endeavor by a statement made in 1597, on the title page of the first Quarto edition of the Bard's plays, that *Romeo and Juliet* had been performed for the public both often and successfully by a group of players referred to as Hunsdon's Men. Research what background you can on this archaic group, then prepare a short presentation in which you consider the early stage history of the play, highlighting how exactly this reference to Hunsdon's Men aids scholars in pinpointing the dates of *Romeo and Juliet*'s composition and first presentations to the public.

- Although long thought historically accurate, the feud between the Montagues and Capulets, as dramatized by Shakespeare, actually never occurred. In fact, although the historical Montecchi family did live in Verona, the Capelletti family was located in Cremona, Italy, and scholars have over the years unearthed no connection between these two households. The cause of this misinformation perhaps can be found in the *Inferno* of Dante, Italy's most revered and prestigious poet. Examine the *Inferno* in order to locate the snippet of text that mentions the Montecchi and Capelletti, then try to unearth other sources that over the years further spread inaccurate news of the apocryphal feud. Present your findings to the class in a short, well-organized presentation.

- *Romeo and Juliet* has been adapted and set to music almost as many times as it has been portrayed on film. In the last 200 years, it has been the inspiration for operas by Vincenzo Bellini and Charles Gounod, symphonic works by Hector Berlioz and Peter Tchaikovsky, a ballet by Sergei Prokofiev, and even a Broadway musical, *West Side Story*. The diversity of these adaptations suggests the variety of emotions that Shakespeare's drama can inspire in its audience. Gather at least two of these musical interpretations of the play, then compare and contrast their portrayals of some of the plot's critical moments, such as the balcony scene of Act II. How are their interpretations of these moments similar to or different than one another? How are they similar to or different than Shakespeare's original diction and syntax? Which of these adaptations do you feel is most true to the spirit of the Bard's *Romeo and Juliet*? Present your findings and conclusions in a well-developed multimedia presentation.

- The Prince is identified in the play's first scene by his name, Escalus, a Latinized version of the surname Della Scala. The Della Scala family was actually a historical monarchy that ruled Verona, Italy, in the past. Research this royal family in order to place the setting of *Romeo and Juliet* at a fairly specific point in

Italian history, then be sure to retrace your investigative steps as you offer your scholarly conclusion in a short presentation to your classmates.

The consummation of a passionate love in shared death is an archetypal literary crescendo, found in stories from all ages and cultures the world over. The most commonly used name for this archetypal phenomenon is the German term *liebestod*, which, when translated, approximately means "love-death." Research how sociologists and psychologists, especially Sigmund Freud, interpret the *liebestod* and its emotional meaning or impact upon an artistic audience, then apply their opinions in an interpretive way to *Romeo and Juliet*. Present your research findings and conclusions in a short, well-organized presentation.

Situated between Milan and Venice, Verona is a rather small, yet vibrant city in central Italy. Using both printed and electronic resources, research the physical layout and appearance of Verona, including the prominence of bridges in its landscape and the materials out of which its most historical buildings and other structures were made. If you are able, find pictures of various parts of the city, in both its present and its past. Finally, organize your information into a short presentation to your classmates, helping their realistic visualization of *Romeo and Juliet*'s geographic and urban setting.

Prior to 1576, professional theaters were outlawed in Puritan-controlled London; by extension, they were rare, if extant at all, throughout all of England at that time. In that year, however, James Burbage, a former carpenter and professional actor himself, obtained permission to construct in the northern London suburb of Shoreditch the first permanent playhouse, a structure devoted wholly to the staging of plays. Appropriately, it was simply called the Theatre. Following its construction, Puritan and otherwise governmental opposition to playhouses lessened, and Burbage's Theatre was soon followed by many similar edifices, constructed to satisfy the public's rising demand for staged entertainment. Research the events leading up to and surrounding the construction of the Theatre, including preconstruction civic attitudes and statutes, Burbage's stated motivations for his playhouse's erection, and its immediate impact on London's artistic scene; likewise, research the rise of theatergoing as a socially and/or morally acceptable pastime in pre-Elizabethan England. Share your findings with the rest of your class in a well-organized presentation.

Grading Rubric

Figure 23 is an original grading rubric that you may use to assess students' research presentations. In order to adapt the rubric's point values to a 100-point grading scale, simply multiply students' scores by 6.25. Please note that the final assessment criterion considers predetermined presentation parameters such as

Romeo and Juliet

	4	3	2	1
Content	The project's content is totally legitimate and highly detailed, exhibiting a strong research base.	The project's content is legitimate and detailed, although not exceedingly deep, exhibiting a solid research base.	The project's content is mostly legitimate, but less detailed overall, exhibiting solid research in only some areas.	The project's content is largely illegitimate and lacks detail and depth, exhibiting major deficiencies in the research base.
Organization	The project's organization is outstandingly logical, and the flow between ideas or sections is superbly smooth, demonstrating much forethought and preparation.	The project's organization is logical, with fluid transitions between most ideas or sections, demonstrating good preparation.	The project's organization is logical to some extent, but the flow between ideas or sections would benefit from stronger transitioning; overall, solid, but not exceptional, preparation is evidenced.	The project's organization is largely illogical, and the flow between ideas or sections is awkward and/or jumpy in many places, demonstrating haphazard preparation.
Engagement of Audience/ Theatricality	The presentation to the audience is cleverly creative, highly original, and thoroughly engaging, exhibiting strong theatricality.	The presentation to the audience is creative, somewhat original, and engaging at many points, exhibiting present, but limited, theatricality.	The presentation to the audience is solid, but lacks creativity and originality at most points; the audience is engaged sporadically, but the presentation overall lacks theatricality.	The presentation to the audience is largely mundane or routine, greatly lacking originality; the audience's response is generally indifferent to the presentation's banality.
Adherence to Project Parameters	The presentation fits perfectly all of the assignment's parameters, such as time limit and/or included elements. *or* The presentation exceeds the assignment's parameters through the use of additional resources or elements.	The presentation fits most of the assignment's parameters, such as time limit and/or included elements.	The presentation fits only a limited amount of the assignment's parameters, such as time limit and/or included elements.	The presentation fits none of the assignment's parameters, such as time limit and/or included elements.

Total Score (Out of 16 Possible): _____

Figure 23. Grading rubric for research presentations.

time limits, which obviously are malleable according to your own instructional purposes and the abilities and talents of your pupils.

Individualized Creative-Interpretive Projects

Another of my own educational beliefs is that the most truly valuable learning that students accomplish in schools occurs not in an academic vacuum, but in an intellectual or emotional synthesis of scholastic theory and real-world relevance. We all are more apt to remember events, details, and facts that hold personal meaning for us, that relate in some way to the occurrences and details of our own lives. Our favorite poems or novels are our *favorites*, of course, because they hold personal significances for us; their ascension to that title is not arbitrary, nor should students' engagement of classic works and themes of literature be. As teachers, if we want our lessons and our students' learning to last, to impact their lives beyond the finite boundaries of classroom walls and school calendars, then we must help our pupils to personalize their learning.

I likewise believe that in high school English classes nationwide, students commonly are asked to recognize, interpret, and understand the artistic intentions and products of canonical authors and poets in a largely vacuous context, without being given the opportunity to reflect upon or reframe those authors' and poets' visions and themes as they relate to students' own lives. Among the most common questions that I ask my AP students in consideration of our literary studies are "So what?" "Why should you care?" and "Why is this stuff relevant to your life?" Students who can answer such questions, regardless of the given work of literature being considered, are able to find, digest, and personalize a work's humanness, the true and lasting reasons why the posterity of canonical artists is timelessly relevant.

Yes, we can utilize *Romeo and Juliet* as a tool to teach classes of young people about Veronese culture, iambic pentameter, figurative language, and dramatic tradition, but unless some theme, idea, conflict, or character in the play connects powerfully with an individual student somehow, then few if any of those academic details are liable to stay with that child beyond his or her classroom experience. In brief, isn't the point of reading literature at all—or studying anything, for that matter—to help you understand more clearly yourself, your life, and your world? Your assignment that students create individualized creative-interpretive projects aims to augment just those understandings.

I have required such original products from my own AP students for years, and the great diversity of submissions that I have received from them testifies to their profound, entertaining, and too often untapped creative talents. One former student composed, utilizing a marimba and toms, a suite portraying *Hamlet's* implication that knowledge and intelligence are a burdensome curse; another wrote, sang, and recorded a song concerning the abandonment of Frankenstein's monster, expressing how that betrayal mirrors her own felt experience as the daughter of divorcees. One year, someone related King Lear's obstinate hubris to modern athletics, designing and filming a mock sports report concerning the misguided blindness of arrogance and greed; others have painted and drawn thematic visualizations, skinned and tanned leather and molded wood for a *Hamlet* dream catcher, designed and compiled photographic essays, and composed original narrative poems, short stories, or one-act plays. I've received shadow boxes, works of stained glass, mobiles and marionettes, computerized short films, and interpretive dances! And, of all of the assignments that I require of my AP students, these creative-interpretive projects are by far the most enjoyable to grade; I look forward to their creative expressions every year.

The following assignment sheet (see Figure 24) is one that you may distribute to your own students if you choose to engage them in this taxing, yet profoundly rewarding endeavor. It is important that students understand the difference between creatively interpreting (i.e., reframing), aspects of *Romeo and Juliet*, and simply regurgitating the plot or its characters in an alternative, albeit extremely similar, setting or situation; the former is the goal of this project, for personalized learning occurs when students are freed from the constraints of Shakespeare's original to focus instead on the truly human, universal heart of the story.

In order to encourage students' honest consideration of themes, emotions, and other elements of both their own artwork (self-reflection) and Shakespeare's original (critical interpretation), I require them to submit short explanations of their artistic products, their interpretive and creative goals in producing them, and the relative success that they feel they achieved in this undertaking. This explanatory portion of the project ensures that students both submit original works that truly are relevant to the literature being studied and verbalize the intertextual ties between that literature and themselves.

Rather than a rubric highlighting gradients of success on various criteria, I assess students' creative-interpretive projects using the "numerical checklist" in Figure 25, which allows for the tremendous—and thus somewhat irreconcilable with the idea of concrete project parameters—diversity of products. The grading criteria defined by this checklist are malleable enough that no matter what a student produces and submits, it is assessable using this instrument. Moreover, its comparatively holistic focus contrasts with the fastidious nature of most hierarchical rubrics; considering students' products that are themselves works of art, I personally see this wide-angle view as optimal.

Creative-Interpretive Project Guidelines

In higher level English classes nationwide, students too often are asked to reflect upon, interpret, and digest the artistic intentions of famous authors without being given the opportunity to reflect upon, interpret, and digest the importance of those authors' visions and themes as they relate to students' own lives. If you cannot relate a theme or philosophical concept to your world, then why bother to study it? Such an idea, an idea without personal utility, becomes inherently useless. In brief, the point of reading literature at all—or any idea, for that matter—is to help you understand better yourself, your own life, and your own world. I hope that this assignment provides you with an opportunity to do just that!

Requirements
1. You are going to submit and reflect upon a creative interpretation—wholly of your own design—of one of *Romeo and Juliet*'s major themes.
2. This interpretation can take any artistic shape that you wish, including (but not limited to):
    a. self-made movie,
    b. narrative poem,
    c. one-act play,
    d. song (sung and/or played),
    e. series of related photographs,
    f. painting,
    g. interpretive dance,
    h. short story,
    i. symbolic marionette or collage,
    j. mock news broadcast,
    k. sculpture, or
    l. some amalgamation of many of the above or some other product of your choice.
3. Your artistic piece does not need to mirror the story of *Romeo and Juliet* in any way, nor does it have to represent any of the literature's characters, settings, situations, etc. What it *must* do is represent in some tangible way one of the work's major *themes* or philosophical ideas (e.g., the futility of fighting one's fate, the emotional difficulty of divided loyalties, the timeless clashes of generations, or the self-destructive nature of hatred).
4. Your creation is to be accompanied by a 400–600-word analysis, a self-reflection, upon both your creative work of art and the play that influenced its creation, explaining just what theme(s) are portrayed in your own work, plus how and why they are important to you not just as a reader of literature, but also as a living, breathing, emotional human being.

Figure 24. Creative-interpretive project guidelines for *Romeo and Juliet*.

Project Grading Checklist

Conceptual Validity
- The interpretive concept underlying the work of art is well thought-out, as explicated either by the work of art itself or by the accompanying analytical paper.

  _____/10

- It is clear, either upon viewing the work of art itself or after reading the accompanying paper, that at least one major theme of *Romeo and Juliet* is present and central to the concept of the newly created work of art.

  _____/10

- The artist's conceptualization of both this major theme and its representation in the new work of art is *not* contrary to Shakespeare's original conceptualization of the same theme, but parallel to it.

  _____/10

Accompanying Reflective Analysis
- The analytical paper that accompanies the work of art is between 400 and 600 words, and there are no major grammatical errors in it.

  _____/10

- The analytical paper reflects clearly and validly upon both the original work of literature and its inspirational effect upon the new work of art, explicating such important factors as their thematic bond, their philosophical views, and/or their sameness of mood.

  _____/10

- It is clear from the paper that the artist/student has thought about the original work of literature, its themes, and his or her own art not only thoroughly, but also well.

  _____/10

Overall Impression
- After viewing the work of art, I as the assessor feel that the artist/student has worked hard on this project, both intellectually and artistically.

  _____/20

- After viewing the work of art, I as the assessor am impressed both with the student's capacity for analyzing and reflecting upon philosophical, thematic literature and with his or her ability to correlate that literature with the "real world" of his or her life.

  _____/20

  Total Score (Out of 100): _____

Figure 25. Grading "checklist" for creative-interpretive project for *Romeo and Juliet*.

Conclusion

This chapter's contents present the diversity of ways in which students, at the end of their study of *Romeo and Juliet*, can demonstrate their mastery, their ownership, and their synthesis of the many disparate threads woven into the play's coherent whole. Although any of the five writing styles included in this chapter might legitimately serve to engender an end-of-unit assessment, I recommend that you overlap several of them at once, helping your students to interpret and reshape the play for themselves in a variety of useful, textual ways.

Finally, although I propose here that you conclude your unit of literary study with a writing product, this book's five core pedagogical chapters, of which this one is the last, do not need to be followed in order. I personally believe that the most effective teachers, and thus the most memorable and effective classes, interweave numerous and various activities simultaneously: a Socratic seminar discussion one day, a performance activity on another, followed by a written assessment and item analysis, then a self-reflective dose of bibliotherapy, all capped off with a virtual field trip to end the week. In this way, I invite you to use the contents of this book not as a step-by-step recipe for instructional success, but as a cabinet of potential ingredients. At its root, the most personal and energetic teaching, like the most personal and energetic learning, is creative and individual. I hope that these activities and techniques inspire your own creative and unique instruction, and that they provide you with license and resources to make the guided study of *Romeo and Juliet* your own, adding a pinch of this and a dash of that to create one very memorable, satisfying course.

Chapter Materials

AP-Style Essay Prompt
Romeo and Juliet, Act I

Read carefully the following interchange and subsequent monologue, in which Mercutio describes Queen Mab, the fictional fairies' midwife. Then compose a well-organized essay in which you analyze how Mercutio's diction and syntax indicate, to either readers or actors of the play, the pacing and tone with which this scene should be performed on stage. **Time limit: 40 minutes.**

Romeo: I dreamt a dream tonight.
Mercutio: And so did I.
Romeo: Well, what was yours?
Line **Mercutio:** That dreamers often lie.
5 **Romeo:** In bed asleep while they do dream things true.
Mercutio: O, then I see Queen Mab hath been with you.
    She is the fairies' midwife, and she comes
    In shape no bigger than an agate stone
    On the forefinger of an alderman,
10   Drawn with a team of little atomi
    Over men's noses as they lie asleep.
    Her wagon spokes made of long spinners' legs,
    The cover of the wings of grasshoppers,
    Her traces of the smallest spider web,
15   Her collars of the moonshine's wat'ry beams,
    Her whip of cricket's bone, the lash of film,
    Her wagoner a small gray-coated gnat,
    Not half so big as a round little worm
    Pricked from the lazy finger of a maid.
20   Her chariot is an empty hazelnut,
    Made by the joiner squirrel or old grub,
    Time out o' mind the fairies' coachmakers.
    And in this state she gallops night by night
    Through lovers' brains, and then they dream of love;
25   On courtiers' knees, that dream on cur'sies straight;
    O'er lawyers' fingers, who straight dream on fees;
    O'er ladies' lips, who straight on kisses dream,
    Which oft the angry Mab with blisters plagues
    Because their breaths with sweetmeats tainted are.

30   Sometime she gallops o'er a courtier's nose,
    And then dreams he of smelling out a suit.
    And sometime comes she with a tithe-pig's tail,
    Tickling a parson's nose as he lies asleep;
    Then he dreams of another benefice.
35   Sometime she driveth o'er a soldier's neck,
    And then dreams he of cutting foreign throats,
    Of breaches, ambuscadoes, Spanish blades,
    Of healths five fathom deep, and then anon
    Drums in his ear, at which he starts and wakes
40   And, being thus frighted, swears a prayer or two
    And sleeps again. This is that very Mab
    That plats the manes of horses in the night
    And bakes the elflocks in foul sluttish hairs,
    Which once untangled much misfortune bodes.
45   This is the hag, when maids lie on their backs,
    That presses them and learns them first to bear,
    Making them women of good carriage.
    This is she—
Romeo: Peace, peace, Mercutio, peace.
50   Thou talk'st of nothing.
Mercutio: True, I talk of dreams,
    Which are the children of an idle brain,
    Begot of nothing but vain fantasy,
    Which is as thin of substance as the air
55   And more inconstant than the wind, who woos
    Even now the frozen bosom of the North
    And, being angered, puffs away from thence,
    Turning his side to the dew-dropping South.

AP-Style Essay Prompt
Romeo and Juliet, Act II

Read carefully the two soliloquies found below, both spoken in Act II of *Romeo and Juliet*. Then compose a well-organized essay in which you compare and contrast the two speakers' apparent points of view regarding the relationship between human beings and inhuman nature. Consider such elements as diction, imagery, tone, and figurative language. **Time limit: 40 minutes.**

Spoken by Romeo
Act II, scene ii

But soft, what light through yonder window breaks?
It is the East, and Juliet is the sun.
Arise, fair sun, and kill the envious moon,
Line Who is already sick and pale with grief
5   That thou, her maid, art far more fair than she.
Be not her maid since she is envious.
Her vestal livery is but sick and green,
And none but fools do wear it. Cast it off.
It is my lady. O, it is my love!
10   O, that she knew she were!
She speaks, yet she says nothing. What of that?
Her eye discourses; I will answer it.
I am too bold. 'Tis not to me she speaks.
Two of the fairest stars in all the heaven,
15   Having some business, do entreat her eyes
To twinkle in their spheres till they return.
What if her eyes were there, they in her head?
The brightness of her cheek would shame those stars
As daylight doth a lamp; her eye in heaven
20   Would through the airy region stream so bright
That birds would sing and think it were not night.
See how she leans her cheek upon her hand.
O, that I were a glove upon that hand,
That I might touch that cheek!
25   . . . She speaks.
O, speak again, bright angel, for thou art
As glorious to this night, being o'er my head,
As is a wingèd messenger of heaven
Unto the white-upturnèd wond'ring eyes
30   Of mortals that fall back to gaze on him
When he bestrides the lazy puffing clouds
And sails upon the bosom of the air.

Spoken by Friar Lawrence
Act II, scene iii

The gray-eyed morn smiles on the frowning night,
Check'ring the eastern clouds with streaks of light,
And fleckled darkness like a drunkard reels
Line From forth day's path and Titan's fiery wheels.
5   Now, ere the sun advance his burning eye,
The day to cheer and night's dank dew to dry,
I must upfill this osier cage of ours
With baleful weeds and precious-juicèd flowers.
The earth that's nature's mother is her tomb;
10   What is her burying grave, that is her womb;
And from her womb children of divers kind
We sucking on her natural bosom find,
Many for many virtues excellent,
None but for some, and yet all different.
15   O, mickle is the powerful grace that lies
In plants, herbs, stones, and their true qualities.
For naught so vile that on the earth doth live
But to the earth some special good doth give;
Nor aught so good but, strained from that fair use,
20   Revolts from true birth stumbling on abuse.
Virtue itself turns vice, being misapplied,
And vice sometime by action dignified.
Within the infant rind of this weak flower
Poison hath residence and medicine power:
25   For this, being smelt, with that part cheers
     each part;
Being tasted, stays all senses with the heart.
Two such opposèd kings encamp them still
In man as well as herbs—grace and rude will;
30   And where the worser is predominant,
Full soon the canker death eats up that plant.

AP-Style Essay Prompt
Romeo and Juliet, Act III

Read carefully the following excerpt from Act III of *Romeo and Juliet*. Then compose an essay in which you analyze Shakespeare's techniques for conveying both direct and indirect characterization. Consider such elements as tone, syntax, meter, and irony. **Time limit: 40 minutes.**

Benvolio: I pray thee, good Mercutio, let's retire.
The day is hot, the Capels are abroad,
And if we meet we shall not 'scape a brawl,
Line   For now, these hot days, is the mad blood stirring.
5 **Mercutio:** Thou art like one of these fellows that, when he
enters the confines of a tavern, claps me his sword
upon the table and says "God send me no need of
thee" and, by the operation of the second cup,
draws him on the drawer when indeed there is no
10 need.
Benvolio: Am I like such a fellow?
Mercutio: Come, come, thou art as hot a jack in thy mood
as any in Italy, and as soon moved to be moody,
and as soon moody to be moved.
15 **Benvolio:** And what to?
Mercutio: Nay, an there were two such, we should have
none shortly, for one would kill the other. Thou—
why, thou wilt quarrel with a man that hath a hair
more or a hair less in his beard than thou hast.
20 Thou wilt quarrel with a man for cracking nuts,
having no other reason but because thou hast hazel
eyes. What eye but such an eye would spy out
such a quarrel? Thy head is as full of quarrels as
an egg is full of meat, and yet thy head hath been
25 beaten as addle as an egg for quarreling. Thou
hast quarreled with a man for coughing in the
street because he hath wakened thy dog that hath
lain asleep in the sun. Didst thou not fall out with
a tailor for wearing his new doublet before Easter?
30 With another, for tying his new shoes with old
ribbon? And yet thou wilt tutor me from
quarreling?
Benvolio: An I were so apt to quarrel as thou art, any man
should buy the fee simple of my life for an hour
35 and a quarter.
Mercutio: The fee simple? O simple!

Enter Tybalt, Petruchio, and others.

Benvolio: By my head, here comes the Capulets.
Mercutio: By my heel, I care not.
Tybalt, *to his companions*:
40 Follow me close, for I will speak to them.—
Gentlemen, good e'en. A word with one of you.
Mercutio: And but one word with one of us? Couple it
with something. Make it a word and a blow.
Tybalt: You shall find me apt enough for that, sir, an you
45 will give me occasion.
Mercutio: Could you not take some occasion without giving?
Tybalt: Mercutio, thou consortest with Romeo.
Mercutio: Consort? What, dost thou make us minstrels?
An thou make minstrels of us, look to hear
50 nothing but discords. Here's my fiddlestick;
here's that shall make you dance. Zounds,
consort!
Benvolio: We talk here in the public haunt of men.
Either withdraw unto some private place,
55 Or reason coldly of your grievances,
Or else depart. Here all eyes gaze on us.
Mercutio: Men's eyes were made to look, and let them gaze.
I will not budge for no man's pleasure, I.

Enter Romeo.

Tybalt: Well, peace be with you, sir. Here comes my man.
60 **Mercutio:** But I'll be hanged, sir, if he wear your livery.
Marry, go before to field, he'll be your follower.
Your Worship in that sense may call him "man."

AP-Style Essay Prompt

Romeo and Juliet, Act IV

Read carefully these two speeches, both spoken by Juliet in Act IV of *Romeo and Juliet*. Then compose a well-organized essay in which you consider Juliet's use of imagery in both speeches. Consider especially how her choice of imagery helps to convey emotional intensity, as well as ways in which the contents of these speeches compare and/or contrast. **Time limit: 40 minutes.**

Monologue Spoken to Friar Lawrence
Act IV, scene i

O, bid me leap, rather than marry Paris,
From off the battlements of any tower,
Or walk in thievish ways, or bid me lurk
Line Where serpents are. Chain me with roaring bears,
5 Or hide me nightly in a charnel house,
O'ercovered quite with dead men's rattling bones,
With reeky shanks and yellow chapless skulls.
Or bid me go into a new-made grave
And hide me with a dead man in his shroud
10 (Things that to hear them told have made me tremble),
And I will do it without fear or doubt,
To live an unstained wife to my sweet love.

Soliloquy Spoken in Juliet's Bedroom
Act IV, scene iii

What if this mixture does not work at all?
Shall I be married then tomorrow morning?

[*She takes out her knife and puts it down.*]

No, no, this shall forbid it. Lie thou there.
Line What if it be a poison which the Friar
5 Subtly hath ministered to have me dead,
Lest in this marriage he should be dishonored
Because he married me to Romeo?
I fear it is. And yet methinks it should not,
For he hath still been tried a holy man.
10 How if, when I am laid into the tomb,
I wake before the time that Romeo
Come to redeem me? There's a fearful point.
Shall I not then be stifled in the vault,
To whose foul mouth no healthsome air breathes in,
15 And there die strangled ere my Romeo comes?
Or, if I live, it is not very like
The horrible conceit of death and night,
Together with the terror of the place—
As in a vault, an ancient receptacle
20 Where for this many hundred years the bones
Of all my buried ancestors are packed;
Where bloody Tybalt, yet but green in earth,
Lies fest'ring in his shroud; where, as they say,
At some hours in the night spirits resort—
25 Alack, alack, it is not like that I,
So early waking, that with loathsome smells,
And shrieks like mandrakes torn out of the earth,
That living mortals, hearing them run mad—
O, if I wake, shall I not be distraught,
30 Environèd with all these hideous fears,
And madly play with my forefather's joints,
And pluck the mangled Tybalt from his shroud,
And, in this rage, with some great kinsman's bone,
As with a club, dash out my desp'rate brains?
35 O look, methinks I see my cousin's ghost
Seeking out Romeo that did spit his body
Upon a rapier's point! Stay, Tybalt, stay!
Romeo, Romeo, Romeo! Here's drink. I drink to thee

[*She drinks and falls upon her bed within the curtains.*]

AP-Style Essay Prompt
Romeo and Juliet, Act V

Read carefully the following excerpt from Act V of *Romeo and Juliet*. Then compose a well-organized essay in which you analyze Shakespeare's pacing techniques throughout this brief scene. Consider elements such as tone, syntax, meter, and punctuation. **Time limit: 40 minutes.**

Enter Friar Lawrence with lantern, crow, and spade.

Friar Lawrence: Saint Francis be my speed! How oft tonight
Have my old feet stumbled at graves!—Who's there?
Balthasar: Here's one, a friend, and one that knows you well.
Line **Friar Lawrence:** Bliss be upon you. Tell me, good my friend,
5 What torch is yond that vainly lends his light
To grubs and eyeless skulls? As I discern,
It burneth in the Capels' monument.
Balthasar: It doth so, holy sir, and there's my master,
One that you love.
10 **Friar Lawrence:** Who is it?
Balthasar: Romeo.
Friar Lawrence: How long hath he been here?
Balthasar: Full half an hour.
Friar Lawrence: Go with me to the vault.
15 **Balthasar:** I dare not, sir.
My master knows not but I am gone hence,
And fearfully did menace me with death
If I did stay to look on his intents.
Friar Lawrence: Stay, then. I'll go alone. Fear comes upon me.
O, much I fear some ill unthrifty thing.
20 **Balthasar:** As I did sleep under this yew tree here,
I dreamt my master and another fought,
And that my master slew him.
Friar Lawrence: [*moving toward the tomb*] Romeo!—
25 Alack, alack, what blood is this that stains
The stony entrance of this sepulcher?
What means these masterless and gory swords
To lie discolored by this place of peace?
Romeo! O, pale! Who else? What, Paris too?
30 And steeped in blood? Ah, what an unkind hour
Is guilty of this lamentable chance!

Advanced Placement Classroom: Romeo and Juliet © Prufrock Press • This page may be photocopied or reproduced with permission for classroom use.

Glossary

🌺 *alliteration:* Alliteration is the name for repeated sounds—not necessarily letters—at the beginnings of words in proximity, such as, "Chronological queens created many kaleidoscopes."

🌺 *allusion:* In a work of literature, an allusion is a reference to characters, events, or elements from a separate literary work. William Blake's (1789/1979) "The Tyger," for example, alludes to the myths of Icarus and Prometheus, respectively, in lines 7–8: "On what wings dare he aspire? / What the hand dare seize the fire?"

🌺 *analogy:* An analogy is a comparison of things by way of their similarities. If William Shakespeare were the European continent, one might analogize, then *Romeo and Juliet* would be Paris, France, its seat of romance and drama.

🌺 *anecdote:* An anecdote is a short, humorous story. The adjective "short" is, of course, only meaningful relative to other stories, but while *A Midsummer Night's Dream* is too long to be considered an anecdote, a 2-minute synopsis of that play is not.

🌺 *antagonist:* The antagonist of any story is the character, institution, or force that opposes the tale's protagonist. It is a common misconception that one should be able to identify in any work of literature a singular antagonist; the collective antagonists at the end of Dickens's *A Tale of Two Cities*, for example, are the rebelling Parisian Jacquerie. Moreover, in Orwell's *1984*, Big Brother is an institutional antagonist, while the truest antagonist to be found in William Golding's *Lord of the Flies* is the intangible, half-imagined Beast.

🌿 *archaism:* An archaism is something archaic (old and outdated). Both criteria must be met, so while the English language, for example, is quite old, it is not yet outdated, and thus not archaic; on the other hand, the particular word "thee" is both old and outdated, so it is classifiable as an archaism.

🌿 *aside:* There are two different types of dramatic commentary classifiable as asides. Firstly, moments arise in a scripted performance when a character briefly ceases speaking to others on stage and instead speaks directly to the audience, apparently the only people who can hear these comments; this type of aside is common in television sitcoms. Secondly, asides can be brief speeches wherein an actor on stage speaks only to him- or herself, inaudible to any other characters, as if he or she is simply thinking out loud; muttering under one's breath is a common example of this type of aside.

🌿 *assonance:* Assonance is the repetition of vowel sounds, as in the sentence "About the town the owl could not be found," wherein the words "About," "town," "owl," and "found" all contain identical vowel sounds, regardless of their distinct spellings.

🌿 *cacophony:* The word *cacophony* describes harsh, discordant, probably loud noises, and it only is rarely applicable to textual writing, especially polished works of art. Nevertheless, sometimes authors and poets do piece together words that are cacophonous if read aloud to make a particular point; Charles Dickens's (1859/1981) description of the storming of the Bastille, from *A Tale of Two Cities*, is a clear example of his attempt to replicate an aural cacophony:

> Everywhere was tumult, exultation, deafening and maniacal bewilderment, astounding noise, yet furious dumb-show. "The Prisoners!" "The Records!" "The secret cells!" "The instruments of torture!" "The Prisoners!" Of all these cries, and ten thousand incoherencies, "The Prisoners!" was the cry most taken up . . . (p. 200)

🌿 *characterization, direct and indirect:* Characterization is the way in which an author illuminates a character's personality; it has less to do with someone's size or physical appearance than with his or her personality. Direct characterization occurs when the audience explicitly is told something about a character, such as, "Brett was really friendly and energetic." Indirect characterization requires that the audience infer characteristics from someone's actions, dialogue, or decisions, or from another's description; one can infer from this sentence, for example, the student's shy, scholarly personality: "Kristen always arrived early to class, but rarely contributed even a word to the goings-on of the group, though the concentration of her eyes, sometimes compounded with a contented slight smile, consistently demonstrated her intellectual engagement."

climax: The climax of any narrative is the moment of highest suspense, excitement, and drama, the last possible moment when it might be possible for the characters to "turn back the clock," so to speak, and return to the ways that they were at the beginning of their story. At the climax of Homer's *The Odyssey*, he finally arrives home in Ithaca, sheds his beggarly disguise, thereby revealing his true identity, and enacts violent and long-overdue vengeance upon the indignant, panicked suitors.

complication: A story's complication is the plot twist that actually makes the rest of the narrative interesting, exciting, or dramatic; it commonly is confused with the inciting incident, which is the moment of time when the complication arises. In *Romeo and Juliet*, the complication is the love at first sight felt by Romeo and Juliet at the Capulets' ball, for if the lovers never actually love one another, well, then there's no rest of the story.

conceit: A conceit is a metaphor that just does not work or fit very easily. The statement that "The United States of America is a venerable sea turtle, silently gliding through the blue depths" is a metaphor, yes, but it's a bit of a stretch. The word *conceited*, describing someone who makes or thinks too much of him- or herself, is related to this noun.

conflict: Generally defined as a clash or struggle between opposing characters or forces, there are six major types of literary conflict: human vs. human (as Tybalt vs. Mercutio), human vs. nature (as in *Lord of the Flies*), human vs. self (exemplified clearly by both Hamlet and Lady Macbeth), human vs. the supernatural (portrayed strongly in *The Odyssey*), human vs. society (as in *1984*), and human vs. technology (as in Shelley's *Frankenstein*). As a rule, the greater the variety of conflicts in a story, the more engaging it will be.

consonance: Consonance is the repetition of consonant sounds in close proximity, as in the sentence, "The archetypal arachnid attacked the critical acrobat's katydid," where the hard "k" sound is repeated six times.

contraction: Shakespeare's iambic pentameter, like all lines of metrical verse, requires a set number of syllables per line. Often, the Bard needed to say something within a line of verse, but could do so no better than to contract a word into fewer syllables. "For I ne'er saw true beauty till this night" is an example, as the contraction of the two-syllable "never" into one syllable retains the necessary 10 syllables (1.5.60).

couplet, rhyming and unrhymed: A poetic couplet is a series of two successive lines. They need not rhyme, but when they do, they are classified as a rhyming couplet: "Tyger! Tyger! burning bright / In the forests of the night" (Blake,

1789/1979, ll. 1–2). Otherwise, a couplet is simply unrhymed: "Shall I compare thee to a summer's day? / Thou art more lovely and more temperate" (Shakespeare Sonnet 18, 1609/1997a, ll.1–2).

❧ *dialect:* A dialect is a form of language that is characteristic of a particular regional (or otherwise homogenized) group of people. Portrayals of dialects are common among regionalist writers such as Twain or Faulkner.

❧ *dialogue:* A true dialogue is a conversation between two persons, but the word also describes any conversation among three or more individuals. Any portion of a staged drama (that is neither a monologue nor a soliloquy) is a dialogue.

❧ *diction:* Diction is one's choice of words. I explain to my own students the differences among vocabulary, diction, and syntax as per this three-step process: one's vocabulary is his or her treasure chest of all the words that he or she knows; diction is the process of rummaging through that chest in order to choose words to use at any given moment; and syntax is the arrangement of them in a logical way, thereby creating linguistic meaning.

❧ *denouement:* The *denouement* of any story, also known as resolution, is the end result, where the characters, conflicts, and situations stand on the last page, so to speak. The word itself is French, and means "the unwinding" or "unknotting"; thus, the *denouement* of *Romeo and Juliet* is that both eponymous lovers are dead, as are four other persons, but the Capulet and Montague families have resolved to make peace with one another.

❧ *enjambment:* Enjambment is a poetic device whereby syllables, within lines of patterned verse, run over into subsequent lines, making the lines of regularized, syllabic verse "irregular." For example, Dr. Seuss' (1960) famous couplet, "I do not like green eggs and ham. / I do not like them, Sam-I-Am," is written in iambic tetrameter (p. 16). Were he to utilize enjambment, however, then the lines might read instead, "I will not eat green eggs / And ham, I will not eat them, Sam I Am." Poets often use enjambment to highlight or emphasize certain words or phrases over others.

❧ *enunciation:* In metrical poetry, to enunciate is to read as a separate syllable one part of a word that normally would not be. For example, the word "martyred" is normally spoken as a two-syllable word; to enunciate the final suffix, "martyrèd," is to make it a three-syllable word. Poets commonly enunciate syllables to retain metrical regularity, and they often indicate enunciated syllables through the use of an *accent grave* ("è").

❧ *epithet:* An epithet is a phrase that is commonly used to describe a certain individual or characteristic, sort of like a cultural code. To describe someone as being "under the weather," for example, is a coded way of saying that he or she is ill.

euphony: The opposite of cacophony, euphony is the grouping together of harmonic, pleasing sounds. Much poetry is naturally euphonic, engendered by such devices as alliteration and consonance, such as in these lines from Robert Frost's (1923/1969) "Nothing Gold Can Stay": "Nature's first green is gold, / Her hardest hue to hold. / Her early leaf's a flower; / But only so an hour. / Then leaf subsides to leaf" (ll. 1–5).

exposition: In any chronological narrative, the exposition occurs prior to the introduction of the major complication via the inciting incident. It contains a near-complete lack of tension and excitement—its purpose, after all, is to explicate basic elements such as characters and setting—so any story's suspense rises only after its exposition's conclusion, hence the rising of the graph in Figure 26 toward the climax. Almost the entirety of *Romeo and Juliet*'s Act I qualifies as its exposition, in which we meet the Capulets and Montagues, learn about their feud, identify where and when the story takes place, and so on. Until Romeo meets Juliet at the Capulets' ball, which is the inciting incident of the play, there really is no suspense, hence the flatness of the exposition's depiction.

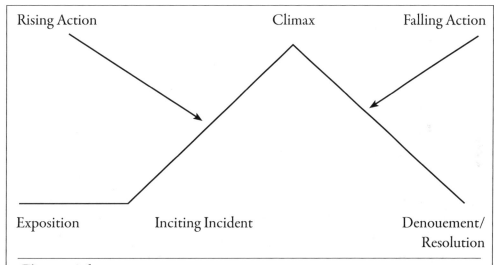

Figure 26. Basic plot diagram. This is an illustration of any chronological narrative's plot; the progress of time is depicted horizontally, while the story's incorporation of suspense, excitement, and drama is represented vertically.

falling action: A story's falling action occurs after the passage of its climax. For example, at the top of any rollercoaster's first hill, up which the cars go slowly and steadily, there is that last possible moment when the ride could be stopped mechanically, when the cars would cease their progress and nobody would have to speed downhill; after the passage of that last possible moment of stoppage, however, gravity takes over, and the cars must speed inevitably downward. If that last moment before gravity takes over is the story's climax, then the speeding downhill is the falling action, during which it is literally impossible to stop the plot's action and return to the narrative's beginning unaltered.

🙖 *figurative language:* Figurative language describes one thing in terms of something else, although it is not meant to be understood literally. It is the larger categorical umbrella under which metaphors, similes, analogies, allegories, symbols, and the like all fit. The statement that "it's raining cats and dogs" often is called a "figure of speech," a phrase derived from the description, "figurative language."

🙖 *foils:* Foils are, widely speaking, opposites in one or more characteristic ways; foils need not be total opposites, and they need not be characters, which are more particularly classified as "character foils." In *Romeo and Juliet*, Tybalt and Mercutio are both young, both male, and both antagonistic toward their perceived rival family, yet they qualify as foils because of their opposite temperaments and approaches to that antagonism: while Mercutio is most of the time mockingly fun-loving, Tybalt is constantly, aggressively belligerent, incapable of even a whit of humor.

🙖 *foreshadowing:* Authors foreshadow future events when they hint or suggest at what may be to come. As Romeo leaves Juliet's bedroom, descending from her balcony in Act III, scene v, she prophetically remarks, "O God, I have an ill-divining soul! / Methinks I see thee, how thou art so low, / As one dead in the bottom of a tomb," a clear example of foreshadowing (ll. 54–56).

🙖 *hyperbole:* Hyperbole is extreme exaggeration, often used to emphasize the power or depth of emotions. Saying, "I'm so hungry that I could eat a horse!" is an example.

🙖 *idiom:* An idiom is a common expression in a particular language that means, connotatively, something quite different than the individual denotations of its words do. For example, the sayings "the early bird gets the worm" and "if you can't stand the heat, then get out of the kitchen" communicate much more than their simple, commonplace words do at face value.

🙖 *imagery:* Imagery is language that appeals to or enlivens one's senses, recreating sensations of sight, touch, taste, smell, and hearing. Consider this excerpt from *Lord of the Flies* as an example:

> Toward noon, as the floods of light fell more nearly to the perpendicular, the stark colors of the morning were smoothed in pearl and opalescence; and the heat—as though the impending sun's height gave it momentum—became a blow that they ducked,

running to the shade and lying there . . . (Golding, 1954/2006, p. 58)

- *implied metaphor:* An implied metaphor is a symbolic comparison that the author does not state outright, but instead simply suggests by using words connotative of the comparison. In Coleridge's (1798/1973a) "Kubla Khan," for instance, phrases such as "oh! that deep romantic chasm" (l. 12), "woman wailing for her demon lover" (l. 16), "this earth in fast thick pants were breathing" (l. 18), and "a mighty fountain momently was forced" (l. 19) imply a sexual subtext quite distinct from Kubla's attempt to build a riverside home in Xanadu.

- *inciting incident:* The moment when a story's complication is introduced, an inciting incident follows the narrative's exposition and begins the rising action.

- *internal rhyme:* Internal rhyme occurs, apropos of its name, internally within individual lines of poetry. Consider this description of ice from line 61 of Coleridge's (1798/1973b) "The Rime of the Ancient Mariner": "It cracked and growled, and roared and howled." There is no need to look at any other lines for evidence of rhyme, since "growled" and "howled" here fit the bill within their own singular line.

- *irony:* Irony generally is defined as a difference between expectation and reality. If one walks into a restaurant, then he or she expects the presence of food, dishes, and utensils, so a restaurant devoid of these staples is an example of irony. There also are specific variants, including dramatic irony, occurring when an audience knows something that characters on stage do not, and verbal irony, whereby what a person says is different than what he or she actually means.

- *jargon:* Jargon is diction that is characteristic of a particular group of people or an activity. It commonly is confused with the term *dialect*, which refers to larger patterns of speech, rather than to individual words. Many of the words and terms in this small glossary are themselves the jargon of literary scholars and students.

- *legend:* A legend is a story that has some basis, however small, in historical fact, but that has grown over time. The famous story of George Washington cutting down his father's cherry tree is one such tale.

- *loaded language:* Diction that conveys strong emotional, social, or political connotations is called loaded language; such words and phrases are effectively loaded with meaning beyond that conveyed by a dictionary. Denotatively, the word *sissy*, for example, is simply a shortened form of "sister," but as any boy on the playground can tell you, it is connotatively loaded with much more social and emotional meaning.

🙞 *metaphor:* A metaphor is a figurative comparison between two things or their qualities, made without the words "like" or "as." "Pete is a riot!" is a simple metaphor describing a humorous student.

🙞 *meter:* A thorough explication of poetic meter, including all of its potential variations and subtleties, requires much more space than this short entry allows, perhaps even than this entire book provides. Nevertheless, it is important not to neglect the fact that Shakespeare wrote the majority of his dialogue in metrical verse, predominantly in iambic pentameter. An iamb is a two-syllable pattern wherein the second syllable is more strongly or highly stressed than the first; its converse is the trochee. Examples of iambic words are "forget," "regard," "askew," and "around," all of which are naturally said with greater stress on the last syllable. The word "pentameter" is just a simple way to denote the fact that there are five iambs in one line of verse, as "penta-" comes from the Greek word for five. Thus, one line of iambic pentameter contains 10 syllables, the even-numbered of which are stressed; a clear example of iambic pentameter occurs in the second line of *Romeo and Juliet*'s Prologue: "In fair Verona, where we lay our scene."

🙞 *metonymy:* A figure of speech with which an author refers to something indirectly, metonymy references the name of something else with which it is associated; it differs from a regular symbol in its reliance on a name, not an object, as the associative link. Uncle Sam is a clear use of metonymy, for rather than being an actual person, Uncle Sam is simply a name with which the United States Government is associated.

🙞 *monologue:* A monologue is a long speech by one person to an audience of any number of people. Any extended speech to another character qualifies. In Shakespeare, Antony's "Friends, Romans, countrymen, lend me your ears" speech from *Julius Caesar* (1599/1971a) is a fine example of a monologue, as is every political speech ever made (3.2.73).

🙞 *oxymoron:* A phrase that seems to contradict itself, composed of contrasting parts, is an oxymoron. The phrases "jumbo shrimp," "black light," and even "Biggie Smalls" are clear examples of such self-contradictory construction.

🙞 *paradox:* A paradox (often called a catch-22) is a close cousin of the oxymoron, yet they differ in that an oxymoron is strictly linguistic in nature, while a paradox is actually a situation, a combination of factors in life, that is seemingly self-contradictory. A paradox to which many teenagers can relate concerns the quest for employment: one needs work experience to get a job, but one needs a job to gain work experience.

parallelism: Parallelism is a word that describes the construction of a piece of writing in some kind of repetitive or otherwise logically structured way. Compare-and-contrast essays generally are written utilizing parallelism, for they tend to alternate extendedly and repetitively between two considered items.

personification: When a writer attributes human characteristics to inhuman things, it is called *personification.* A very simple example is an "angry storm."

prose: The opposite of verse, prose is most easily described as "normal" sentence-and-paragraph-style writing. Novels and newspapers are written in prose, while poems are written in verse.

protagonist: The protagonist of any narrative is the main character around whom the story revolves. I like to think of the protagonist as the central hub around which all of the spokes of a story's wheel rotate; remove that hub from the plot, and the story simply falls apart. By this calculus, Charles Dickens explicitly identifies Lucie Manette-Darnay, rather than any of his male characters granted considerably more dialogue, as the protagonist of *A Tale of Two Cities*; if Lucie were not present, then the story's concentration of characters, and thus its plot, would simply never cohere.

proverb: A proverb is an old, common saying that makes a wise observation about life. "A bird in the hand is worth two in the bush" is an English proverb; ironically enough, many of Shakespeare's more quotable observations about life have actually reached proverbial status, such as King Claudius's poignant observation in *Hamlet* (1600/1970), "When sorrows come, they come not single spies, / But in battalions" (4.5.78–79), which actually echoes another, much more common, proverb: "when it rains, it pours."

pun: A pun is a play on like-sounding, but distinctly meaningful words (homonyms). Much of the sexual humor extant in *Romeo and Juliet* arises from characters' punning, as does its introductory banter concerning coals, choler, and colliers (1.1).

redundancy: Although technically not a literary device, but a syntactical error, redundancy is an element of dialogue that is somewhat common in Shakespeare's plays, usually to emphasize some point. Mercutio's description of Queen Mab's chariot, "drawn by a team of little atomi," is redundant, because atoms naturally are little (1.4.62).

refrain: Anything that is repeated or returned to constantly can be called a *refrain.* If asked, many teenagers are likely to identify daily refrains of showering and brushing their teeth, weekly refrains of Saturday sleep-ins, monthly refrains of full and new moons, and annual refrains of holiday celebrations.

A strong example of a literary refrain is Charles Dickens's continued mention of the golden thread in *A Tale of Two Cities*.

🌼 *rhetorical question:* A rhetorical question is one to which the inquirer actually expects no response. "What's up?" is a standard rhetorical question, often asked in passing, as is the affixation of "you know?" at the ends of sentences.

🌼 *rhyme, feminine and masculine:* Children learn about rhyme as they learn to talk and read. Few students, however, recognize the difference between the two major types of rhyme. Masculine rhyme occurs when multiple syllables at the ends of words are rhymed, such as "toaster" and "roaster," or "pigeon" and "religion." Feminine rhyme, by contrast, occurs when only the last syllable shared by words is rhymed, such as "principal" and "recital," or "Shakespeare" and "dear." The effect of masculine rhyme often is more comedic than feminine rhyme, which is more graceful and natural.

🌼 *rhyme scheme:* A poem or dramatic excerpt's rhyme scheme is the pattern created by an author's use of end rhyme. The first rhyme used in any pattern is labeled rhyme A, the second rhyme used, regardless of the line on which it arises, is labeled rhyme B, and so on. Thus, poems written strictly in rhyming couplets utilize a rhyme scheme labeled AABBCC, while lines of alternating rhyme, such as the first three quatrains of any Shakespearean sonnet, are classifiable according to an ABAB scheme. Not all verse, of course, rhymes according to regularized schemes, such as blank verse, which by definition incorporates no rhyme scheme.

🌼 *rising action:* The rising action of any plot occurs after the inciting incident's introduction of the main complication. This name, rising action, effectively describes the period of any story between its inciting incident and climax, wherein tension, drama, and action supposedly rise parallel to the progress of time. In *Macbeth*, every event that occurs following Macbeth's midnight murder of King Duncan qualifies as part of the rising action, leading the power-hungry, paranoid Scotsman ultimately and inevitably to his climactic confrontation with Macduff.

🌼 *setting:* Details regarding where and when a story takes place contribute to that story's setting. *Romeo and Juliet* is set in Verona, Italy, circa 1590, while the setting of *The Great Gatsby* is New York City during the Roaring Twenties. Not all narratives require clearly distinguishable settings (e.g., *Waiting for Godot*), and it is certainly possible for a story to have more than one.

🌼 *simile:* Like a metaphor, a simile is a figurative comparison between two things or their qualities, although a simile makes that comparison more explicit, incorporating the comparative words "like" or "as." Describing students, I might say that "Ashlee is as sharp as a tack," and "Corinne has a memory like a steel trap."

slant rhyme: Slant rhyme, also known as approximate rhyme, occurs when authors attempt to rhyme words that, well, simply do not rhyme exactly. "What immortal hand or eye / Could frame thy fearful symmetry?" Blake (1789/1979) asks in an infamous example of slant rhyme from "The Tyger" (ll. 3–4). Readers generally are supposed to overlook slant rhyme's inexactness, granting the poet or author artistic license for the sake of making his or her literary point.

soliloquy: Commonly confused with monologue, a soliloquy is a long speech wherein a person speaks to no one but himself or herself, thinking privately but aloud. The two most famous soliloquies in all of Shakespeare occur in *Romeo and Juliet*'s balcony scene and *Hamlet* (1600/1970)—"To be or not to be—that is the question" (3.1.56).

sonnet, Shakespearean or English: My experience is that high school students somehow pick up the misconception that Shakespeare "invented" the sonnet. Although he may have perfected it, depending on one's literary tastes, the poetic form itself arose long before the Bard ever took his first breath. Moreover, the form known as the Shakespearean or English sonnet, written in iambic pentameter and incorporating the rhyme scheme ABABCDCDEFEFGG, is far from the only style extant; technically, all that a poet requires in order to pen a sonnet is 14 lines, a rhyme scheme, and a regularized metrical pattern. Thus, there are potentially as many sonnet forms in the world as there are creative sonneteers. Nevertheless, Shakespeare's is by far the most recognizable and common type of sonnet in English, three examples of which he incorporated into *Romeo and Juliet*, the two speeches spoken by the Chorus and the initial 14-line exchange between Romeo and Juliet at the Capulets' feast.

stage directions: Stage directions in Shakespearean plays are scant, which is one reason why directors and actors so love the creative license afforded them by the Bard. In his dramas, however, they serve the same purposes that they do in other plays: to direct actors' movements and emotions, as well as to describe stage settings. The most famous stage direction in all of Shakespeare occurs in Act III, scene iii of *The Winter's Tale* (1611/1971b), where Antigonus is directed to "*Exit, pursued by a bear.*"

stereotype: It is perhaps easier for teenagers to identify examples of stereotypes than it is for them to define exactly what they are. Specifically, a stereotype is a belief that all members of a given group share a certain characteristic, in terms of which they can be described homogeneously. The beliefs that all stereotypes concern people and that no stereotypes are true actually are stereotypes themselves; to wit, the belief that all coffee is caffeinated is a stereotype that has nothing to do with people, and the statement that all licensed high school teachers graduated high school themselves is a true stereotype.

- *stream of consciousness:* Stream of consciousness is a style of writing aimed at imitating the discursive meanderings of human thought patterns, rather than following any kind of tightly focused organizational pattern. Beat writers, such as Jack Kerouac, commonly utilized stream of consciousness in their works, as did Walt Whitman in many of his longer poems.

- *suspense:* Everything from fearful anxiety and apprehension to pleasant excitement, suspense is the quality felt by a reader or audience that is engaged in a narrative, unknowingly anticipating its outcome. We can imagine the suspense that *Romeo and Juliet*'s first audiences felt as Romeo descended into the Capulets' crypt in Act V, scene iii, ready to take his own life just as Juliet was about to wake up from her intoxication.

- *synecdoche:* Synecdoche is a figure of speech whereby something is identified only by mention of a smaller part of itself. "I soared into the air as the wheels left the runway" is an example of synecdoche used to describe an airplane's departure, for while the entire aircraft became airborne, only its wheels are mentioned.

- *syntax:* The placement of words in a logical order to create communicative meaning, syntax follows diction as the next step in the linguistic process; once one has chosen the words "dog," "ran," "my," "door," "to," and "the," they need to be placed syntactically into a sensible order to communicate meaning.

- *tone:* The word *tone* usually is associated with speaking voice, but a person's tone can come across on paper just as easily as it can face-to-face. What someone's tone illuminates is his or her attitude toward a subject; on the printed page, that attitude is communicated via a writer's choice of words. One author's description of the "banal, anachronistically cute soiree" differs significantly from another's "enjoyably lighthearted picnic," although both writers may be describing the same event, toward which their attitudes obviously differ.

- *verse, blank and rhymed:* Verse is a synonym for metrical poetry (i.e., poetic lines that adhere strictly to patterns of meter). Because all verse, therefore, must by definition contain meter, the only issue is whether that verse rhymes (rhymed verse) or does not rhyme (blank verse). Percy Shelley's "Ozymandias" is an example of a near-sonnet written in blank verse, for while it contains 14 lines and is written in iambic pentameter, there is no regularized rhyme scheme to be found.

Appendix A

Literary Elements and Devices in Act I of *Romeo and Juliet*

Prologue		
Literary Device	*Lines*	*Why?*
Shakespearean, aka English, sonnet	The entire Prologue (1–14)	The Chorus's speech follows the rhyme scheme, ABABCDCDEFEFGG, and is written in iambic pentameter.
alliteration	"From forth the fatal loins of these two foes / A pair of star-crossed lovers take their life" (5–6)	The repetition of the initial "f" and, in line 6, "l" sounds.

Scene i		
Literary Device	*Lines*	*Why?*
puns	". . . we'll not carry coals." ". . . then we should be colliers." ". . . an we be in choler, we'll draw." ". . . draw your neck out of the collar." (1–5)	Sampson and Gregory play with the similar-sounding, but distinct, words *coal*, *collar*, *choler*, etc.
dialogue	The entirety of the scene, especially lines 1–33	Sampson and Gregory, in lines 1–33, banter between themselves; there is no narration at all, nor a long speech by anyone.

Scene i		
Literary Device	*Lines*	*Why?*
indirect characterization	"What, art thou drawn . . . / Turn thee, Benvolio; look upon thy death." "I do but keep the peace. Put up thy sword, / Or manage it to part these men with me." (67–70)	Tybalt shows himself to be hot-headed and malevolent, while Benvolio demonstrates his inclination toward concord and level-headedness.
foils	"What, art thou drawn . . . / Turn thee, Benvolio; look upon thy death." "I do but keep the peace. Put up thy sword, / Or manage it to part these men with me." (67–70)	Tybalt and Benvolio are contrary characters here, for while both represent their respective families more distinctly than do other characters presently on stage, their opposite interests and dispositions are evident.
antagonism	"What, drawn and talk of peace? I hate the word / As I hate hell, all Montagues, and thee. / Have at thee, coward!" (71–73)	Tybalt attacks Benvolio, who has himself heretofore demonstrated no inclination to fight.
stage directions	*"Enter Benvolio."* *"Enter Tybalt, drawing his sword."* *"Enter old Capulet in his gown, and his Wife,"* etc.	Such directions indicate arrivals and actions on stage, plus props and, in some cases, costuming.
monologue	"Rebellious subjects, enemies to peace . . . Once more, on pain of death, all men depart." (83–105)	In a relatively long speech, the Prince addresses the assembled crowd.
blank verse	"Rebellious subjects, enemies to peace, / Profaners of this neighbor-stainèd steel— / Will they not hear?—What ho! You men, you beasts . . ." (83–105)	The Prince speaks in iambic pentameter, although his speech utilizes no regularized rhyme scheme.
conflict	"Three civil brawls bred of an airy word / By thee, old Capulet, and Montague, / Have thrice disturbed the quiet of our streets . . ." (91–93)	We learn that the barely averted street brawl in this scene is not an isolated incident, but emblematic of one of the play's major sources of tension.
assonance	"Here were the servants of your adversary" (108)	Benvolio repeats the same vowel sounds, both the "*er*" and the "*ad*" sounds, in "were," "servants," and "adversary."
personification	"He swung about his head and cut the winds / Who, nothing hurt withal, hissed him in scorn." (113–114)	Benvolio attributes physical vulnerability and scorn, both human traits, to the inhuman wind.
rhyming couplet	"O, where is Romeo? Saw you him today? / Right glad I am he was not at this fray." (118–119)	Lady Montague rhymes the last syllable of both adjacent lines.
blank verse	"Madam, an hour before the worshiped sun / Peered forth the golden window of the east, / A troubled mind drove me to walk abroad . . ." (120–133)	Benvolio addresses Lord and Lady Montague in iambic pentameter, yet utilizes no regularized rhyme scheme.

Scene i		
Literary Device	*Lines*	*Why?*
direct characterization	"Many a morning hath he there been seen, / With tears augmenting the fresh morning's dew, / Adding to clouds more clouds with his deep sighs." (134–136)	Benvolio clearly explicates Romeo's melancholy character in this description of him.
alliteration	"Away from light steals home my heavy son / And private in his chamber pens himself . . . Black and portentous must this humor prove, / Unless good counsel may the cause remove." (140–145)	Montague repeats the "s," "h," "p," and "c" sounds at the beginnings of various words in close proximity.
archaism	"Ere he can spread his sweet leaves to the air . . . Could we but learn from whence his sorrows grow . . ." (155–157)	Montague's usage of "Ere" and "whence" were common in the late 16th century, but these words are not used anymore today, thus their description as archaic.
rhyming couplets	"See where he comes. So please you, step aside. / I'll know his grievance or be much denied." "I would thou wert so happy by thy stay / To hear true shrift.—Come, madam, let's away." (159–162)	Benvolio and Montague, respectively, each rhyme the final syllables of their adjacent lines of verse.
consonance	"It was. What sadness lengthens Romeo's hours?" (168)	Benvolio repeats the "s" and "z" sounds six times in this one line of verse.
personification	"Alas that love, so gentle in his view, / Should be so tyrannous and rough in proof!" (174–175)	Intangible love is described as "gentle" and "tyrannous," both human characteristics.
consonance	"Alas that love, whose view is muffled still, / Should without eyes see pathways to his will!" (176–177)	Romeo repeats the "l" and "w" sounds often in this couplet, not necessarily as the initial sounds of words.
oxymorons	" . . . O brawling love, O loving hate . . . O heavy lightness . . . Misshapen chaos of well-seeming forms, / Feather of lead, bright smoke, cold fire, sick health . . ." (181–185)	Romeo juxtaposes numerous images and adjectives that simply contradict one another (e.g., "heavy lightness").
implied metaphor	"Griefs of mine own lie heavy in my breast, / Which thou wilt propagate to have it pressed . . ." (193–194)	Romeo implies that his previous griefs are birthing more, engendered by Benvolio's inquiries; the key to this implication are the words *lie*, *breast*, *propagate*, and *pressed*, which suggest both sex and impregnation.
consonance	"A sick man in sadness makes his will—" (210)	Romeo repeats the "s" sound five times in this one line.
internal slant rhyme	"A word ill urged to one that is so ill." (211)	The words *word* and *urged* do not rhyme exactly, but approximately, and within one line of verse.

Scene i		
Literary Device	*Lines*	*Why?*
allusions	"She'll not be hit / With Cupid's arrow. She hath Dian's wit . . ." (216–217)	Romeo describes Rosaline by referring to Cupid and Diana, both ancient mythological figures.
assonance	"She hath and in that sparing makes huge waste . . ." (226)	In this one line of verse, Romeo repeats the short "a" sound four times, and the long "a" sound twice.
masculine rhyme	"For beauty starved with her severity, / Cuts beauty off from all posterity." (227–228)	Romeo here rhymes the last *two* syllables of each line, rather than just the last one.
metaphor	"He that is strucken blind cannot forget / The precious treasure of his eyesight lost." (241–242)	Romeo describes Rosaline, for whom he has pined but in pursuit of whom he has failed, not literally, but as "precious treasure of . . . eyesight lost" by "He that is strucken blind" and must now examine other women's less-perfect attractiveness.

Scene ii		
Literary Device	*Lines*	*Why?*
blank verse	"My child is yet a stranger in the world. / She hath not seen the change of fourteen years." (8–9)	Capulet and Paris speak in iambic pentameter throughout their dialogue, though they do not utilize a regularized pattern of end rhyme.
personification	"Earth hath swallowed all my hopes but she . . ." (14)	Capulet describes the Earth as "swallow[ing]" his other children, thereby endowing it with the human traits of eating and digesting.
internal rhyme	"This night I hold an old accustomed feast . . ." (20)	The words *hold* and *old* rhyme within this one line of verse.
slant rhyme	"This night I hold an old accustomed feast, / Whereto I have invited many a guest . . ." (20–21)	The final words of these lines, *feast* and *guest*, do not rhyme exactly, but approximately.
consonance	"One more, most welcome, makes my number more." (23)	Capulet repeats the "m" sound seven times in this one line, and not only at the beginnings of words.
conceit	"At my poor house look to behold this night / Earth-treading stars that make dark heaven light." (24–25)	Capulet describes the women that are to attend his ball this evening as "Earth-treading stars," illuminating heaven itself; this is certainly a rather strained metaphor.

Scene ii		
Literary Device	*Lines*	*Why?*
euphony	"Among fresh fennel buds shall you this night / Inherit at my house. Hear all, all see, / And like her most whose merit most shall be; / Which, on more view of many, mine, being one, / May stand in number, though in reck'ning none." (29–33)	Capulet's use of alliteration, repeated "soft" consonant sounds, parallelism, and refrains makes these five lines pleasing to the ear when heard.
archaism	"Go, sirrah, trudge about . . ." (35)	The word *sirrah* was common during the Elizabethan era, but is no longer used or even recognized by most people.
prose	"Find them out whose names are written here! . . . I must to the learned. In good time!" (39–46)	The Servingman's small soliloquy is not written in lines of verse at all, but in standard sentences in one paragraph.
soliloquy	"Find them out whose names are written here! . . . I must to the learned. In good time!" (39–46)	The Servingman speaks to no one but himself, basically thinking aloud.
stereotype	"But I am sent to find those persons whose names are here writ, and can never find what names the writing person hath here writ. I must to the learned." (43–45)	The Servingman, a commoner, is illiterate, unable even to read the names upon Capulet's guest list.
paradox	"Tut man, one fire burns out another's burning; / One pain is lessened by another's anguish . . . Take thou some new infection to thy eye, / And the rank poison of the old will die." (47–52)	Benvolio's statements here seem self-contradictory or illogical, but are in fact potentially true.
hyperbole	"Not mad, but bound more than a madman is, / Shut up in prison, kept without my food, / Whipped and tormented . . ." (57–59)	Romeo, still pining after Rosaline, describes his amorous frustration as akin to a starving prisoner's torturous condition.
contraction	"God gi' good e'en. I pray, sir, can you read?" (61–62)	The Servingman contracts the phrase "give you" into "gi'," and the word "evening" into "e'en," thereby allowing his one line to be spoken in iambic pentameter.
analogy	"Compare her face with some that I shall show, / And I will make thee think thy swan a crow." (93–94)	Benvolio states that compared to some of the beautiful women that will attend the Capulets' ball, Rosaline will appear more like a crow than a swan.
rhyme scheme	"When the devout religion of mine eye / Maintains such falsehood, then turn tears to fire . . . The all-seeing sun / Ne'er saw her match since first the world begun." (95–100)	Romeo's statement on Rosaline's unmatchable beauty follows the rhyme scheme ABABCC.

Scene ii		
Literary Device	*Lines*	*Why?*
slant rhyme	"That I will show you shining at this feast, / And she shall scant show well that now seems best." (105–106)	The final words of this couplet, *feast* and *best*, do not rhyme exactly, but approximately.
cacophony	"That I will show you shining at this feast, / And she shall scant show well that now seems best." (105–106)	Arguably, Benvolio overuses the alliteration of the "sh" sound, making this couplet difficult to say and awkward to hear.

Scene iii		
Literary Device	*Lines*	*Why?*
anecdote	"Marry, I remember it well. / 'Tis since the earthquake now eleven years . . . I should live a thousand years, / I never should forget it." (24-51)	The Nurse relates a short, humorous story regarding Juliet's youth and an earthquake.
dialect	"Marry . . . my dug . . . tetchy . . . by th'rood . . . by my holidam," etc. (24–47)	The Nurse tells her story using diction characteristic of such a person as herself.
personification	"'Shake,' quoth the dovehouse." (35)	The Nurse's story includes a dovehouse that talks, albeit figuratively.
refrain	"Wilt thou not, Jule?" "Ay." (47–48, 51–53, and 62)	The Nurse repeats the punchline to her anecdotal joke three full times.
tone	"I warrant, an I should live a thousand years, / I never should forget it. 'Wilt thou not, Jule?' quoth he. / And, pretty fool, it stinted and said 'Ay.'" "Enough of this. I pray thee, hold thy peace." (50–54)	The Nurse's and Lady Capulet's contrary attitudes toward both Juliet and the story regarding her youth are evident from the diction that each uses: the Nurse's lighthearted and sentimental, and Lady Capulet's impatient and commanding.
alliteration	" . . . it had upon its brow / A bump as big as a young cock'rel's stone . . . " (57–58)	Juliet's Nurse repeats the "b" sound at the beginnings of three words out of a consecutive five.
refrain	"Marry, that 'marry' is the very theme / I came to talk of.—Tell me, daughter Juliet, / How stands your disposition to be married?" (68–70)	The word *marry* is repeated three times within these three lines, and many more times in this scene as a whole, emphasizing to the audience its importance to the plot.
alliteration, consonance, and assonance	"Well, think of marriage now. Younger than you / Here in Verona, ladies of esteem, / Are made already mothers. By my count / I was your mother much upon these years / That you are now a maid." (75–79)	This statement by Lady Capulet contains both assonant and consonant alliteration, as both the "m" and "y" sounds are repeated at the beginnings of words; additionally, the assonant phrase "By my count" repeats the long "y" sound.

Scene iii		
Literary Device	*Lines*	*Why?*
epithet	"... why, he's a man of wax." (82)	The Nurse's description of Paris requires interpretation by modern readers, but it was perhaps a common way during the Elizabethan era to describe a person as "the mold" against whom others are to be judged.
figurative language, conceit, analogy, and metaphor	"Read o'er the volume of young Paris' face, / And find delight writ there with beauty's pen.... That book in many's eyes doth share the glory / That in gold clasps locks in the golden story." (87–98)	Lady Capulet describes Paris figuratively as a beautifully written, though uncovered (by a wife), book, emphasizing their various similarities to expand the metaphor, which gets stretched pretty thin after a while.
feminine rhyme	"Examine every married lineament / And see how one another lends content ..." (89–90)	Lady Capulet rhymes only the last syllable of each line in this couplet.
masculine rhyme	"This precious book of love, this unbound lover, / To beautify him only lacks a cover.... That book in many's eyes doth share the glory / That in gold clasps locks in the golden story." (93–94, 97–98)	Lady Capulet here rhymes multiple, successive syllables at the ends of lines.
euphony	"For fair without the fair within to hide." (96)	The repetitive soft "f" and "w" sounds lend this line a pleasing sound when spoken.
pun	"By having him, making yourself no less." "No less? Nay bigger. Women grow by men." (100–101)	The Nurse either mistakes or plays with Lady Capulet's statement that Paris, if possessed, would make Juliet "no less" in social status; the Nurse refers to the physical size implied by "no less," meaning growth by pregnancy instead of social rank.
cacophony	"I'll look to like, if looking liking move." (103)	In contrast to the soft "f" and "w" sounds repeated in line 96, the hard "k" and alliterated "l" sounds make this line both difficult to say and awkward to hear aloud.
verse vs. prose	"But no more deep will I endart mine eye / That your consent gives strength to make it fly." *Enter Servingman.* "Madam, the guests are come, supper served up, you called, my young lady asked for, the Nurse cursed," etc.	The educated, upperclass Juliet speaks in iambic verse, followed immediately by the unpoetic prose of the lowerclass Servingman; this moment provides a good example of the way in which Shakespeare altered the forms of his dialogue to suit the speakers in question.

Scene iv		
Literary Device	*Lines*	*Why?*
assonance	"Nor no without-book prologue, faintly spoke / After the prompter, for our entrance." (7–8)	Both the long and short "o" sounds are repeated numerous times in this couplet.
allusion	"You are a lover. Borrow Cupid's wings / And soar with them above a common bound." (17–18)	Mercutio refers to the Roman god of love here.
puns	"Borrow Cupid's wings / And soar with them above a common bound." "I am too sore enpiercèd with his shaft / To soar with his light feathers, and so bound / I cannot bound a pitch above dull woe." (17–21)	Romeo responds to Mercutio's romantic advice by punning upon the meanings of *bound* as "tied up" and "leap," as well as of *sore* as hurt and *soar* as to fly.
loaded language	"I am too sore enpiercèd with his shaft . . . Is love a tender thing? It is too rough, / Too rude, too boist'rous, and it pricks like thorn." "If love be rough with you, be rough with love. / Prick love for pricking . . ."	Romeo and Mercutio banter back and forth using words and phrases like "enpiercèd with [Cupid's] shaft," "tender," "rough," and "prick," all of which have easily understood sexual connotations.
parallelism	"It is too rough, / Too rude, too boist'rous . . ." (25–26)	Romeo describes love via this list of parallel characteristics.
alliteration	"Here are the beetle brows shall blush for me." (32)	Mercutio begins three words with "b" in this line.
proverbs	"For I am proverbed with a grandsire phrase: / I'll be a candle holder and look on; / The game was ne'er so fair, and I am done." "Tut, dun's the mouse, the constable's own word." (37–40)	Romeo and Mercutio banter back and forth, alluding to three separate common Elizabethan proverbs, as Romeo states in line 37.
pun	"The game was ne'er so fair, and I am done." "Tut, dun's the mouse . . . If thou art dun, we'll draw thee from the mire. . . ." (39–41)	Mercutio cleverly plays with the similar-sounding but distinct words *done* and *dun*.
idiom	"Come, we burn daylight, ho!" (44)	This common idiomatic saying is difficult to translate directly, conveying more figuratively than its literal diction does.
redundancy	"Drawn with a team of little atomi . . ." (62)	"Atomi," aka atoms, are little by nature, so the statement "little atomi" is redundant.
imagery	" . . . she comes / In shape no bigger than an agate stone / On the forefinger of an alderman . . . Her wagon spokes made of long spinners' legs . . . Her collars of the moonshine's wat'ry beams, / Her whip of cricket bone . . ." (59–74)	Mercutio describes Queen Mab's physical appearance and entourage utilizing much language that appeals to or enlivens the reader's five senses.

Scene iv		
Literary Device	*Lines*	*Why?*
stereotypes	"And in this state she gallops night by night / Through lovers' brains, and then they dream of love; / On courtiers' knees, that dream of cur'sies straight; / O'er lawyers' fingers, who straight dream on fees; / O'er ladies' lips, who straight on kisses dream . . ." (75–79)	Queen Mab is described as engendering in each sleeping person dreams that portray the common stereotype of that particular person's station (e.g., "lawyers . . . straight dream on fees").
consonance	"Which oft the angry Mab with blisters plagues . . ." (80)	The "g," "s," and "b" sounds are repeated numerous times each in this line of verse.
archaism	"Of healths five fathom deep, and then anon / Drums in his ear . . ." (90–91)	The word *anon*, common in Elizabethan speech, is not used today.
internal rhyme	"And, being thus frighted, swears a prayer or two / And sleeps again." (92–93)	The words *swears* and *prayer* rhyme within one line of verse.
monologue	"O, then I see Queen Mab hath been with you. . . . This is she—" (58–100)	Mercutio describes to his companions the fictional Queen Mab over 40 lines, in an entertaining, inventive speech.
stream of consciousness	"O, then I see Queen Mab hath been with you. . . . This is she—" (58–100)	Mercutio's monologue concerning Queen Mab follows no directed pattern, but meanders as he apparently thinks of ways to describe her.
loaded language	"This is the hag, when maids lie on their backs, / That presses them and learns them first to bear, / Making them women of good carriage." (97–99)	Mercutio describes Queen Mab's nocturnal visitations using language that clearly suggests sex and subsequent pregnancy.
simile	". . . I talk of dreams, / Which are the children of an idle brain, / Begot of nothing but vain fantasy, / Which is as thin of substance as the air . . . " (103–106)	Mercutio directly compares insubstantial dreams to the air, using the word *as*.
personification	"And more inconstant than the wind, who woos / Even now the frozen bosom of the North / And, being angered, puffs away from thence, / Turning his side to the dew-dropping South." (107–110)	Mercutio describes the wind as a male and as "angered," which is a human reaction to events.
foreshadowing	"I fear too early, for my mind misgives / Some consequence yet hanging in the stars . . . By some vile forfeit of untimely death." (113–118)	Romeo imagines that the events of this night, at the Capulets' ball, will lead him to an "untimely death"; of course, they ultimately do.
metaphor and figurative language	"But he that hath the steerage of my course / Direct my sail." (119–120)	Romeo describes himself as a ship, steered by an unnamed "he" upon the "course" of his life.

Scene iv		
Literary Device	*Lines*	*Why?*
synecdoche	"But he that hath the steerage of my course / Direct my sail." (119–120)	Not only would Romeo's "sail" be directed on "course" by his metaphoric captain, but his entire "ship" would as well; hence, a small part stands in this sentence for the larger entity.
aside	"I fear too early, for my mind misgives / Some consequence yet hanging in the stars . . . By some vile forfeit of untimely death." (113–118)	Romeo's statement of foreshadowing is said not to any other character on stage, presumably, but to himself and, by extension, to the audience.

Scene v		
Literary Device	*Lines*	*Why?*
prose	"Where's Potpan that he helps not to take away? He shift a trencher? . . . Cheerly, boys! Be brisk awhile, and the longer liver take all." (1–17)	The Servingmen who open the scene, as per Shakespearean dialogic tradition, speak not in verse, but in "common" prose.
jargon	"He shift a trencher? He scrape a trencher?" (2–3)	The words *shift* and *trencher*, in this case, are particular to the Servingmen's occupation; they would not be used otherwise in this play.
verse	"Welcome, gentlemen. Ladies that have their toes / Unplagued with corns will walk about with you. . . . Nay, sit, nay, sit, good cousin Capulet, / For you and I are past our dancing days." (18–36)	Lord Capulet speaks (perhaps excitedly) in somewhat imperfect iambic pentameter, in contrast to the Servingmen whom he follows in this scene.
enjambment	"Ah, my mistresses, which of you all / Will now deny to dance? She that makes dainty . . . " (21–22)	Though these two lines are considered iambic pentameter, the first line of this couplet contains only 9 syllables, while the second line contains 11. Probably Shakespeare bumped this lone syllable down in order to maintain the iambic rhythm of the second line.
exposition vs. inciting incident, plus complication and rising action	"Will you tell me that? / His son was but a ward two years ago." "What lady's that which doth enrich the hand of yonder knight?" (46–49)	The very moment at which Romeo notices Juliet marks the narrative's transition from the exposition to the inciting incident, for it introduces the complication, which begins the play's rising action.
consonance and alliteration	"O, she doth teach the torches to burn bright!" (51)	Romeo repeats the "t," "ch," and "b" sounds in this line, often at the beginnings of words.

Scene v		
Literary Device	*Lines*	*Why?*
simile	"It seems she hangs upon the cheek of night / As a rich jewel in an Ethiop's ear—" (52–53)	Romeo directly compares Juliet's beauty to a rich jewel, using the word *as*.
personification	"It seems she hangs upon the cheek of night . . ." (52)	Night does not have cheeks, which are parts of the human face.
internal slant rhyme	"So shows a snowy dove trooping with crows. . ." (55)	The words *so*, *shows*, *crows*, and arguably *snowy* rhyme (approximately) within this one line of Romeo's verse.
rhetorical question	"Did my heart love till now?" (59)	Romeo asks this question of nobody in particular, expecting, therefore, no response to it.
contraction	"For I ne'er saw true beauty till this night." (60)	Romeo contracts the two-syllable "never" into a one-syllable word, thereby retaining the 10 syllables required for iambic pentameter.
aside	"What, dares the slave / Come hither covered with an antic face / To fleer and scorn at our solemnity? / Now, by the stock and honor of my kin, / To strike him dead I hold it not a sin." (63–67)	Tybalt speaks these lines concerning Romeo to himself alone, yet the utterance is too short to qualify as a full-fledged soliloquy.
indirect characterization	"Fetch me my rapier, boy. / What, dares the slave / Come hither with an antic face. . . . He shall be endured. / What, Goodman boy? I say he shall. Go to. / Am I the master here or you? Go to." (62–88)	Although never explicitly described, Tybalt's and Capulet's fiery tempers are visible in this exchange; Tybalt moreover portrays himself, through his dialogue, as belligerent, while Capulet is ostensibly more concerned with public decorum, at least initially.
assonance	"Content thee, gentle coz. Let him alone." (74)	Lord Capulet repeats the short "e" sound three times in this line, in "Content," "gentle," and "Let."
hyperbole	"I would not for the wealth of all this town / Here in my house do him disparagement." (78–79)	Stating that he would not disparage Romeo for "the wealth of all this town" is quite exaggerated, surely. After all, Romeo is a Montague, and Verona surely held much wealth that could entice Capulet to disparage him.
consonance	"An ill-beseeming semblance for a feast." (83)	The "b," "s," and "m" sounds are all repeated in close proximity here.
idioms	"You will set cock-a-hoop, you'll be the man!" (91)	These phrases are both culturally contextualized, although the latter idiomatic phrase is still used today, albeit with perhaps a slightly more positive connotation.

Scene v		
Literary Device	*Lines*	*Why?*
aside	"Patience perforce with willful choler meeting / Makes my flesh tremble in their different greeting. / I will withdraw, but this intrusion shall, / Now seeming sweet, convert to bitt'rest gall." (100–103)	Tybalt makes this remark to no one but himself, although the audience can of course overhear it; this commentary of only four lines is far too short, moreover, to be considered a soliloquy.
masculine rhyme	"Patience perforce with willful choler meeting / Makes my flesh tremble in their different greeting." (100–101)	Tybalt rhymes the last two syllables of these lines.
feminine slant rhyme	"I will withdraw, but this intrusion shall, / Now seeming sweet, convert to bitt'rest gall." (102–103)	Tybalt here rhymes only the last syllable of each line, "shall" and "gall," which rhyme approximately, not exactly.
metaphor	*Romeo, taking Juliet's hand*: "If I profane with my unworthiest hand / This holy shrine, the gentle sin is this: / My lips, two blushing pilgrims, ready stand / To smooth that rough touch with a tender kiss." (104–107)	Romeo refers to Juliet's hand as "This holy shrine," which is a metaphoric comparison of the two; likewise he symbolically calls his "lips, two blushing pilgrims."
Shakespearean, aka English, sonnet	"If I profane with my unworthiest hand / This holy shrine, the gentle sin is this: / My lips, two blushing pilgrims, ready stand.... Saints do not move, though grant for prayers' sake." "Then move not while my prayer's effect I take." (104–117)	Famously, Romeo and Juliet's first verbal interchange follows the rhyme scheme, ABABCDCDEFEFGG, and is written in iambic pentameter, a perfect Shakespearean sonnet.
analogy	"My lips, two blushing pilgrims, ready stand . . . Good pilgrim, you do wrong your hand too much, / Which mannerly devotion shows in this: / For saints have hands that pilgrims' hands do touch, / And palm to palm is holy palmers' kiss . . . O then, dear saint, let lips do what hands do. / They pray: grant thou, lest faith turn to despair." (106–115)	Romeo and Juliet compare their lips to the hands of praying saints and pilgrims; the commonality is that they potentially touch in what Romeo refers to as amorous "prayer."
direct characterization	"Her mother is the lady of the house, / And a good lady, and a wise and virtuous." (126–127)	Juliet's Nurse explicitly describes Lady Capulet's personal characteristics to Romeo; no inference is required.
idiom	"I tell you, he that can lay hold of her / Shall have the chinks." (129–130)	The phrase "have the chinks" is highly ambiguous, but is a culturally particular way of saying "will become rich."
rhyming couplets	"Is she a Capulet? / O dear account! My life is my foe's debt." "Away, begone. The sport is at the best." "Ay, so I fear. The more is my unrest." (131–134)	In contrast to the graceful lines of alternating rhyme present in Romeo and Juliet's previously improvised sonnet, Romeo and Benvolio here rhyme every pair of adjacent lines.

Scene v		
Literary Device	*Lines*	*Why?*
allusion	"The sport is at the best." (133)	Benvolio here refers to the proverb that Romeo cited in Act I, scene iv, on line 39, "When game is best, it is time to leave," indicating his belief that it's time for their departure.
contraction	"Is it e'en so? Why then, I thank you all." (137)	Capulet contracts the two-syllable word "even" into one syllable, thereby retaining the 10 syllables required of iambic pentameter.
enunciation	"Go ask his name. If he be marrièd. . . ." (148)	In contrast to Capulet's contraction of "even" in line 137, Juliet here makes the two-syllable word *married* into a three-syllable word by enunciating the "èd" separately, similarly creating the 10 syllables required of iambic pentameter.
paradoxes	"My grave is like to be my wedding bed. . . . My only love sprung from my only hate! . . . Prodigious birth of love it is to me / That I must love a loathèd enemy." (149, 152, and 154–155)	All three situations described by Juliet seem self-contradictory, but in fact are apparent truths.
enunciation	"That I must love a loathèd enemy." (155)	Another example of Juliet's elongation of a word, the one-syllable "loathed," by enunciating an extra syllable, thereby meeting the syllabic requirement of iambic pentameter.

Literary Devices That Overarch the Entire Act	
Literary Device	*Explanation*
legend	The feud between the Capulet and Montague families has some historical verity in Italian history, at least apocryphally. It certainly has been elaborated upon over time, if it ever really occurred, thereby qualifying *Romeo and Juliet* as based in some fact, but largely fictional.
setting	The play takes place in Verona, Italy, a town between Milan and Venice, circa the 1590s.
verse and meter	Much of this act and the play as a whole is written in verse (poetic meter), whereby only a set number of syllables—10 in one line of iambic pentameter—are allowed per line of dialogue, unlike prose, which utilizes standard English sentences.
rhyme	Much of the characters' verse in this act is spoken according to rhyme schemes (i.e., regularized patterns of rhymes at the ends of lines); the most common examples are rhyming couplets, AABB, and quatrains of alternating rhymed lines, ABAB.
protagonists	The central figures of this work of literature, around whom the action of the plot revolves and without whom this particular story would not exist, are of course Romeo and Juliet themselves.

Literary Devices That Overarch the Entire Act	
Literary Device	*Explanation*
diction/syntax	The characters in this act and the play as a whole choose words for particular purposes (diction), then place them in particular orders for various reasons, poetic, common, or otherwise (syntax).
conflict	The major conflicts in this act concern the feud between the Montague and Capulet families, the feuding clans and the government that wishes to suppress their vehement public outbursts, and Romeo and Juliet's love for one another in opposition to their respective familial loyalties.
suspense	At the conclusion of Act I, the audience is excited by the prospect of Romeo and Juliet's illicit love affair, yet anxious at the prospect of their families' reactions to it.
figurative language	Actually, every time that a metaphor, simile, or analogy arises in any form, it also is an example of figurative language, which is the large umbrella under which those three particular devices rest.

References

Blake, W. (1979). The Tyger. In M. L. Johnson & J. E. Grant (Eds.), *Blake's poetry and designs* (pp. 29–30). New York: W. W. Norton. (Original work published 1789)

Bloom, H. (1995). *The western canon: The books and school of the ages.* New York: Riverhead Books.

Bloom, H. (1998). *Shakespeare: The invention of the human.* New York: Riverhead Books.

Center for Gifted Education. (1998). *Guide to teaching a language arts curriculum for high ability learners* (pp. 49–51). Dubuque, IA: Kendall/Hunt.

Chaucer, G. (1987). The Miller's tale. In L. D. Benson (Ed.), *The Riverside Chaucer* (3rd ed., pp. 68–77). Boston: Houghton Mifflin. (Original work written circa 1387)

Coleridge, S. T. (1973a). Kubla Khan. In H. Bloom & L. Trilling (Eds.), *Romantic poetry and prose* (pp. 254–257). New York: Oxford University Press. (Original work written 1798)

Coleridge, S. T. (1973b). The rime of the ancient mariner. In H. Bloom & L. Trilling (Eds.), *Romantic poetry and prose* (pp. 238–254). New York: Oxford University Press. (Original work written 1798)

College Board: Advanced Placement Program. (2007). *English language and composition, English literature and composition: Course description.* Princeton, NJ: Author. Retrieved December 4, 2007, from http://apcentral.collegeboard.com/apc/public/repository/52272_apenglocked5_30_4309.pdf

Constable, H. (2002). My lady's presence makes the roses red. In J. Beaty, A. Booth, J. P. Hunter, & K. J. Mays (Eds.), *The Norton introduction to literature*

(8th ed., pp. 1048–1049). New York: W. W. Norton. (Original work published 1592)

Dickens, C. (1981). *A tale of two cities.* New York: Bantam Books. (Original work published 1859)

Frost, R. (1969). Nothing gold can stay. In E. C. Lathem (Ed.), *The poetry of Robert Frost* (pp. 222–223). New York: Holt, Rinehart and Winston. (Original work published 1923)

Frye, N. (1986). *Northrop Frye on Shakespeare* (R. Sandler, Ed.). New Haven, CT: Yale University Press.

Golding, W. (2006). *Lord of the flies.* New York: Penguin. (Original work published 1954)

Marlowe, C. (1995). Doctor Faustus. *Complete plays and poems* (Rev. ed., E. D. Pendry, Ed.). London: Everyman. (Original work published 1604)

National Council of Teachers of English & International Reading Association. (1996). *Standards of learning for the English language arts.* Urbana, IL: Author.

Seuss, D. (1960). *Green eggs and ham.* New York: Random House.

Shakespeare, W. (1970). *Hamlet* (Rev. ed., W. Farnham, Ed.). New York: Penguin. (Original work written 1600)

Shakespeare, W. (1971a). *Julius Caesar* (Rev. ed., S. F. Johnson, Ed.). New York: Penguin. (Original work written 1599)

Shakespeare, W. (1971b). *The winter's tale* (Rev. ed., B. Maxwell, Ed.). New York: Penguin. (Original work written 1611)

Shakespeare, W. (1992). *Romeo and Juliet* (Rev. ed., B. A. Mowat & P. Werstine, Eds.). Washington, DC: Folger Shakespeare Library. (Original work written 1594)

Shakespeare, W. (1997a). Sonnet 18. In H. Vendler (Ed.), *The art of Shakespeare's sonnets* (p. 119). Cambridge, MA: Harvard University Press. (Original work published 1609)

Shakespeare, W. (1997b). Sonnet 116. In H. Vendler (Ed.), *The art of Shakespeare's sonnets* (p. 487). Cambridge, MA: Harvard University Press. (Original work published 1609)

VanTassel-Baska, J. (1986). Effective curriculum and instructional models for the gifted. *Gifted Child Quarterly, 30,* 164–169.

VanTassel-Baska, J., & College of William and Mary Center for Gifted Education. (2007). *The Integrated Curriculum Model (ICM).* Retrieved February 25, 2008, from http://cfge.wm.edu/curriculum.htm

Willson, D. H. (1972). *A history of England* (2nd ed.). Hinsdale, IL: Dryden Press.

Resources for Further Study

Abbott, E. A. (1972). *A Shakespearean grammar* (Rev. ed.). New York: Haskell House. (Original work published 1870)

Baskin, B. H., & Harris, K. H. (1980). *Books for the gifted child.* New York: Bowker.

Bentley, G. E. (1961). *Shakespeare's life: A biographical handbook.* New Haven, CT: Yale University Press.

Boyce, C. (1990). *Shakespeare A to Z: The essential reference to his plays, his poems, his life and times, and more.* New York: Laurel.

Brooke, N. (1968). Romeo and Juliet. In N. Brooke, *Shakespeare's early tragedies* (pp. 80–106). New York: Methuen.

Brown, J. R. (1995). *Oxford illustrated history of theatre.* New York: Oxford University Press.

Clark, S. (1997). *The Shakespeare dictionary.* Lincolnwood, IL: NTC Publishing Group.

Davis, G. A., & Rimm, S. B. (1998). *Education of the gifted and talented* (4th ed.). Needham Heights, MA: Allyn & Bacon.

Drakakis, J. (Ed.). (1985). *Alternative Shakespeares.* New York: Methuen & Company.

Dutton, R. (1989). *William Shakespeare: A literary life.* New York: St. Martin's Press.

Gurr, A. (1987). *Playgoing in Shakespeare's London.* Cambridge, UK: Cambridge University Press.

Harrison, G. B. (1991). *Introducing Shakespeare* (4th ed.). London: Penguin Books.

Lace, W. W. (1995). *Elizabethan England*. San Diego: Lucent Books.

McMurtry, J. (1989). *Understanding Shakespeare's England: A companion for the American reader*. Hamden, CT: Archon Books.

Morley, J. (1994). *Shakespeare's theater*. New York: Peter Bedrick Books.

Novy, M. (1984). Violence, love, and gender in *Romeo and Juliet* and *Troilus and Cressida*. In M. Novy (Ed.), *Love's argument: Gender relations in Shakespeare* (pp. 99–124) Chapel Hill, NC: University of North Carolina Press.

Onions, C. T. (1986). *A Shakespeare glossary*. Oxford, England: Clarendon Press.

Paul, R. (1992). *Critical thinking: What every person needs to survive in a rapidly changing world*. Rohnert Park, CA: Foundation for Critical Thinking.

Singman, J. L. (1995). *Daily life in Elizabethan England*. Westport, CT: Greenwood Press.

Vendler, H. (1997). *The art of Shakespeare's sonnets*. Cambridge, MA: Harvard University Press.

Wells, S. (Ed.). (1986). *The Cambridge companion to Shakespeare studies*. Cambridge, UK: Cambridge University Press.

Adaptations of Romeo and Juliet on Film

Brabourne, J., Goodwin, R. B., & Havelock-Allan, A. (Producers), & Zeffirelli, F. (Director). (1968). *Romeo and Juliet* [Motion picture]. United States: Paramount Pictures.

Czinner, P. (Producer), & Czinner, P. (Director). (1966). *Romeo and Juliet* [Balletic motion picture]. United States: Embassy Pictures Corporation.

Ghenzi, S., Janni, J., & St. John, E. (Producers), & Castellani, R. (Director). (1954). *Romeo and Juliet* [Motion picture]. United States: United Artists.

Jencíková, N., & Venza, J. (Producers), & Sweete, B. W. (Director). (2002). *Roméo et Juliette* [Operatic motion picture]. Germany: Arthaus Musik.

Luhrmann, B., & Martinelli, G. (Producers), & Luhrmann, B. (Director). (1996). *Romeo + Juliet* [Motion picture]. United States: Twentieth Century Fox Film Corp.

Parkhomenko, A. (Producer), & Armstram, L., & Lavrovsky, L. (Directors). (1955). *Romeo I Zhulietta* [Balletic motion picture]. United States: Kultur International Films Ltd.

Thalberg, I. (Producer), & Cukor, G. (Director). (1936). *Romeo and Juliet* [Motion picture]. United States: MGM/UA Home Entertainment.

Internet Resources

Alchin, L. K. (2005). *Elizabethan era: Elizabethan theatre.* Retrieved December 4, 2007, from http://www.elizabethan-era.org.uk/elizabethan-theatre.htm

America Online. (2007). *The Shakespearean homework helper.* Retrieved December 4, 2007, from http://hometown.aol.com/liadona2/shakespeare.html

Bates, A. (Ed.). (1906). Romeo and Juliet: An analysis of the play by Shakespeare. In A. Bates (Ed.), *The drama: Its history, literature and influence on civilization* (Vol. 14; pp. 6–13). London: Historical Publishing Company. Retrieved December 4, 2007, from http://www.theatrehistory.com/british/romeoandjuliet001.html

Bellinger, M. F. (1927). Elizabethan playhouses, actors, and audiences. In M. F. Bellinger (Ed.), *A short history of the theatre* (pp. 207–213). New York: Henry Holt. Retrieved December 4, 2007, from http://www.theatrehistory.com/british/bellinger001.html

Cambridge University Press. (2007). *An introduction to Shakespeare's life and times: Seminar introduction.* Retrieved December 4, 2007, from http://www.fathom.com/course/28701903

Charles, G. (1998). *Romeo and Juliet: World premiere of David Nixon's BalletMet, Columbus, April 23, 1998.* Retrieved December 4, 2007, from http://www.balletmet.org/Notes/ROMEOAND.HTM

Community Learning Network. (2007). *Romeo and Juliet theme page.* Retrieved December 4, 2007, from http://www.cln.org/themes/romeo_juliet.html

Degas, E. (1858–1867). *The Bellelli family.* Retrieved January 22, 2008, from http://www.hermitagemuseum.org/html_En/04/2006/hm4_1_145.html

Folger Shakespeare Library. (2007). *Lesson plan archive.* Retrieved December 4, 2007, from http://www.folger.edu/eduLesPlanArch.cfm

Folger Shakespeare Library. (2007). *Teaching resources.* Retrieved December 4, 2007, from http://www.folger.edu/template.cfm?cid=618

Foret, K., & Weber, K. (1999). *Rewriting Romeo and Juliet: A Shakespearean webquest for high school English students.* Retrieved December 4, 2007, from http://oncampus.richmond.edu/academics/education/projects/webquests/shakespeare

istockphoto.com. (n.d.). *Stock Photo: London antique view.* Retrieved February 28, 2008, from http://www.istockphoto.com/file_closeup.php?id=2289462

The Kennedy Center. (2007). *Artsedge: Romeo and Juliet.* Retrieved December 4, 2007, from http://artsedge.kennedy-center.org/exploring/randj/artsedge.html

Larque, T. (2001). *Shakespeare and his critics: A lecture on Elizabethan theatre.* Retrieved December 4, 2007, from http://shakespearean.org.uk/eliztheal.htm

The Louvre. (2008). *Louvre museum official Web site.* Retrieved January 22, 2008, from http://www.louvre.fr

Metropolitan Museum of Art. (2008). *Homepage.* Retrieved January 22, 2008, from http://www.metmuseum.org

New Internet Shakespeare Editions. (2007). *Sites on Shakespeare and the Renaissance.* Retrieved December 4, 2007, from http://internetshakespeare. uvic.ca/Annex/links/index.html

Public Broadcasting Service. (2007). *For educators: Shakespeare in the classroom.* Retrieved December 4, 2007, from http://www.pbs.org/shakespeare/ educators

Public Broadcasting Service. (1995–2007). *The Shakespeare mystery: Who, in fact, was he?* Retrieved December 4, 2007, from http://www.pbs.org/wgbh/pages/ frontline/shakespeare

Rusche, H. (2007). *Shakespeare illustrated.* Retrieved December 4, 2007, from http://www.english.emory.edu/classes/Shakespeare_Illustrated/Shakespeare. html

Shakespeare Oxford Society. (1995–2007). *A beginner's guide to the Shakespeare authorship problem.* Retrieved December 4, 2007, from http://www. shakespeare-oxford.com/?p=35

ThinkQuest Team. (2000). *Literature: Elizabethan theatre.* Retrieved December 4, 2007, from http://library.thinkquest.org/C006522/literature/eliztheatre. php

Web English Teacher. (2007). *William Shakespeare, Romeo and Juliet: Lesson plans and other teaching ideas.* Retrieved December 4, 2007, from http://www. webenglishteacher.com/romeoandjuliet.html

Wild, L. (2007). *Renaissance theatre: England.* Retrieved December 4, 2007, from http://www.northern.edu/wild/th100/CHAPT15B.HTM

William Shakespeare info: Site map. (2007). Retrieved December 4, 2007, from http://www.william-shakespeare.info/site-map.htm

Wyeth, A. (1948). *Christina's world.* Retrieved January 22, 2008, from http:// www.moma.org/collection/browse_results.php?object_id=78455

About the Author

R. Brigham Lampert, a National Board Certified Teacher of English Language Arts, teaches at Jamestown High School in Williamsburg, VA, where he chairs the English department, serving as its Curriculum Leader. An AP English Literature teacher for most of his career, Lampert has been nominated for various recognitions as an instructor, including a 2006 Disney Teacher Award for outstanding creativity in the classroom. He has written and published numerous works, both creative and scholarly, including six Shakespearean *Navigator* teachers' guides for the Center for Gifted Education at the College of William and Mary, as well as original poems in national publications such as *Möbius* and the *Parnassus Literary Journal*.

Lampert currently is pursuing his Ed.D. in curriculum leadership at the College of William and Mary, where he was awarded an Excellence in Gifted Education scholarship and received his M.Ed. in educational policy, planning, and leadership, with an emphasis on administering gifted education services; previously, he received his B.A. in English from Haverford College. He resides with his wife and two sons in Williamsburg, VA.

Common Core State Standards Alignment

Grade Level	Common Core State Standards
Grade 7 ELA-Literacy	RL.7.1 Cite several pieces of textual evidence to support analysis of what the text says explicitly as well as inferences drawn from the text.
	RL.7.2 Determine a theme or central idea of a text and analyze its development over the course of the text; provide an objective summary of the text.
	RL.7.3 Analyze how particular elements of a story or drama interact (e.g., how setting shapes the characters or plot).
	RL.7.4 Determine the meaning of words and phrases as they are used in a text, including figurative and connotative meanings; analyze the impact of rhymes and other repetitions of sounds (e.g., alliteration) on a specific verse or stanza of a poem or section of a story or drama.
	RL.7.5 Analyze how a drama's or poem's form or structure (e.g., soliloquy, sonnet) contributes to its meaning
	RL.7.6 Analyze how an author develops and contrasts the points of view of different characters or narrators in a text.
	RL.7.7 Compare and contrast a written story, drama, or poem to its audio, filmed, staged, or multimedia version, analyzing the effects of techniques unique to each medium (e.g., lighting, sound, color, or camera focus and angles in a film).
	W.7.2 Write informative/explanatory texts to examine a topic and convey ideas, concepts, and information through the selection, organization, and analysis of relevant content.

Grade Level	Common Core State Standards
Grade 7 ELA-Literacy, *continued*	W.7.9 Draw evidence from literary or informational texts to support analysis, reflection, and research.
	SL.7.1 Engage effectively in a range of collaborative discussions (one-on-one, in groups, and teacher-led) with diverse partners on grade 7 topics, texts, and issues, building on others' ideas and expressing their own clearly.
	SL.7.4 Present claims and findings, emphasizing salient points in a focused, coherent manner with pertinent descriptions, facts, details, and examples; use appropriate eye contact, adequate volume, and clear pronunciation.
	L.7.5 Demonstrate understanding of figurative language, word relationships, and nuances in word meanings.
Grade 8 ELA-Literacy	RL.8.1 Cite the textual evidence that most strongly supports an analysis of what the text says explicitly as well as inferences drawn from the text.
	RL.8.2 Determine a theme or central idea of a text and analyze its development over the course of the text, including its relationship to the characters, setting, and plot; provide an objective summary of the text.
	RL.8.3 Analyze how particular lines of dialogue or incidents in a story or drama propel the action, reveal aspects of a character, or provoke a decision.
	RL.8.4 Determine the meaning of words and phrases as they are used in a text, including figurative and connotative meanings; analyze the impact of specific word choices on meaning and tone, including analogies or allusions to other texts.
	RL.8.6 Analyze how differences in the points of view of the characters and the audience or reader (e.g., created through the use of dramatic irony) create such effects as suspense or humor.
	RL.8.7 Analyze the extent to which a filmed or live production of a story or drama stays faithful to or departs from the text or script, evaluating the choices made by the director or actors.
	W.8.2 Write informative/explanatory texts to examine a topic and convey ideas, concepts, and information through the selection, organization, and analysis of relevant content.
	W.8.9 Draw evidence from literary or informational texts to support analysis, reflection, and research.
	SL.8.1 Engage effectively in a range of collaborative discussions (one-on-one, in groups, and teacher-led) with diverse partners on grade 8 topics, texts, and issues, building on others' ideas and expressing their own clearly.

Grade Level	Common Core State Standards
Grade 8 ELA-Literacy, *continued*	SL.8.4 Present claims and findings, emphasizing salient points in a focused, coherent manner with relevant evidence, sound valid reasoning, and well-chosen details; use appropriate eye contact, adequate volume, and clear pronunciation.
	L.8.5 Demonstrate understanding of figurative language, word relationships, and nuances in word meanings.
Grade 9-10 ELA-Literacy	RL.9-10.1 Cite strong and thorough textual evidence to support analysis of what the text says explicitly as well as inferences drawn from the text.
	RL.9-10.2 Determine a theme or central idea of a text and analyze in detail its development over the course of the text, including how it emerges and is shaped and refined by specific details; provide an objective summary of the text.
	RL.9-10.3 Analyze how complex characters (e.g., those with multiple or conflicting motivations) develop over the course of a text, interact with other characters, and advance the plot or develop the theme.
	RL.9-10.4 Determine the meaning of words and phrases as they are used in the text, including figurative and connotative meanings; analyze the cumulative impact of specific word choices on meaning and tone (e.g., how the language evokes a sense of time and place; how it sets a formal or informal tone).
	RL.9-10.5 Analyze how an author's choices concerning how to structure a text, order events within it (e.g., parallel plots), and manipulate time (e.g., pacing, flashbacks) create such effects as mystery, tension, or surprise.
	RL.9-10.9 Analyze how an author draws on and transforms source material in a specific work (e.g., how Shakespeare treats a theme or topic from Ovid or the Bible or how a later author draws on a play by Shakespeare).
	RL.9-10.10 By the end of grade 9, read and comprehend literature, including stories, dramas, and poems, in the grades 9-10 text complexity band proficiently, with scaffolding as needed at the high end of the range. By the end of grade 10, read and comprehend literature, including stories, dramas, and poems, at the high end of the grades 9-10 text complexity band independently and proficiently.
	W.9-10.2 Write informative/explanatory texts to examine and convey complex ideas, concepts, and information clearly and accurately through the effective selection, organization, and analysis of content.
	W.9-10.9 Draw evidence from literary or informational texts to support analysis, reflection, and research.

Grade Level	Common Core State Standards
Grade 9-10 ELA-Literacy, *continued*	W.9-10.10 Write routinely over extended time frames (time for research, reflection, and revision) and shorter time frames (a single sitting or a day or two) for a range of tasks, purposes, and audiences.
	SL.9-10.1 Initiate and participate effectively in a range of collaborative discussions (one-on-one, in groups, and teacher-led) with diverse partners on grades 9–10 topics, texts, and issues, building on others' ideas and expressing their own clearly and persuasively.
	SL.9-10.6 Adapt speech to a variety of contexts and tasks, demonstrating command of formal English when indicated or appropriate. (See grades 9–10 Language standards 1 and 3 here for specific expectations.)
	L.9-10.5 Demonstrate understanding of figurative language, word relationships, and nuances in word meanings.
	L.9-10.6 Acquire and use accurately general academic and domain-specific words and phrases, sufficient for reading, writing, speaking, and listening at the college and career readiness level; demonstrate independence in gathering vocabulary knowledge when considering a word or phrase important to comprehension or expression.
Grade 11-12 ELA-Literacy	RL.11-12.1 Cite strong and thorough textual evidence to support analysis of what the text says explicitly as well as inferences drawn from the text, including determining where the text leaves matters uncertain.
	RL.11-12.2 Determine two or more themes or central ideas of a text and analyze their development over the course of the text, including how they interact and build on one another to produce a complex account; provide an objective summary of the text.
	RL.11-12.3 Analyze the impact of the author's choices regarding how to develop and relate elements of a story or drama (e.g., where a story is set, how the action is ordered, how the characters are introduced and developed).
	RL.11-12.4 Determine the meaning of words and phrases as they are used in the text, including figurative and connotative meanings; analyze the impact of specific word choices on meaning and tone, including words with multiple meanings or language that is particularly fresh, engaging, or beautiful. (Include Shakespeare as well as other authors.)
	RL.11-12.5 Analyze how an author's choices concerning how to structure specific parts of a text (e.g., the choice of where to begin or end a story, the choice to provide a comedic or tragic resolution) contribute to its overall structure and meaning as well as its aesthetic impact.

Grade Level	Common Core State Standards
Grade 11-12 ELA-Literacy, *continued*	RL.11-12.6 Analyze a case in which grasping a point of view requires distinguishing what is directly stated in a text from what is really meant (e.g., satire, sarcasm, irony, or understatement).
	RL.11-12.7 Analyze multiple interpretations of a story, drama, or poem (e.g., recorded or live production of a play or recorded novel or poetry), evaluating how each version interprets the source text. (Include at least one play by Shakespeare and one play by an American dramatist.)
	W.11-12.2 Write informative/explanatory texts to examine and convey complex ideas, concepts, and information clearly and accurately through the effective selection, organization, and analysis of content.
	W.11-12.9 Draw evidence from literary or informational texts to support analysis, reflection, and research.
	W.11-12.10 Write routinely over extended time frames (time for research, reflection, and revision) and shorter time frames (a single sitting or a day or two) for a range of tasks, purposes, and audiences.
	SL.11-12.1 Initiate and participate effectively in a range of collaborative discussions (one-on-one, in groups, and teacher-led) with diverse partners on grades 11–12 topics, texts, and issues, building on others' ideas and expressing their own clearly and persuasively.
	SL.11-12.6 Adapt speech to a variety of contexts and tasks, demonstrating a command of formal English when indicated or appropriate. (See grades 11–12 Language standards 1 and 3 here for specific expectations.)
	L.11-12.5 Demonstrate understanding of figurative language, word relationships, and nuances in word meanings.
	L.11-12.6 Acquire and use accurately general academic and domain-specific words and phrases, sufficient for reading, writing, speaking, and listening at the college and career readiness level; demonstrate independence in gathering vocabulary knowledge when considering a word or phrase important to comprehension or expression.